Humanitarians on the Frontier

Identity and Access along the Borders of Power

Alasdair Gordon-Gibson

ROWMAN & LITTLEFIELD
Lanham • Boulder • New York • London

Executive Editor: Dhara Snowden
Assistant Editor: Rebecca Anastasi
Marketing Manager: Kim Lyons

Credits and acknowledgments for material borrowed from other sources, and reproduced with permission, appear on the appropriate page within the text.
Published by Rowman & Littlefield

An imprint of The Rowman & Littlefield Publishing Group, Inc.
4501 Forbes Boulevard, Suite 200, Lanham, Maryland 20706
www.rowman.com

Copyright © 2022 by The Rowman & Littlefield Publishing Group, Inc.

British Library Cataloguing in Publication Information Available

Library of Congress Cataloging-in-Publication Data

ISBN: 978-1-5381-5103-7 (cloth)
ISBN: 978-1-5381-5105-1 (paper)
ISBN: 978-1-5381-5104-4 (electronic)

For my daughters

Contents

Contents

Acknowledgements

Throughout the process of researching and writing I have received professional guidance from numerous people, notably, Alexander Bellamy, Fabrizio Bensi, John Black, Eleanor Burt, Mark Cutts, Roy Dilley, Antonio Donini, Denis Dragovic, Kristin Eggeling, Ed Schenkenberg, Jo Fox, Caron Gentry, Patrick Hayden, Daniel Herrera-Kelly, Raymond Hinnebusch, John Humphreys, Omar Imadi, Mukesh Kapila, Anthony Lang Jr, Iain Logan, Fiona McCallum Guiney, David Miles, Kurt Mills, Nicholas Morris, Jeffrey Murer, Mateja Peter, Julia Prest, Tilman Schwarze, Hugo Slim, Andrew J. Williams, as well as anonymous reviewers of my manuscript. All have provided me with a valuable mix of academic theory and practical experience that form the foundations of this book. I am grateful to the British Red Cross for providing funding of my initial research, and for the access to archived material provided by the International Committee of the Red Cross and the International Federation of Red Cross and Red Crescent Societies.

Outside the immediate environment of study, great support was given by friends. There are too many names to mention here, and many would prefer the anonymity. I must especially say thank you to David Horobin and Catherine Blum, who were always generous with their friendship and hospitality during my visits to Geneva. The late John Joly has been a constant inspiration and his wisdom kept me secure through many difficult times. And of course, a special thanks to my family: my parents drove a spirit to challenge and enquire, my wife has kept me balanced, and our daughters have kept me aware of the opportunities from being young in the modern world. I extend my gratitude to the production unit at Rowman & Littlefield for their patience and support during the conclusion of this publication. But most of all, I want to thank the people who have inspired me most throughout this journey: the staff and volunteers of the national Red Cross and Red Crescent Societies, local humanitarian organisations and the thousands of people in communities affected by crisis. Any wisdom that emerges from this book is a tribute to them.

Introduction

This book explores the humanitarian sector's relationship with authority. Emerging from my work as a professional and as a volunteer in humanitarian responses to situations of complex emergency, where a lack of access to affected populations was a growing concern, it combines a blend of practical experience and theoretical reflection on the contemporary humanitarian identity. Whilst the investigation follows an orthodox approach, looking at principles and practice amidst the swirl of stakeholder politics, its arguments focus on two fundamental humanitarian concepts not commonly explored in studies of the topic: voluntary service and universality.[1] Together with a review of documentation in the Red Cross and Red Crescent archives, and using examples in case studies on the contested humanitarian responses to the tsunami in Sri Lanka, 2004–2005 and the conflict in Syria which began in 2011, it questions assumptions that common themes have a universal expression, prescribed and regulated outside of the socio-political contexts in which they take place.

The focus on voluntary service was triggered by a conversation with a senior British journalist with extensive experience in reporting from scenes of conflict and natural disaster and had consistently been struck by the motivation and dedication of national Red Cross and Red Crescent Society volunteers. She questioned why mainstream constructions in the international media, of which she formed a part, drew on narratives from the aid and development sectors that echoed the conversations of the international elite but ignored the voices of national volunteers and voluntary structures. She concluded that this exclusive discussion was driven by the assumption of a universal, uncontested humanitarian identity that encompassed all stakeholders in the sectors and brooked no further engagement – an assumption contradicted by experiences on the ground but that was pervasive in the corridors of authority and copied by those searching for participation.

Most practitioners struggle with confusion of meaning and identity, with the tensions poignantly expressed to me by a colleague on the field as those emerging from conflicting interpretations of 'job' and 'duty': Volunteering in emergency response for whom? Why? To whom are we accountable and for whom is the impact directed? This swirl of forces in the humanitarian arena question pairings of purpose and practice; of allegiances and alliances; of community and state, and lead to anxious introspection amongst many practitioners about the humanitarian identity. Too often, anxiety turns to cynical reflection on how the instrumental forces of politics and society serve to compromise an independent humanitarian identity and undermine the spirit of voluntary service that, I argue here, is an essential part of its functional space.

Throughout my work, the beacon that lit a path away from the trap of cynicism is what I refer to in my book as the 'creative messiness of humanity'. In the midst of chaos, and despite the hardship and suffering evident in all the complex emergencies in which I was engaged, was the emergence of order from disorder. This was more often the result of ordinary human interaction in extreme situations than the product of institutional and organisational efficiency. This spirit of spontaneous engagement to cooperate in the face of hardship finds frequent expression in practitioner reports and anecdotal accounts of life in the field, often with examples of humour and tolerance in the worst of crisis: a dynamic that is often absent from the official narratives.[2] Personal diaries and mission reports remark on the creative energy that comes from a situation of chaos in which there are no clear lines anymore, but undefined frontiers for interaction. These are 'opportune spaces' that allow humanity to function and provide an opportunity to return the human to humanitarian in actions along these frontiers.[3]

BACKGROUND TO THE BOOK

My book is the culmination of a journey which began over thirty years ago. Following graduation from university in 1982, I joined a shipping and insurance company based in Beirut, Lebanon, where a significant portion of work was linked to the national and international humanitarian response to the civil war which had begun in 1975. As well as informal daily exposure to the conflict environment, the practical logistics of work in the operational sector of a shipping company meant formal engagement with state authorities and the multiple non-state authorities who determined access. This raised awareness of the commercial, political and social influences of what I refer to in this book as the established and unestablished power that determine access in the environment – not only at a physical, material level, but, as importantly, at a conceptual, metaphorical level: one that directs access to participation in these spaces. I experienced first-hand the practical strategies of 'negotiating' participation in discussions and the daily process of navigating physical access across frontlines and military checkpoints that were everyday realities for a population coping with conflict. This period of eight years in the commercial sector was followed by twenty-three years working in the humanitarian sector, mainly within the Red Cross and Red Crescent Movement. Beginning with technical positions as a relief and logistics administrator with the International Committee of the Red Cross (ICRC) in Iraq, in 1991, this period culminated in positions as a senior manager for the International Federation of Red Cross and Red Crescent Societies (IFRC), in 2011. Work included the operational management of humanitarian responses to complex emergencies in Goma (1994), Bosnia and Herzegovina (1997), Sri Lanka (2004), Myanmar (2008) and Syria (2006; 2009; 2011) all of which inform the arguments in this study. Periods were also spent at the head offices of both ICRC and IFRC in Geneva.

This breadth of experience working within the institutional and organisational structures of the humanitarian sector, as well as within the commercial structures of the business sector, sparked an interest in the way the narratives of each component construct differing spaces for discourse and interaction, influencing the way communities in crisis navigate paths for participation within them. The personal experiences of having to adapt and adopt context-specific strategies of political and social interaction to gain the trust of stakeholders in the humanitarian environment were pivotal for operational and organisational effectiveness and led me to reflect on how transferable this was as a strategy to engage trust and access across all stakeholders in a contested environment. This enquiry led to a period of academic research in the United Kingdom which introduced me to the theoretical and philosophical approaches that frame scholarship in these topics. The result was a master's thesis examining mis-readings of humanitarian space, to which this study makes occasional reference, and then a doctoral study on questions of identity and access on which this book is based.

Exposure to the differing environments of theory and practice, grounded by a working life spent in the turbulent dynamics of conflict and natural disaster, has enabled me to focus my book on topics which have relevance across the broad community of stakeholders. The opening chapters begin by situating some of the historical background and academic approaches to contemporary interpretations of a humanitarian identity. These include an examination of social scientific and psychological theories on social identity and consider the risks and opportunities that bonds of influence can present. Recognition of the social and political relationship in a humanitarian identity directs the study towards an exploration of documents in the archives of the Red Cross and Red Crescent Movement, focusing on the institutional and organisational debates around understandings of Voluntary Service and Universality. The empirical examinations continue with case studies on the discourse surrounding the humanitarian response to the tsunami in Sri Lanka, where assumptions of familiarity with the environment and easy access to resources led to deterioration in the socio-political relationship. A comparative study is made on the conflict in Syria which began in 2011, in an environment that was less familiar and from the outset was more restrictive. In counterpoise to both case studies, a short reflection is made on the response to the cyclone that struck Myanmar in 2008 which presented unexpected opportunities for engagement and cooperation. These three operational environments involved close cooperation with volunteers as members of affected communities and with internal and external stakeholders as voluntary respondents in the environments of crisis. In all cases, questions of identity, trust and representation were paramount to determine the success or failure of humanitarian action. A summary of the arguments and proposals for new direction towards a pro-social discourse are presented in the concluding chapters.

Recasting the Gaze

The focus of analysis is confined to humanitarian action undertaken by the group of front-line responders in the 'minimalist' frame,[4] whose primary focus is on saving lives and protecting a minimum level of dignity for survivors of complex emergencies.[5] My study narrows the focus further to consider those actors who – in a loosely defined way – can be considered as auxiliary to the provision of public services at times of complex emergencies, inhabiting a limited and restricted humanitarian space, or 'niche'. It might be argued that any actor providing life-saving support in complex emergencies is, through the existential nature of its practices, in some way an auxiliary to the provision of public services. However, the critical nuance that my book wants to bring to the discussions are interpretations which consider such humanitarian auxiliaries as *voluntary representatives* of established public services, performing a complementary role in support of existing capacities, or providing them in case these are absent or dysfunctional. These actors are explicitly not agents of the state, nor act in a direct capacity dependent on the state, but voluntarily perform emergency humanitarian functions of protection, search and rescue in support of critical public services.

The idea of representation is complex. 'Representing people has been one of the primary functions of modern states – however great the problems with how they do it'.[6] Outside of the state, or state-like forms of governance, there is a risk that representation of peoples becomes arbitrary, where there is no anchor on which to determine an identity. By framing this representation with what I argue is the stable identity of a humanitarian niche, it locates a place of mutual commitment that unites its stakeholders across a range of different aims and identities,[7] offering opportunities for forms of solidarity that render representation less arbitrary and more a matter of choice. The ability to choose is an important element in my discussion, and variant understandings of the representational character of these actors are presented in the chapters that follow. By presenting an orientation that positions voluntary service as an autonomous, freely chosen auxiliary to the provision of public humanitarian services, and by illustrating the sense of social obligation attending actions in this humanitarian space, this offers the opportunity to chart new pathways to better understand the cohesion and complementarity that cooperative humanitarian action can bring. The sense of humanity invoked coalesces around a common purpose enacted with variable practices that are shaped, defined, legitimated and protected in this humanitarian niche, whose spatial properties derive from the cultural, historical and ideational norms of the community it serves. This challenges an assumption amongst the dominant paradigms of humanitarian action constructed by the Global North[8] that there is a form of externally formed, non-contestable 'best practice' which must be firmly in place to achieve the humanitarian purpose.[9] However, while contesting the idea of a *universal* humanitarian blueprint, my book indicates opportunities that *a universalist* idea of common humanity could bring.

The case studies analyse the discourse in the narratives surrounding the humanitarian response to the Indian Ocean tsunami in Sri Lanka and to the conflict in Syria. There are many types of discourse analysis, but all ask common questions of the way discourse structures are deployed in the reproduction of social dominance and make common references to 'power'; 'dominance'; 'legitimacy' and 'social order' at the macro-level of the state, as well as verbal interaction at the micro-level of the community and individuals within it. This value-conscious approach to analysis is especially pertinent to my study of discourse and narrative across multiple stakeholders situated in diverse environments in which ideals and attitudes are influenced by the contexts. Whereas Critical Discourse Analysis traditionally looks at understandings of social power as *control*,[10] my study chooses to look for opportunities of social power as *cooperation*. My analysis of the discourse in this book is focused accordingly, examining whether auxiliary voluntary service in environments of complex emergencies can be the bridge between discourse at the macro-level and micro-level in the contexts under study. It seeks to determine whether a revised comprehension of the auxiliary role in certain spaces can act as a representative – or a replacement – of public services yet remain autonomous from the coercive structures normally associated with power. Are there opportunities for independent humanitarian auxiliaries to be trusted within a system of state but not seen to be wholly part of it? Does the discourse identify separations between humanitarian emergency actors at the minimalist end of the aid spectrum and the rights-based actors at the maximalist end, where there may be differences in purpose as well as in practice? Central to this competing discourse are the tensions often seen to be inherent in notions of volunteers as auxiliaries to public services, emerging from contested approaches towards their relationship with the state or state-like authority, when their purpose and practices are seen to be an adjunct to political power. In the Movement debates examined in chapter 6, the association of a humanitarian identity as an auxiliary is a dominant theme. The prominence of an auxiliary role in these internal discussions between members of the Movement makes the absence of its reference more noticeable in the public discourse examined in chapter 7. By explaining these omissions, there is an opportunity to identify reasons for the absence of a common discourse on its humanitarian principles.

In summary, this book is looking at the concept and the phenomenon of voluntary service as a means of widening access to a shared discourse in environments of humanitarian emergency. It looks at how the humanitarian identity in general, and voluntary service in particular, is interpreted and understood as a means for social bonding, focusing on the community of stakeholders as the unit for analysis of the social nature of this relationship.[11] Arguments that position the humanitarian identity as a critical part of this social relationship are central to my study and so the analysis of the narratives, together with the surrounding discourses which 'manage' these, adopts this broad approach. It is one that goes beyond the immediate text and analyses the motivations behind the phenomenon: an analysis that extends methods to include the study of structures and relationships that foreground the social influence of humanitarian voluntary service. As will become apparent in the discussions that follow, an appreciation of context and the inter-action of these relationships is important to gain understanding of the identities in the humanitarian environment explored here.

Whilst the following chapters refer to classical works of Rousseau and philosophers of the European Enlightenment, seen as informing traditional approaches to contemporary moral philosophy in the Global North, the book is not a guide to a common form of moral authority. Rather, it contests the universal spiritual or secular prescriptions that western interpretations of these studies have presented. However, it does suggest a universalist opportunity that discourse around a shared history and purpose might bring. Freed from the confinement of an exclusive history of (Western) thought and practice it points towards the recognition of diversity, intersectionality and shared identities that are a core feature of contemporary social scientific debates.[12] A monocular view of the literature around classical interpretations of humanitarian principles and practice, focusing on the principles of independence, neutrality and impartiality, might lead to a conclusion that humanitarian and political identities are polar opposites. In an ICRC weblog, Hugo Slim points out the significance of diversity and intersectionality in humanitarian response.[13] He remarks that the modern elaboration of humanitarian norms and policy may have accidentally created a damaging social simplification in human labelling. By foregrounding the importance of intersectionality and an appreciation of differences in human identity, Slim presents a more complex pattern of intersecting power and vulnerability.[14] My book accepts this argument and urges recognition of the complex messiness of humanity. It supports the call for a careful appreciation of the multiple factors that intersect the social and political dimensions of the 'lived experience' of people, which, in crisis as well as in normal life, are experiences that shape our ability to respond.[15] This calls for recognition of the variety of factors that intersect within each of us and shape our socio-political capabilities. Its arguments present opportunities that go beyond the frame of emergency response which is the primary focus of my book. By acknowledging some common goals and collective outcomes, it presents opportunities for a shared discourse that can bridge the humanitarian-development nexus, which is a junction of contestation in contemporary debate that some critics fear will lead to a dead end.[16] In its examination of access and identity, the book confronts the dysfunctions of an identity that appeals to all and appears representative of all which, as cautioned by these debates, risk being lost in a humanitarian no-man's land. By calling for a shift in the discourse, and an acknowledgement of broader influences and stakeholder interests, the book presents a more liminal space: a humanitarian 'niche' that can appeal to all, but which harbours the ability to challenge.

The study is intended to be less a critique of action than as a catalyst for reflection. It does not offer templates for a solution but opens avenues towards a different pattern of cooperation, leading to a less exclusive and more representative space for shared discourse which understands multiple social and political dimensions: a 'new way of thinking' that leads to revitalised engagement and participation, enabled to challenge and confront forces that are seen as antithetical to a common humanitarian purpose. In this, it has links to the works of contemporary philosophers and historians, such as Bertrand Badie and Andrew J. Williams, urging analysis not to focus on the particular, but on the construction of identity and trust in a broad social and political context.[17] My book's reconsiderations of patterns of socio-political engagement can also be seen as a contribution to emerging work on quantum approaches to international relations, which offer exciting and innovative discussions by introducing well-grounded scientific approaches to social theorising that can help us better interpret and address the global issues of our time.[18] Like Stephen Hopgood and his study on human rights,[19] the book urges to cast the gaze away from the institutional typefaces of emergency response and consider more context-based understandings of the humanitarian identity, which are at once more modest and more representative, and so with greater relevance to the communities, it seeks to assist. In the search for a more functional middle ground, this study asks us to reconsider the pairings which lead to accusations of dysfunction in the swirl of political and social forces; job and duty; volunteer and auxiliary; confrontation and compliance – the location of a middle ground emerging from the tensions of competing identities and the creative messiness of humanity struggling to survive.

Outline of the Book

I have located 'identity' and 'trust' as the core elements guiding investigations in the book and these coalesce around an analysis of *purpose* and *practice*. Since practices are seen to operationalise the purpose,[20] the chapters that follow focus on the prominence of purpose and practice in the constructions of social identity. Chapter 1 builds on the background presented in this introduction and proposes directions towards the new way of thinking through understandings of humanitarian action as 'praxis' that directs a discussion around purpose and practice that is less exclusive than the traditional debates allow. These tensions and assumptions are explored in greater detail in chapter 2, focusing on how they are expressed within the differing institutional and organisational constructions in the humanitarian sector.

Chapter 3 examines the foundation of these tensions by reviewing some of the expressions of humanitarian identities in history and across cultures. It considers the way understandings of its purpose and its practice have altered within societies and by the influences of the environments in which they take place. The opening section considers how interpretations of purpose and practice in these differing contexts of space and time share common expressions of 'humanity' in modern environments of complex emergencies which is the focus of this study. It considers linkages between humanity as an ideal and as an ideology, and examines how this relationship has altered or affected its purpose and practice within the broad community of stakeholders in the environments of humanitarian emergency. The next section presents a comparison of voluntary service across cultures where interpretations of voluntary service and the social status of a volunteer have varying expressions. The chapter concludes with analysis of how far these expressions of humanity and voluntary service have provided its members with access to the entitlements of respected and dignified life in the community.

Chapter 4 looks at Social Identity Theory that sees social identity underpinning intergroup behaviour and social context as the key determinant of self-definition.[21] It begins with consideration of what identifies a sense of community membership by exploring the drivers of social bonding and the opportunities for collective intention emerging from constructive interaction between the individual and the group.[22] This chapter includes an examination of the dynamics of power and resistance and introduces the concept of the Shakespearean 'sage-fool' as a figure for legitimated resistance. The next section of this chapter, *'Identity and Practice: a Capability Approach'* focuses on arguments towards a 'tangible' formulation of the theoretical needs for a collective identity and communal trust. Constructions of identity in this section draw upon arguments presented by Martha Nussbaum in her formulations of the Capability Approach that expand on the economic theories for development argued by Amartya Sen[23] and which she offers as an alternative, philosophical approach to traditional social contract theory. These arguments revolve around notions that engage mutual cooperation to render people capable of living a life with dignity (or, in Nussbaum's words, a life 'worthy of living'). The arguments in this chapter define the path towards which my book aims to lead; that is to open a protected space for trusted humanitarian action that will enable communities affected by crisis to access the capabilities to survive and participate with dignity.

Chapter 5 considers the risks and opportunities that emerge from the humanitarian identities argued in chapter 4. These include the risks of co-optation; of reputational discreditation in public/private image and the risks from collective action identified in psychological theory. It considers how far these risks might limit trust in a volunteer auxiliary. It examines the risks from 'over-reach', or over ambition, which exposes the fragility of trust and the irrelevance of certain expressions of humanitarian action to communities in crisis.

Chapter 6 turns to a study of documentation in the archives of the Red Cross and Red Crescent Movement. Accepting the premise that formalisation of the modern humanitarian identity begins with the foundation of the ICRC in 1863 and the promulgation of the first Geneva Convention the following year,[24] this chapter presents an analysis of the debates leading to the official proclamation of the Red Cross Movement's Fundamental Principles in Vienna, 1965. It focuses on the discussions around two of the Fundamental Principles of the Red Cross Movement – Voluntary Service and Universality – but which my study argues have wider relevance and more common representation than the principles of neutrality, impartiality and independence, which form the core of academic debates and are at the centre of contemporary humanitarian discourse. The analysis makes reference to the arguments on the purpose and practice of humanitarian voluntary service presented in chapters 2 and 3 and considers the drive and motivation behind the less tangible expression of a shared 'spirit' behind this identity.

The empirical examinations continue in chapter 7, analysing national and international narratives over a period of six months following the tsunami which struck Sri Lanka on 26 December 2004, and on a six-month period following the start of conflict in Syria in 2011. These are supported by a comparative reflection on the emergency response to the cyclone which struck Myanmar in May 2008. Drawing on the author's own experience in these contexts of humanitarian emergency and acquaintance with the complexities of the socio-political environment in which the responses occurred, this chapter provides both an empirical and a heuristic analysis of the expressions of humanitarian response. All these responses occurred in environments of complex emergency but mis-readings of the nature of discourse in the humanitarian space led to different, unexpected, outcomes.

Making direct reference to the archival research in chapter 6 and the case studies in chapter 7, as well as synthesising the theoretical arguments and discussions presented in the preceding chapters, chapter 8 builds on the formulations of the identities which, I argue, frame the humanitarian space in which auxiliary volunteers might interact and gain collective legitimacy of practice and purpose. Providing examples from experiences in environments of crisis, it expands on discussions presented by the Capability Approach addressing access to procedures which secure human dignity. Combining personal reflection on the conflict in Bosnia and Herzegovina (1992–1995) and its aftermath with the findings from an ethnographic study of the population under siege in Sarajevo,[25] these consider capacities emerging from communities struggling to cope which extend beyond the classical paradigm of humanitarian response of survival and protection. This penultimate chapter returns to discussing elements of 'legitimacy', 'authority' and 'representation' posed by the questions in chapter 1 about the place of humanitarian voluntary service in the social fabric and opportunities for access its formulation can provide, with closer examination of their associations with purpose and practice.

Chapter 9 concludes the book by assessing the legitimacy of the shared identities being proposed and suggesting new strategies for engagement. It links some of the classical philosophical arguments presented in the book with contemporary approaches in policy and practice articulated by guidelines such as the Sphere Charter, and modern humanitarian expressions through global humanitarian platforms, such as the United Nations and the international conferences of the Red Cross and Red Crescent Movement. It addresses the tensions between a 'humanitarian purpose' and its association with the authority of political power and ideology that permeate the arguments throughout this book.

Whilst the arguments presented are influenced by a career spent working in the humanitarian sector, mainly with the Red Cross and Red Crescent Movement, unless explicitly stated, all opinions and conclusions presented are my own. Nevertheless, I hope that the arguments will be familiar and recognisable to members of the Movement, the United Nations agencies, international and national non-government organisations as well as a broad panoply of stakeholders across the aid-development spectrum. Unless otherwise indicated, translations of documents from the archives are my own.

This introduction concludes with a brief presentation of some of the core terms used in the book. In addition to the understandings of the terms 'voluntary service', 'volunteer' and the notions of 'space' which are central to the concepts argued in my book and are explained fully in the following chapters, it is helpful to include the definitions of other words and terminology featuring regularly in this study. First, an understanding of the term 'humanitarian system'. Scholars, practitioners and policymakers are unanimous that there is no uniformly recognised understanding of either the word 'humanitarian' or the term 'system'. As will become apparent, the multiplicity of aims, perceived mandates, positionalities of the stakeholders and the variant contexts in the unstable environments of crisis make any stable and universal definition impossible. The understanding which most closely corresponds to the arguments pursued in this book is the holistic interpretation given by Peter Walker and Daniel Maxwell, describing a system 'that allows those caught up in a crisis to articulate what they need to alleviate their suffering while allowing others in the human family, who are better off, to provide the resources to meet those needs. It is a people-to-people structure with governments, agencies and aid organizations as the go-betweens'.[26] Whilst there is no agreement about definition of a humanitarian system, there is recognition of a spectrum of purposes and practices along the humanitarian-development continuum. These range from the 'classical' emergency response of providing relief and protection at the minimalist end of the spectrum, through the development agencies with a focus on rehabilitation and reconstruction, to the advocates for structural and political change at the maximalist end. The differing interpretations of what the humanitarian system should include and exclude along this spectrum are at the root of debates about the humanitarian identity.[27] References to a 'formal' humanitarian system in this book correspond to the definition provided by Hugo Slim, seen to comprise 'the mainly Western-funded humanitarian system which works closely within or in coordination with the international authority of the United Nations and Red Cross movements'.[28]

The term 'stakeholders' is another much debated term. Most evidently it includes the population affected by a humanitarian crisis, but as Slim observes: 'In any piece of work, an NGO will need to account to different groups of people as stakeholders. These will be the targeted rights-holders, the various duty-bearers and those secondary and tertiary stakeholders beyond the primary stakeholders who operate as interested or critical observers'.[29] Amongst these secondary or tertiary stakeholders, Walker and Maxwell identify these more specifically as 'structured groups of private citizens: community-based organizations (CBOs), which tend to arise from within communities in crisis, or non-governmental organizations (NGOs) which are often external to, but wanting to assist the crisis-affected people'.[30] My study concurs with the broadest understanding of stakeholders and corresponds closely with Michel Agier's remark that 'far from involving only nongovernmental organizations acting in the humanitarian field, it includes all the actors – private and public, governmental, intergovernmental, nongovernmental or affiliated with the UN – who use the label of 'humanitarianism' in order to secure recognition, distinction, or legitimacy for their actions on the ground'.[31] For these reasons, my study purposely engages with the (often contested) concept of a 'community' of stakeholders.

The arguments in the book centre around the meaning of 'trust'. Scholars of trust theory recognise that trust is interpreted according to the nature of trust being examined (e.g. deterrence-based trust, relational trust and institutional trust), as well as the contexts in which relationships of trust take place.[32] Scholarship agrees, however, that risk and interdependence are two invariable conditions.[33] The definition of trust on which arguments in this book are framed is as follows: 'a psychological state comprising the intention to accept vulnerability based upon positive expectations of the intentions or behaviour of another'.[34]

Chapter 1

Humanitarian Relations

The generally accepted position in academic and policy studies is of a traditional, or 'formal'[1] humanitarian system which faces a crisis of legitimacy 'blocked by significant and enduring flaws that prevent it from being effective'.[2] Iterations of a 'humanitarian problem' are prominent in discussions around contemporary responses to crisis. These usually identify a dysfunctional, unrepresentative space where policymakers and practitioners have lost access to populations in need. Resolutions to the problem traditionally focus on the core humanitarian principles of humanity, independence, neutrality and impartiality, and steadfastly maintain a distance from the political sphere. This suggests that there is a 'humanitarian solution' to the problem, allowing it to distance its agency from its political and historical context. However, echoing the remark made by the UNHCR High Commissioner during the height of the conflicts in the former Yugoslavia from 1992–1996, analyses of modern humanitarian responses at the end of the twentieth century and at the start of the twenty-first century have demonstrated that there can be no humanitarian solutions to situations of humanitarian crisis.[3]

Following perceived failures in humanitarian responses to conflict and complex emergencies in the Horn of Africa, the Great Lakes and the Balkans in the 1990s tools emerged that focused on setting guidelines for good practice and accountability, and advocated for greater participation with affected populations.[4] This was a pattern of engagement that grew in the 2000s and became associated with stakeholder discourse on 'localisation'. Localisation featured prominently at the 2016 World Humanitarian Summit called by the UN Secretary General in search of a resolution to the dysfunctions in the humanitarian aid and development sectors. One of the aims of this summit was to agree to a 'new way of working' that would identify a platform from which local voices could be heard. It sought to re-position decision making in a humanitarian response away from international organisations and instead into the hands of affected people who are at the heart of humanitarian action.[5] Following the Summit, statements emerged around a 'Grand Bargain' that committed to change patterns of engagement between stakeholders in a crisis. Questions remained as to how the proposed change would look in practice and how access for participation would improve.

These questions emerge from the paradox that an expansion of actors in the humanitarian arena over the past thirty years has led to diminished access for principled humanitarian action. The confusion of a multiplicity of practitioner identities, with corresponding questioning of their purpose and practices, has led to a loss of trust, and with this loss of trust has come shrinking space for cooperation. This book examines humanitarian identities in environments of crisis that lead to accusations of dysfunction in a sector where norms of cooperation should be evident, and participation in a shared discourse be easily accessible. By reimagining and recasting the identity of humanitarian actors, the book's arguments redefine the places of participation inside the contemporary constructions of humanitarian space. These places are located along the borders of power, situated in a liminal space where a stable yet contingent humanitarian identity is constructed that has agency as an auxiliary to state responsibility in response to humanitarian emergencies, yet is enabled to challenge authority if the norms of humanitarian protection are not met. This argues for a trusted representation that allows the paradox of being a part of the governing space but remaining apart from it.

Confrontation with authority and competition within the stakeholder community feature prominently in debates on dysfunction in the humanitarian environment. These tensions are striking, since humanitarian identities are associated with the phenomena of altruism, helping and social solidarity, seen in psychological science as the essence of prosocial behaviour.[6] However, since these engage with fundamental questions about human nature and humanity's place in the social and political structures of society, the space for contestation is evident. The arguments that follow examine whether the phenomenon and concept of voluntary service provides a shared, least contested, and most universally accepted expression of the humanitarian purpose and its practices in the disordered socio-political spaces of crisis and emergency. Through a combination of practitioner studies of emergency humanitarian action and philosophical reflection on purpose and practice in these responses, the book explores evidence of the dysfunction arising from a confusion of multiple identities that leads to the absence of a common, cooperative discourse. The analysis suggests how new understandings of voluntary service and universality can address this absence.

The 'politics of identity' have become a prominent theme for discussion in the humanities and social sciences over recent years. As distinct from the 'identity politics' that emerged in debates about social justice in the 1960s, and developed as a core theme of social scientific study in the 1980s, the politics of identity refer to practices and values that are based on the voluntary and often involuntary subscription to a variety of overlapping social and political identities.[7] Arguments in the book interpret these as claims to shared experience and common group characteristics.[8] Within the sector of humanitarian aid itself, there is continued reluctance to acknowledge a political identity, though this self-enforced denial may be changing. The failures of global diplomacy in Syria, Libya, Iraq, Yemen and Afghanistan – to name only the most recent examples – mean that humanitarian aid and politics have become increasingly paired to bridge the divisions and to protect the most vulnerable.[9] The central themes in this book focus enquiry on the identity of humanitarian actors and access to the humanitarian space. It considers the significance of a humanitarian identity ready to acknowledge its place in politics, thereby participating in the construction of an inclusive, prosocial discourse that departs from the exceptionalism of dominant humanitarian narratives around 'best practice' and 'good governance', seen by many as blocking access to effective cooperation in contemporary crises.[10]

IDENTITY AND ACCESS

Evidence from academic studies as well as from periods of deep introspection by professionals in the humanitarian sector have indicated significant and persistent unease over its identity and the identities of those working within it. This has been positioned by some scholars as a sign of ontological insecurity around interpretations of purpose and practice in the humanitarian sector[11] and has led to the conduct of wide-ranging studies into the meanings and functions ascribed to the humanitarian system.[12] The call for greater humanitarian access to populations in crisis has been a persistent refrain in contemporary discussions and debates amongst political scientists, policymakers, practitioners and the broad range of stakeholders in the humanitarian arena.[13] However, reaching a shared understanding of what this call means has been difficult. Misappropriations of core humanitarian principles, and miscalculations as to how these principles are practised have fractured presumptions of an impartial space for cooperation and prosocial action in response to complex humanitarian emergencies.

In order to engage coherently with the arguments that follow we must first engage with the problematic understandings of 'community' in the context of the stakeholders in a humanitarian system. Contestations of the term reflect similar critiques on presentations of an 'international community' and question on whether such a 'system' actually exists.[14] A broad and inclusive, comprehension of 'community' is important to understanding the nature of the prosocial space of discourse presented here, since variant interpretations of community lead to the confusion over meanings of identity. In this book, these meanings are entwined within the paradoxical concept of 'voluntary obligation', which I link to understandings of politics of identity, expressed by Jonathan Hill and Thomas Wilson as 'issues of personal and group power, found within and across all social and political institutions and collectivities, where people sometimes choose, and sometimes are forced, to interact with each other in part on the basis of their shared, or divergent, notions of their identities'.[15] It is within the creative tensions of a voluntary obligation where this book finds opportunities for a shared discourse. Community harbours a broader, looser representation of shared identities than the united sense of common practices or defined purpose that many commentaries and analyses present. Dysfunction in the humanitarian sector derives from a sweeping interpretation of the humanitarian identity, with assumptions of a shared acceptance of 'best' practice and a universal purpose that clumsily encompasses a broad range of stakeholders and interests across the sector. I argue that a less prescriptive engagement with what loosely constitutes a 'community' of stakeholders in a crisis will offer a more functional space for cooperation.

WHAT IS AT STAKE?

At stake in a new humanitarian discussion is how – and how far – humanitarian identities can be seen to represent and challenge the broadening stakeholder interests of contemporary humanitarian responses. Today's humanitarian responses are more complex and involve more stakeholders than ever before. In such circumstances, how can humanitarian identities represent the various voices and challenge authority in this new humanitarian space? The answer to this question begins by asking what, and where, are the spaces for humanitarian participation? Scholars and practitioners have agreed that the humanitarian sector has lost its way in recent decades,[16] with this loss of direction rendered more acute in face of the changing environments in which it performs. Incremental growth in the sector since the evolution of a formal humanitarian identity in the nineteenth century, and its institutional development in the twentieth century, has brought with it an increasingly professional profile with global recognition. However, with this professionalisation and institutionalisation has come a growth in organisational self-referral – where each only recognises the other in terms of the system's own 'logic'[17] – that has made the humanitarian sector seen to be more distant and disconnected from the communities it serves. Despite the many steps that have been taken over recent years to try to make the sector more accessible and relevant to the stakeholders it is seen to represent, there is a sense of continued disconnection from them. This raises questions of what has led to this loss of access and how a process of relevance and re-identification can be regained.

A search to understand the sector's perceived lack of relevance and representation to those it seeks to assist means asking whether recognition of a more shared, less exclusive, humanitarian identity can present opportunities to reconnect the divided narratives in the discursive space. The arguments that follow do not rest on a radical re-structuring of the humanitarian architecture or the creation of new laws, principles, codes and guidelines. Rather, they call for a re-direction of the institutional gaze towards existing laws, principles and codes that guide humanitarian action to enable reflection on how these relate and are relevant to the broad community of stakeholders. In order to discover more representative legitimacy in the changed environments of contemporary humanitarian response, this study suggests an exploration of existing but less well-travelled paths along the humanitarian narratives.

Until now, narrative pathways have directed and protected an identity based on the principles of humanity, neutrality, independence and impartiality that form the core of a 'universal' discourse within the network of stakeholders in the formal humanitarian system.[18] The following examination sets out how two of the Fundamental Principles of the Red Cross and Red Crescent Movement seen to be particular to the Movement[19] – Voluntary Service and Universality – have a shared meaning that is relevant across the broader humanitarian system and recognise a more inclusive network of influence in contemporary environments of conflict and complex emergency. To re-focus the lens calls us to step away from the prescriptive gaze that informs much of the contemporary narrative – one that primarily sees principles, codes and guidelines as being the modern codification of pre-existing rules, rather than the aspirational construction of a messier, more human 'spirit' to cooperate and protect. It presents a less exceptional expression of purpose and practice with the aim of providing fresh vitality to a contested discourse and the opportunity to access a prosocial space for effective cooperation in situations of crisis. The search is for ways to 'rehumanise' the humanitarian narratives that can lead to a more inclusive, more representative and more relevant discourse on the meaning and function of the humanitarian identity: in short, ways to establish better humanitarian relations.

In contrast to most studies on questions of the humanitarian space, this book does not argue that there is a loss of space. Rather, it suggests that the loss of relevance, representation and trust has meant that access to the space for discourse has changed. Changed structures in the socio-political environment of humanitarian action, formed from the competing forces of globalisation and increasing state regulation at the turn of the twenty-first century,[20] has meant that entrances and exits to this discursive space have been re-situated, leaving dislocated narratives echoing inside a chamber whose construction was formed by an architectural plan determined by, and contingent on, the authority of its original designers. Over the past thirty years, geopolitical shifts have led to changes in the authorising environment and the actors that respond to them.[21] The institutionalisation of the sector which developed following paradigms of the 'liberal peace' that dominated the Western political narratives in the early years of the twenty-first century[22] has meant the norms and values of the formal system in a changing environment are less readily identified by a larger and more diverse set of stakeholders, and 'are no longer able to instil a sense of relevance and trust in aid recipients'.[23] This book argues that loss of relevance and trust has restricted access to a discursive space for prosocial action, and that exclusion from this space is a key factor driving the dysfunctional humanitarian environment. It seeks to resolve the tensions through transforming what is at present a space of contesting discourse into a space for common articulation,[24] at least along the borders of power and common survival that situations of humanitarian emergency present.

HUMANITARIAN PRAXIS

Whilst the book reflects on the opportunities and challenges embodied by practice in the field, it suggests that resolutions to the problems of access and identity are found through philosophical understandings of 'praxis' that re-orientates the pragmatism of its function and directs the discussion towards a shared meaning that is relevant to all its stakeholders. An engagement with praxis directs access to a conversation that pragmatism shares with theory, 'an extended and open dialogue which pre-supposes a background of inter-subjective agreement and a tacit sense of relevance'[25] that is not the exceptional purview of humanitarian professionals alone. This facilitates discourse in a space that harbours the middle ground between what Richard Bernstein refers to as the traditional philosophical extremes of objectivism and essentialism and the opposite extremes of scepticism, relativism and nihilism[26], leading to a narrative that is more modest: one that is more uncertain and less sure of itself, but which is well-anchored in a shared and stable history. This avoids direction towards some form of humanitarian idealism but instead embraces a discourse that is messier and more human,[27] distanced from the 'argumentative finesse' which Bernstein sees as hobbling the progress of modern approaches. To this end, the book engages with some of the traditional philosophical approaches which endorse and challenge the narratives (Georg Hegel in chapter 3; Immanuel Kant in chapter 6), and acknowledges the 'politics of humanity' which has for long been disowned by the sector[28] but towards which recent scholarship calls for an honest recognition.[29]

To understand praxis as an embodiment of purpose and practice in the niche, the analysis considers arguments presented by Michel Foucault, who sees language as not only a conduit of meaning, but as an enactment or 'discourse practice'.[30] Foucault's ideas endorse the unstable interpretation of practices even when performed within the frames of a common purpose: practices which *represent* the world in specific ways and according to specific interpretations.[31] The differing approaches to theories of identity and practice presented in the book indicate that representations are mediated by the environment and thereby offer opportunities that can change the environment, 'as well as the ideas that individually and collectively people hold about the world'.[32] Practices can change collective thinking, and so 'good' practices can offer 'good' collective thinking.[33] Examinations in the case studies provide evidence of how constructions of the humanitarian narrative can harbour a partisan political direction for 'good' collective thinking.

Chapters 4–5 highlight the opportunities that emerge from a changed discourse about the nature of 'representation' that auxiliary voluntary service might bring if we distance arguments away from the binary nature of the discussions referred to earlier. Once we acknowledge the contingent nature of practices, this opens the possibility for the legitimation of multiple spaces in which the common humanitarian purpose can interact. Emanuel Adler and Vincent Pouliot give the example of a single event (the G8 summit) as a practice which indicates there can be multiple 'practices' or multiple niches, all with a common pattern.[34] The limitations of the humanitarian niche and the role of auxiliary voluntary service within it might be considered as a microcosm of a greater collective practice in the larger humanitarian arena, which by virtue of the restrictions to its purpose may be more functional. This book argues that if the identities of those in the niche become mainstream and part of the macrocosm, then they lose legitimacy and risk becoming absorbed *as* state or corporate 'practice' instead of an independent auxiliary to it.

Whilst the analysis examines influences and searches for solutions that are applicable across the broad humanitarian sector, the lens of study is purposely focused on the national rather than the global environment of humanitarian practice. The assumptions presented are that a 'domestic' scope of action which is relevant, focused and achievable provides greater opportunity for mutual support and the building of trust to enable more confident, secured access to the space for participation and representation.[35] Furthermore, the study looks at volunteering as a specific form of helping behaviour – that of people devoting substantial amounts of time and energy to help others with whom they have no personal or political bonds of obligation. This concept of the un-coerced and non-coercive nature of voluntary service is important to understand the arguments presented in the following chapters and takes precedence over other motivations traditionally associated with voluntary service, such as questions related to a 'free gift'[36] and the absence of financial remuneration. Ontologically linked to this are the understandings of what a volunteer auxiliary represents and how the voluntary profile is represented in the contexts under study here. Scholars of social psychology observe that volunteering can be conceived as being at once both an individual as well as a collective phenomenon.[37] This makes for a complex space, operating within a discourse of *cooperation* rather than *contestation* – a place for prosocial behaviour that is ready to assist across group boundaries.[38] Providing an understanding of the hybrid nature of this space and the opportunities its complexities offer forms the analytical direction of this book. The complexities in this socio-political space of participation must be understood through the lens of lived experience as much as through theoretical consideration. Chapter 2 begins this examination by considering the part that voluntary service and volunteers plays in the complex fabric of this prosocial space.

Chapter 2

Voluntary Service

Volunteering is much more than simply the giving of time for some particular purpose. In fact, as a cultural and economic phenomenon, volunteering is part of the way societies are organized, how they allocate social responsibilities, and how much engagement and participation they expect from citizens.[1]

Formal reference to voluntary service adopted by the UN General Assembly in 2002 states that 'The terms *volunteering, volunteerism* and *voluntary activities* refer to a wide range of activities . . . undertaken of free will, for the general public good and where monetary reward is not the principal motivating factor'.[2] The study by Helmut Anheier and Lester Salamon referred to in the epigraph in the beginning of the chapter defines volunteers as 'individuals who reach out beyond the confines of paid employment and normal responsibilities to contribute in different ways without expectation of profit or reward in the belief that their activities are beneficial to the community as well as satisfying to themselves'.[3] Outside the scope of volunteering for the state and social services (e.g. volunteer armies, village associations and mutual caring work), or for the church (e.g. voluntary laypersons), their study associates the birth of the concept of the modern volunteer movement with the creation of the Red Cross.[4] In his commentaries on the Fundamental Principles of the Red Cross, one of the leading figures in guiding definition and formulation of the Movement's principles, Jean Pictet[5] defends payment for the performance of voluntary work, acknowledging that

> since most people cannot work for nothing and since the Red Cross needs professional and specialized workers, sometimes with very high qualifications, part of the personnel, generally speaking, has to consist of paid employees . . . the work may preserve its voluntary character even though it is paid for. . . . The

21

important thing is that the work carried out for the Red Cross shall be voluntary. Whether it is paid for or not is a secondary consideration.[6]

The shift of emphasis away from interpretations of volunteering seen as primarily motivated by the dismissal of economic gain is key to the ontological reframing of voluntary service argued here. Rather, the emphasis is on uncoerced cooperation to bring help within and across communities in need. Voluntary service is considered a specific form of 'helping behaviour' led by people devoting substantial amounts of time and energy to helping others with whom they have no bonds or connection *to oblige* them to help.[7] Volunteering can be conceived as being an individual as well as a collective phenomenon, combining the agency of both, acting together at the same time for a common goal.[8] This means it occupies a complex and agential space, referred to in this book as a *niche*. The arguments presented here examine the nature and location of this hybrid space and explore a re-framing of its discourse that offers a more nuanced picture of its expression as part of humanity's social nature. More specifically, it considers human sociality in the context of complex humanitarian emergencies in which the driving forces of human sociality remain stable, guided by a common purpose (humanitarian emergency response) and shared cultural-historical narratives (cultural expressions of voluntary service and the history of principled humanitarian action, formalised normatively since the founding of the ICRC in 1863).

INSTITUTION AND ORGANISATION: WHAT IS A VOLUNTEER?

As noted earlier, studies on the voluntary sector have identified that volunteering is much more than simply the giving of time for some particular purpose but is part of the way societies are organised, how social responsibilities are allocated, and a process through which expectations on the level of engagement amongst members of the community are gauged.[9] A report commissioned by the IFRC on the role of volunteers remarks:

> Volunteering is neither a panacea nor a simple proposition. The contributions that volunteering makes needs to be situated in the context of complex and interdependent social, political, economic and cultural forces that are going through dramatic changes and are constantly reshaping who volunteers, why they volunteer, how they are able to engage and what they are able to accomplish.[10]

The standard definition of volunteering in the Global North typically tends to have three pillars: that it is done under free will; that it benefits the community in some way, beyond the personal or family circles of the volunteers;

and that it is not done primarily for material or financial gain.[11] How far these prosocial drivers form a common expression and how far they are transferable across the humanitarian identity are central to my arguments for the construction of a shared discursive space.

For more than 150 years the International Red Cross and Red Crescent Movement has pioneered volunteering and organised volunteers for humanitarian assistance, to alleviate suffering and poverty.[12] Core to guiding the humanitarian work of the RCRC Movement was the adoption of its seven 'Fundamental Principles' at the Vienna Conference in 1965.[13] Jean Pictet defined each principle as 'a rule, based upon judgement and experience, which is adopted by a *community* to guide its conduct'.[14] The Fundamental Principle of 'Voluntary Service' in its contemporary wording states that 'the International Red Cross and Red Crescent Movement is a voluntary relief movement not prompted in any manner by desire for gain'.[15] The first statement highlights the importance of a common consensus based on judgement and experience rather than the prescription of rules. The second emphasises the selfless, or 'disinterested', motivation behind humanitarian voluntary service – the significance of which to arguments in the book are analysed in chapter 6.

In his commentary on the Fundamental Principles of the Movement, Pictet makes it clear that he prefers the English title 'voluntary service' rather than the French title 'caractère bénévole' ('benevolent character') which was adopted at the Vienna Conference.[16] The interpretation of the latter term in French refers to persons who donate their services and work without payment. The English word 'volunteer' ('volontaire' in French) refers to someone who works of his own free will, without external compulsion – and not necessarily one who is not paid.[17] He illustrates the important nuances of this distinction, and refers to the sense of personal responsibility that volunteering takes in the form of a commitment which carries with it obligations from which the volunteer feels committed to in principle and action once he has signed up – that is to say, 'he is obliged to keep his word'.[18]

Historical records give abundant evidence of professional services offered in response to crises that were considered as voluntary but for which these services were paid. In a study of the humanitarian response of the British National Society for the Sick and Wounded in War during the Franco-Prussian War from 1870–1871, Gill states that medical professionals working as volunteers were granted financial recompense for their work.[19] An analysis of internal documents held by Médecins Sans Frontièrs (MSF) France and MSF Switzerland observes that during the first decade after its foundation, the organisation's identity was formed by a collective ethos defined by its original charter that 'required of each of them an individual commitment and seemed to value a spirit of selflessness and vocation'.[20] As with the original French text of the Fundamental Principles of the Movement, the term 'bénévole' was used to convey this spirit of vocation, rather than the term 'volontaire', giving emphasis to a motivation driven not by personal or collective reward, but as a matter of personal choice and collective responsibility. Against a background of growing geopolitical insecurity and expanding membership, the analysis by Abu Sa'da and Crombé marks a growing shift in the debates towards alignment with the institutional identities of the private sector, notably in relation to the demand for an increasingly 'professionalised' duty of care towards its members.[21] These led to a revision of the MSF charter in 1991,[22] where for the first time the word 'volunteer' was officially used in the text, making the distinction between 'bénévole' and the salaried employee.[23] The authors note an incremental lack of distinction in these reports, where the term 'volunteer' came to refer to all professionals who engage with the organisation and become part of its membership.[24] Whilst the focus of the study on MSF relates specifically to managing the balance between institutional and individual responsibility in situations of danger on the field, the underlying call for a return to a sense of social responsibility expressed in its original charter mirrors the direction of arguments presented in this book, towards which further connections are made in chapters 7 and 8.

The question of remuneration is a recurring debate in specialist scholarship on the voluntary sector as well as in organisational policy. The report by Shaun Hazeldine and Matt Baillie Smith observes that the question of how volunteering is remunerated and rewarded is a critical feature of its changing meanings and practices. It also remarks that this issue needs to be approached with care:

> Mainstream definitions of volunteering often require that pecuniary motivation is not the main driver, and there is growing critical commentary on the pitfalls of 'paid' volunteering (e.g. Wilson 2007, Lewis 2014 p. 38). But remuneration of volunteering is more complex than headlines sometimes allow, and needs to [be] explored in its specific contexts.[25]

My arguments acknowledge the tensions in the volunteer identity and the contingencies of context. As the archival studies in chapter 6 and the case studies in chapter 7 make apparent, there is a diverse interpretation of the term volunteer, even within the institutional narratives of the humanitarian sector. The analytical arguments in this book offer to resolve this by considering voluntary service as 'praxis' that presents discussions around a vocational 'spirit' of service and is less concerned with the mechanics of its practice in differing contexts.

As the study by Anheier and Salamon observes, volunteering is much more than simply the giving of time for some particular purpose. Quoting from the IFRC, their study defines volunteers as 'individuals who reach out beyond the confines of paid employment and normal responsibilities to contribute in different ways without expectation of profit or reward in the belief that their activities are beneficial to the community as well as satisfying to themselves'.[26] The authors remark that in European countries, such as Sweden and Germany, volunteers were regarded as amateurish 'do-gooders': 'relics of the past to be replaced by paid professional staff capable of performing tasks more effectively and efficiently'.[27] They note that in the former socialist countries of Central and Eastern Europe, the very concept of volunteering became almost obsolete following the collapse of communism during which period there were involuntary state and party requirements to contribute time and efforts freely for some common social, cultural or political cause. Their study finds that in developing countries, a great diversity of indigenous forms of volunteering coexists with Western ways, citing examples in Nigeria and Ghana where village associations of volunteers can be found in nearly every rural and urban community, '(r)ooted in the local culture, they provide communal services and assistance in times of need'.[28] In their study for the IFRC, Hazeldine and Baillie Smith report that several of the national Red Cross and Red Crescent societies regarded volunteering as an intrinsic part of their culture, naming particular traditions of volunteering that includes *Bayanihan* or *Alayon* in the Philippines, *Siasanana* in Madagascar, *ikibiri* in Burundi and *Al Huda* in Palestine.[29] Anheier and Salamon note the cultural and political differences in their cross-national surveys and observe that one source of confusion is tied to personal motivations and dispositions, especially when volunteers are paid to perform or present advocacy functions.

The importance of context and culture are significant influences on the identities of volunteers in all these reports and this calls for recognition of the position voluntary identities hold in crafting the political and social fabric of the environments where they work. The differing political and social affiliations that are constructed offer a place for both cooperation and contention in the spaces they occupy. My discussions with volunteers on the field have expressed varying understandings of the notion of volunteering. Some have seen this as an exclusive 'club' for those who can afford to be a member. Others are discouraged by the belief that work is unremunerated, as well as by variations in the status of volunteers in their respective communities. In environments of crisis, this was often seen as a factor that united communities across social divides, where everyone was made to feel welcome. In other, less critical, situations, some communities saw volunteers as members of an exclusive 'club', open to those who could afford to be a member. Opportunities emerging from this dynamic are examined in chapter 8. First, the study turns to consider the nature of collaborative spaces in the sector and begins with positioning how it understands the distinction between 'institutions' and 'organisations' in its analysis.

Organisational Spaces for Participation

This book has already made references to the concept of institutions and the mixed associations that the term 'institution' brings. This term is often linked to 'organisation' and the differences between the two are often indistinct. Indeed, the formulations of the Fundamental Principles of the Red Cross and Red Crescent Movement themselves use the two terms almost interchangeably, where the principle of Universality states: 'The Red Cross is a world-wide *institution* in which all Societies have equal status and share equal responsibilities and duties in helping each other', and yet where the principle of Voluntary Service states that 'The Red Cross is a voluntary relief *organization* not prompted in any manner by desire for gain'.[30] But the difference is an important one, which, I argue, lies at the heart of the humanitarian identity in the niche and its relationship with authority. The distinction rests with an understanding of the social nature of the space and the harbouring of a capability to represent and be relevant to both an individual and a collective identity: the organisation of a spirit of social responsibility where the humanitarian purpose and its practices are part of the design of social institutions.

Viewed in realist terms, activities in the niche are transactional and functional, with expectations of reciprocity and more general patterns of social exchange. This is an approach challenged by constructivist and post-modernist interpretations of the motivations behind volunteering, who view its values as being rooted in more selfless motivational drives.[31] My arguments consider a position between the two that explores a 'common humanity' where purposes and practices reify a prosocial bridge to enable inter-group cooperation and trust. Examples from Myanmar presented in chapter 7 give evidence of humanitarian interaction with a state whose authority was seen to focus primarily on its own survival but where recognition of authority at a central level was reciprocated by cooperative access at the regional level. In her study of reciprocity norms, Elinor Ostrom observes that individuals tend to react to the positive actions of others with positive responses, and vice versa. 'Human beings do not inherit reciprocity norms through a biological process (though they may acquire cultural norms through sociological processes). The argument is more subtle. Individuals inherit *a capacity to learn*'.[32] This indicates that agency for cooperation and community cohesion emerges from participation in a prosocial space in which interconnected discussion offers opportunities to learn.[33]

Prosocial motives are rooted in the belief that we share a common bond with the outgroup.[34] The book seeks to identify opportunities to reify this common bond within the boundaries of a defined humanitarian space. The recognition of boundaries in the niche calls for acknowledged limitations to action and authority within this prosocial space. In compensation for accepting these boundaries, my arguments urge a robust acknowledgement of the need for autonomy and the right to challenge on behalf of the community. The arguments for autonomy provided here are not linked to debates around the power-dependency nexus which feature prominently in much of contemporary scholarship on the aid-development divide,[35] but are linked to more normative, human pre-conditions. Predominant amongst these is the demand for mutual respect and trust.[36] Requests for help and the reciprocal offer of a 'helping hand' are seen in this respect as 'solicited support', regarded as an autonomous request for assistance and cooperation, instead of the passive, negative associations of unsolicited aid, seen as antithetical to notions of dignity and self-respect.[37] Therefore, critical to the understandings of voluntary service as an autonomous auxiliary in my study is the ability to choose. The ontological complexity being untangled derives from the contradictions apparent in understandings of a spontaneous, *voluntary obligation* to respond to populations in distress which, I argue, is inseparable from the social organisation of the identities presented in this book. The central aim is to position a narrative that translates this 'niche' of humanitarian space as the place for least-compromise but most cooperation. It searches opportunities for discourse around a status-neutral space that repositions some of the core concepts in humanitarian narratives and places its actors as auxiliaries to public services, but which do not devolve responsibility from the state being what Jennifer Rubenstein terms the 'first best actors' in protecting its citizens.[38] Rather than confronting established power and contesting its authority, the arguments presented here search for the capabilities to participate with it in the humanitarian space and share in the obligation to provide a common good. My reasoning here draws on Martha Nussbaum's interpretation of the Capability Approach, originally presented by Amartya Sen as a philosophical approach to guide work in the sector of international development.[39] This approach accepts hierarchies and imbalances of power but supports the location of a middle ground that gives access to a shared discourse, able to recognise and legitimate the complementary tensions this imbalance presents.

Expressions of this middle ground are evident in practitioner studies and the growing platforms for online discussion where paths of navigation along the complex social and political frontiers in humanitarian action are frequently charted.[40] Documented experiences on the field support the critical identification of a measured and principled engagement with this space, and anecdotal accounts of the engagement of humanitarian volunteers across political boundaries are well verified.[41] Since the English publication of Arnold van Gennep's book *The Rites of Passage* in 1960, academic studies have indicated the existence of a 'liminal' space where trusted interaction occurs,[42] and these arguments form the basis of the humanitarian identity presented in the chapters that follow.

Chapter 3

Evolving Expressions
of Humanitarian Space

In the opening chapter, I argued that an expansion of humanitarian identities in environments of crisis has lost relevance amidst competing tensions and is no longer representative of the community of stakeholders. Then chapter 2 situated the focus on how an identity of voluntary service can shape a common discursive space. This chapter explores this shared identity and the opportunities for a space of common discourse. It considers the nature of spaces for participation.

In his examination of the contingent nature of humanitarianism, Henry Radice engages with the question of humanitarian identity by linking discussions with International Political Theory, revealing the interdependence between the ethical and the political dimensions of humanitarian response.[1] By interpreting the humanitarian identity through a variety of different disciplinary perspectives (international law; development; sociology and anthropology) his study develops new understandings of humanitarians which he sees as 'frequently discussed but little understood'.[2] Radice declares in his study that 'humanitarian debates are really discussions about how best to honour our human identity'.[3] This is a useful way to frame the discussions in the chapters that follow, aiming to identify a human capacity to trust and have access to an honourable discourse: that is to say, one of honest and transparent engagement with all stakeholders in a crisis. This chapter examines expressions of voluntary service across historical and political cultures. It focuses on two competing frames which are at the foundation of the tensions in identity inside humanitarian space: (1) notions of power and authority in the arena of humanitarian action and (2) notions of free choice as a driver towards action to protect the welfare and dignity of fellow humans. The opening section reviews some of the historical antecedents that inform contemporary debates about the nature of humanitarian voluntary service and which position the context in which arguments in my book towards a space for prosocial action take place. It begins with an overview of this historical-cultural expression through the interpretive lenses of Western scholarship and practice which dominate the construction of contemporary paradigms of humanitarian action.

EARLY IDENTIFICATIONS

Understanding the historical narratives is an essential tool for the sound evaluation and analysis of any examination in the social sciences. This is especially important when analysing the complex and contesting drivers of humanitarian action in modern environments, where 'cultural and religious crises have helped undermine the fundamental humanitarian principles by contesting their universality' and where humanitarian action has suffered as a result.[4] Many working in the sector of humanitarian aid see the principles of neutrality, impartiality and independence as being an essential and pre-existing part of the expression of 'humanity' and are universally applicable regardless of context or culture. However, to many analysts, they were established – like the organisations themselves – at a particular historical juncture and so may represent an ethos that is questioned or rejected by stakeholders outside of the traditions wherein they were established.[5]

The growth in the unestablished power of the market in the second half of the twentieth century that was formerly part of the political-economic strategies in foreign affairs, and framed the agenda in a post-colonial period of international development has to some extent been uncoupled from the narratives of contemporary aid and development.[6] However, the reality of some recent practices in the sectors has meant that associations remain closely linked, with private contractors engaged instead by elements of established power seen to be acting with their own commercial interests in the environments of humanitarian emergency.[7] Changes in the authorising environment mentioned earlier, together with dynamic alterations in the way news and information is shared in our digital age, have meant a growing consciousness of practice and consequences across the broader stakeholder community. Bertrand Taithe remarks on the growing awareness of how history informs humanitarian practices and observes that this historical consciousness has constructed semantic obstacles to inclusive understandings of the term 'humanitarian'.[8] He argues that associations of the term with exceptional identities in history present the appearance of a quasi-ideology in its modern expression, adding to the blurred relationship between humanitarianism and human rights. In my study, this translates as a call for engagement with a more modest iteration of the humanitarian identity that is aware of this ideological risk. This call is different from a return to some imagined golden age of universal humanitarian expression, which has never existed.[9] As indicated in chapter 1, scholars dispute the existence of any universally recognised understanding of the term 'humanitarian', or of any formal and uniform 'system' that houses it.[10] The recent report by ALNAP on the State of the Humanitarian System defines the humanitarian system as 'the network of inter-connected institutional and operational entities that receive funds, directly or indirectly from public donors and private sources, to enhance, support or substitute for in-country responses in the provision of humanitarian assistance and protection to a population in crisis'.[11] However, whilst recognising this diversity of stakeholder interests, my study argues that a shared and universal 'spirit' to attend to the welfare and rescue of humans in distress is a universal expression across history and cultures.

Associations with modern notions of humanitarianism lead back to the earliest times. There are documented examples of acts of human welfare in ancient Assyrian history, and accounts of the spontaneous human urge to help others in distress appear frequently in the earliest written records.[12] For the Romans, 'humanity' was linked to education and knowledge and was used in this sense to distinguish the human being from others in the animal world.[13] Other accounts in scholarship trace the origins of modern humanitarianism back to the Spanish colonisation of the Americas in the late fifteenth century and to the moral and theological debates provoked in reaction to the genocidal violence inflicted upon indigenous populations under the *encomienda* system of slavery.[14] Modern expressions of the African philosophy of 'ubuntu',[15] described as 'the capacity in an African culture to express compassion reciprocity, dignity, humanity and mutuality in the interests of building and maintaining communities with justice and mutual caring',[16] have their origins in ancient cultural practices of the continent long pre-dating modern times. In 'The Humanity of Thucydides', Clifford Orwin reconsiders Thucydides's work as characterised by a deep humanity, which he defines as a sympathy for the victims of power and fortune.[17] Within the ancient classical philosophies, it is the 'cosmopolitanism' of the Stoics that is often represented as most closely associated with modern conceptions. However, as Samuel Moyn notes, 'neither the cosmopolitanism of the Stoics nor the original concept of humanity were remotely similar to current versions'.[18]

Taithe argues that the development of the humanitarian narrative cannot be separated from its religious sources, notably in their formulations from an emotional response to pain, pity and compassion. He observes that, to the ancients, pity was essentially a 'cognitively assessed' emotion 'overriding the initial repulsion or desire to avoid the undeserved misfortune of others'.[19] He considers that the theme of pity, later Christianised and modified as compassion or sympathy, became a central theme in eighteenth-century philosophy.[20]

Here a focus is often brought to the political movements of the Protestant Reformation, and the movement for the abolition of slavery by the Quakers and religiously inspired philanthropists in the eighteenth and nineteenth centuries, protesting against the cruelties done to slaves and against structural injustices violating principles of human dignity.[21] Dunant's vision after the Battle of Solferino, in 1859, invoked a more universalist expression compared with the texts produced by slavery abolitionists, breaking away from the individualism of compassion and its single purpose (the abolition of slavery in one place, at one time), 'to redefine the parameters of a new universalism embarking on an open-ended quest'.[22] The Humanitarian Policy Group report into the history of the humanitarian system concurs that, in its broadest sense, 'humanitarian' action can be traced through hundreds of years of history across the world.[23] It includes religion amongst the two most widely cited forces of influence, the other being around articulation of the laws of war:

> Christian ideas of charity have been particularly important in Europe and North America, and scholarship has emphasised the importance of charitable gestures in other religions, including notably the tradition of *zakat* in Islam, one of several ways in which Islamic duty involves assisting others (Ghandour, 2002; Benthall and Bellion-Jourdan, 2003; Krafess, 2005). Laws of war or limits on the acceptable conduct of war were adopted in ancient Greece and Rome; articulated in The Art of War ascribed to Sun Tzu in Warring States China; promoted by Saladin in the Middle East in the 1100s; taught to Swedish soldiers by Gustavus Adolphus in the 1600s; and recognised in the tenets of Hinduism, Islam and Judaism.[24]

It is important to note that, while historians agree that expressions of 'humanitarianism' and associated identities in the Global North have its origins in ideas of Christian pity and Enlightenment sympathy, crafted during the period of colonial expansion in the nineteenth century, this developed independently from modern understandings of rights talk.[25] Such expressions entered into the language of the international system in the inter-war years following the establishment of the League of Nations in 1920, with its concern over the trafficking of women and the cause of refugees, but Moyn considers it mistaken to conceive of these as human rights organisations.[26] He observes that an external codification of *Human Rights* is recent and contingent, linked to the history of the utopian approaches and 'the heartfelt desire to make the world a better place'[27] and not historically linked to nineteenth-century expressions of humanitarianism understood following the founding of ICRC in 1863 and the League of Red Cross Societies, in 1919. Michael Barnett and Thomas Weiss see the development of modern notions of humanitarianism in three phases, first from 1859 to 1945, then the post-war period from 1945 to 1989, and from 1989 to present, with the first period of humanitarian reforms following the Treaty of Versailles which regulated the end of the First World War.[28] The League of Nations established at that time initiated the creation of international organisations to address humanitarian issues and was a central part of US President Woodrow Wilson's vision of international reform. As well as being the first permanent international organisation whose mission was to maintain world peace through collective security, the League's Covenant and related treaties covered issues including labour conditions, the treatment of indigenous inhabitants in colonial territories and the protection of minorities and displaced people in Europe.[29]

Discussions now turn to the nature of the universal spirit which I have outlined earlier. This considers how the emotional forces of pity, compassion and sympathy have been harnessed by authority to appoint a sense of shared identities in the changing historical environments and are harnessed within the socio-political fabric of the community.

The Enchanted Ages of Humanitarianism

Scholars such as Charles Taylor and Iain Wilkinson[30] see modern humanitarianism in the Western traditions being narrowly conceived as a specific form of civil action, guided by core principles drawn up from expressions of the Protestant Reformation in the sixteenth century, and whose antecedents Taylor dates to the 'proto-Reformation' of the Lollards in fourteenth-century Britain.[31] This was a period when profound changes in spiritual outlook in medieval and early-modern Europe meant that the space for 'magical practices' as a form of human power were seen to have no role in the secular world of modern western philosophies.[32] According to Taylor, this marked a fundamental re-orientation in terms of understanding who we are and who we represent, leading to ontological reconsiderations of the moral space humanity inhabits. It dismissed notions of the cosmic forces that were a translation of the meaning of life in the Graeco-Roman Classical Age, and sought out a more humble, less enchanted, quest to explain the human condition. This new space shifted fatalist thinking of the pre-modern age towards reflection on what an ordinary (non-cosmic) life means and what agency the human individual plays in creating for itself a life worth living: 'a space in which questions arise about what is good or bad, what is worth doing and what not'.[33]

Michael Barnett's study on the history of humanitarianism in the modern period considers the tensions that arose from the legacies of earlier articulations of humanitarian action, formed from the background of the eighteenth-century philosophy of the European Enlightenment and the processes of Western colonisation in the nineteenth century.[34] He refers to this as the 'first age' of humanitarianism, marked by a sense of superiority and paternalism which drove the mission to educate and 'civilise' the populations of the territories they occupied.[35] This was followed by what he calls a 'second age' of liberal humanitarianism arriving in the wake of decolonisation and the end of the Second World War. This marked a more democratic, inclusive phase of international aid and development, but whose benefits were tempered by a growing culture of institutionalisation that gave rise to rules for professional practice and accountability which reinforced a distancing of the agency of affected populations. Barnett criticises the way in which contemporary international humanitarian action has retained much of the imperialist and colonialist legacies of its earlier expression. He concludes with definition of a 'third age', characterised by the equally destructive forces of the intra-state conflicts following the end of the Cold War, and the clash of ideas which has drawn the civilian populations into being an unwilling but crucial part in the struggle for power. My earlier study remarks on how this changed environment influenced the planning and practice of humanitarian assistance to affected populations in the period following the end of the Cold War, and suggests that we have now entered a 'fourth age' marked by a growing dissatisfaction with the statist formations that have framed power and authority in the previous periods.[36] Recent scholarship has emphasised the need to recognise the existence of other approaches than the 'classical' paradigm that frame the dominant narrative. Dorothea Hilhorst cites evidence from surveys of war in Angola that most humanitarian assistance fell outside of the dominant classical paradigm and was local and non-traditional.[37] Her study refers to the 'resilience' paradigm which she sees as occupying an important but unrecognised place in the contemporary narratives. Dualta Roughneen argues for a 'subsidiarity' approach which calls for priority to be given to supporting a local response to crisis.[38] In all of these, the concern is around the lack of trust and representation in contemporary models of international humanitarian response.

With particular significance to discussions around trust in a moral platform in the chapters that follow, Taylor sees that the force of two moral ideas developed in the modern period: the significance of ordinary life and the idea of universal benevolence. He considers that the first has made issues of life itself and the avoidance of suffering of supreme importance, while the second imposes the obligation to secure them universally: both have become deeply anchored in our moral culture.[39] Chapter 1 has indicated the mistrust and questioned legitimacy of a universally defined moral platform arising from the confused identities of humanitarian responses seen to be driven by the political forces spearheading the conflicts at the turn of this century. Critics of the monocular approaches to America's 'war on terror' and the overthrow of autocratic regimes from which these conflicts arose urged a turning of the lens whereby 'the fundamental principles of humanitarian action should offer a framework for principled engagement with governments in situations of conflict'.[40] This calls for recognition of national authority and state responsibility[41] and a re-identification of the space in which all those responding to humanitarian emergencies use legitimised practice and principles to inform their engagement with national actors in times of crisis. The difficulties of engagement are emphasised by Barnett's arguments about the evolution of the increasingly diverse nature of 'humanitarianisms', defined by the tensions of destruction, production and compassion, interacting in different ways, and each with its own dominance at different times, giving changing shapes to the environment and its humanitarian space.[42] These humanitarian philosophies extended beyond the traditional confines of urgent care and survival towards expressions in the growing arena of rights-based entitlements, framed within the political democracies of the liberal peace.

This expansion of the humanitarian arena beyond the emergency response of urgent care and survival was problematic for these frontline humanitarian agencies, whose minimalist aims were obscured by the maximalist aims of the rights-based arena. Scholars such as David Rieff and Kurt Mills consider that the classical humanitarian identity became absorbed within the utopian ambitions of the larger humanitarian arena.[43] Its inhabitants are no longer seen to be independent or neutral and have lost the moral authority that lies in the 'modesty' of the classical humanitarian idea – a recognition of the fundamental dignity and value of common humanity. I argue that a loss of this 'moral space' – which Taylor sees critical to identifying 'a sense of ourselves'[44] – has restricted access to a common discourse, having been excluded by the institutional hierarchies formed from its earlier historical expressions, and alienated by less readily shared formulations of modern rights-based narratives. Wilkinson asserts that contemporary debates remain stifled by the way 'humanitarianism' is institutionalised or incorporated into the apparatus of state and global international organisations and urges a refreshment of the discussion by focusing on a broader recognition of the local agencies which give relevance to the humanitarian expression.[45] It is towards a re-acknowledgement of the *humility* of expression of the classical humanitarian idea that the arguments in this chapter direct attention and suggests that in the modesty of its expectations, there lies a more egalitarian space for shared action. Modern scholarship has argued that in order for there to be popular legitimacy, the locus of this space must move away from the exceptional formations of contemporary humanitarian response towards a place that prioritises responsibility towards local people[46] – a direction endorsed by practitioners and policymakers at the World Humanitarian Summit in 2016, convened by the UN Secretary General in response to the increasing inability of the international arena to protect populations in environments of contemporary conflict and complex emergency.[47] The debate needs to extend its analysis beyond the confines of institutionalised Western

humanitarian practices and look at the swirl of forces defining expressions
of humanitarianism in our own era.[48]

Whilst religious associations remained prominent in the literature of
the Global North until the Second World War, over the post-war period,
contemporary western scholarship and policy documents rarely referred
to the role of religion in aid and development literature, and this absence
remained true until the turn of the twenty-first century.[49] It was foreseen
that as societies modernise, religious institutions would lose their social
significance and become an irrelevance to work and studies in the sector of
international development. Whilst this absence was less pronounced in the
literature of some faith-based agencies in the humanitarian sector, where
religious drivers towards notions of charity was a less self-conscious part
of their organisational history, issues of religion and faith remained a
taboo subject for most donors and policymakers at an institutional level.[50]
This started to change with the rise of the politics of identity, which gained
expression following the 1979 Iranian Revolution and the concomitant
rise in evangelical conservatism in the United States.[51] Religion as an
identity trend was consolidated following the collapse in communism and
the rise in religious institutions following the democratic transitions in
Eastern Europe, the Americas and Southern Africa. Religious identity as
a political force was brought to global prominence following the terrorist
bombings in the United States in 2001 and American declarations of a
'war on terror'.

Wilkinson suggests that in order to set contemporary expressions of
humanitarianism into analytical relief, there needs to be a carefully elaborated
account of their histories. He criticises the tendency for IR scholarship to
treat humanitarianism as no more than a form of ideology or politics which
see its influence resting primarily in the way its practices and ideals are
incorporated into the design of social institutions. Instead, he prefers to adopt
the sociological approaches of theorists which see modern humanitarianism
and its cultures being an embodiment of the social life of communities and
expressions of human sociality.[52]

In addressing the criticism presented in chapter 1 that humanitarian identities have become institutionalised or incorporated into the apparatus of state,
it is necessary to examine the intersubjective nature of these places of interaction. This requires consideration of the different semantic understandings
of an institution and an organisation that connect the tensions of formal and
informal – the control and accountability of the professional with the goal-
driven vocation of the amateur[53] – and provide shared access to the space. It
means a redirection of the institutional gaze to locate space for a common
discourse relatively free from the institutional biases referred to in chapter 1.
A report for the IFRC compiled by the Feinstein International Center points

out the difference between the prescriptive rigidity of an institutional or corporate structure, and the membership dynamic of the IFRC, where 'open relationships, conversations and chatter are the oil in the federal machine. And this IFRC, with its multiplicity of languages, cultures and geography, needs to be constantly encouraging and inventing new ways to talk'.[54] This echoes the call for recognition of the value and 'creative messiness' such a membership structure can bring, recognising its strength in the contexts of its functional environment.

In a sociological study of the nature of institutions and organisations, Peter Rogers observes the interchangeability of the terms and critiques the lack of clarity from unexplained variations in their meaning. He sees understandings of 'institution' as most often falling into two groups. The first treats institutions as a broad process – an act of creation wherein institutions 'bring order to a thing' and become seen as an 'arrangement' or 'regulation' of an established order that is common-place and assumed.[55] They are also seen as an organisation or establishment with some form of charge. According to Rogers, 'The institution can thus also be defined in its general meaning as an association of people coming together as a group; but more than that, a grouping created for the promotion of some common object or collective outcome'.[56] This suggests the creation of a common outlook, but one that is regulated and regulatory. Rogers lists a number of institutions in his study, amongst which he includes charities and NGOs.[57]

A categorisation of identities is not the focus of my study, but rather the understanding of a space for particular humanitarian identities to be housed and protected. For this, a distinction is made between 'institutional space' and its 'organisational space', though both are closely interlinked. Rogers points to two semantic groups emerging from the term 'institution'. One he sees comprising a set of 'processual' relationships of individual and collective ideas 'which are commonly known'.[58] The other he sees as a grouping of individuals coming together into an organisational structure, with behavioural norms which are often messier in practice but more social, organic and dynamic. As an example of the way these two concepts are confused, Rogers uses this distinction to position the concept of 'family' as a semi-organised social unit, distinct from the characteristics of an institution with its more general 'institutional' ideas: what Ernest Burgess and Harvey Locke described as 'a varied and complex series of companionship oriented social relations'.[59] These oblige a commitment to formal and informal consensus that must not be conflated with the decision-making of individuals within the group. This requires recognition of its social-human agency, identified as being more *socially organised* than *institutionally regulated* and is a dynamic which my study sees as critical in determining the nature of cooperative interaction in the space being examined here.

Consideration of the humanitarian space occupied by the Red Cross and Red Crescent Movement provides a useful comparison in this regard. As indicated earlier, the RCRC Movement is a worldwide institution, currently comprising 192 National Societies,[60] with their own autonomy and separate management and governance structures (it is notable that the Movement is commonly referred to as the Red Cross or Red Crescent 'family' within both the institutional and organisational narratives). Under the institutional umbrella of the IFRC Secretariat, there is regulatory and governance authority to facilitate common approaches and share complementary capacities.[61] The success of this interaction relies on a formal recognition of the agency of its membership and the informal willingness of its members to follow a shared direction. The constructions of identity in the humanitarian niche presented in this book follow this location of a middle ground that balances the collective regulation of an institution with the dynamic nature of an organisation. This argues that organised humanitarian space must not be seen as the extension of a dominant trend, nor seen to be dominated by one. Rather, it is the organisation of an autonomous expression of individual and collective interests – a social organisation of the humanitarian institution. Within the disciplines of management and linguistics, this corresponds to a view of organisations as a form of institutionalised governance structures but with distinctive ways of doing, and with 'a specific character reflecting the value of the firm'.[62] This expression of a humanitarian community is mirrored across many of the international NGOs and organisational structures in contemporary aid and development environments, seen by them to be spaces for collaboration.[63]

The United Nations Volunteers (UNV) programme report on the International Year of the Volunteer, 2015 discusses the opportunities for new collaborative spaces which volunteers working in society can open up, and the variations in form and access through which the spaces offer participation.[64] The report divides these into 'invited spaces', 'closed spaces' and 'claimed spaces', each with their own rules of access and qualification for membership. Invited spaces are those where governance actors (public authority) invite participation and therefore are tasked to adopt some measures of the governance spaces they occupy. 'Closed' spaces are where rules of access are defined, and only certain people or groups qualify. 'Claimed' spaces are where those who are less powerful or excluded may claim space informally or through formal community associations. The UNV surveys show that when governments take the initiative to leverage volunteerism, most volunteer engagements take place in invited spaces. When people seize the initiative, the greater part of such engagements takes place in claimed spaces, at least in the beginning. In later stages some of the action may move to invited spaces. In both cases, whilst activities occur in all three spaces, volunteers seek to influence decision-making in closed spaces.[65] The significance of these multiple spaces becomes evident in the discussions on the discourse and empirical evidence in the case studies presented in chapter 7, which present the complex understandings of purpose and practice and the contesting narratives that differing interpretations of the contexts engage. The humanitarian identities being represented in this book acknowledge these multiple spaces and occupy a middle ground capable of organising individual and collective interests. This social organisation of the humanitarian initiative and its recognition of multiple spaces has special relevance to interpretations of the auxiliary identity and its relationship with political and institutional authority in the space. They raise questions about the nature of a humanitarian engagement with narratives that drive political and institutional (donor and policy) interests.

Amongst these multiple spaces, my arguments locate opportunities arising from the conflicting tensions that voluntary service and the notion of voluntary obligations entail. By acknowledging the place of voluntary service in the political identity of the contemporary humanitarian system, it recognises the legitimacy of its engagement with authority (the state) and its obligation to represent it as an auxiliary for protecting a principled humanitarian response in situations of complex emergency. By accepting that the 'spirit' of voluntary service entails an obligation to perform – to 'keep his word' to use Pictet's expression – then the nature of the relationship with an authority shifts from being independent, to a relationship of mutual dependence which embodies a shared purpose.[66] In his study of the social space of communities affected by gang violence, Tilman Schwarze engages with arguments presented by Henri Lefebvre and scholars of the 'spatial turn' that consider space as a social product, defined and produced through social relationships. This sees the concept of space not as a fixed and pre-defined 'container' that exists in and of itself, or as an a priori fact, but a place for the production of meaning and representation.[67] 'Abstract space' is a political as well as an ideological concept in Lefebvre's understanding, producing spaces of representation of both the political and the everyday life in its construction. This concept of the social construction of space and its place for producing meaning and representation helps inform the identity of the auxiliary relationship with state and other stakeholders. The social organisation of this relationship is discussed at the end of this chapter and further pursued in chapter 8. It is to the nature of the state, and considerations of how voluntary service can be understood in the frame of an autonomous auxiliary to certain public services of state, able to bridge the growing divide in trust and confidence in public authority, to which the following arguments in the book turn. This pays attention to its identification with community membership which this study sees as an essential expression of voluntary service.

The Auxiliary Identity of Voluntary Service

Arguments for an identity of the volunteer seen as auxiliary to authority and able to bridge divisions of trust may appear counterintuitive. Scholarship sees much of the tension in the spaces for voluntary action to stem from the conceptual twinning of volunteerism and social activism that mirrors the tensions of passion and compassion identified by Barnett in his 2011 study, referred earlier. The identification of volunteers with political authority is nothing new. After the Franco-Prussian War, aid work had achieved definition as a distinct vocation. ' "Expert" relief practices and protocols were increasingly regulated and conceived in official circles as auxiliaries to the regular army medical services, while a sense that aid work was a form of national duty threatened any notion that it sprung from the voluntarist dictates of conscience'.[68] Associations extended beyond the field of conflict into contexts of civil society, notable in the same period by the activism of the abolitionist movement mentioned earlier, and the charitable organisations working with governments to improve the dignity and welfare of citizens.

The UNV Report on volunteering observes that the terms 'volunteerism' and 'social activism' are not mutually exclusive and warns against limiting voluntary service to the performance of charitable acts, which would provide only a superficial line of difference that does not consider other related acts of social welfare. It does, however, acknowledge that volunteering is highly context-specific, and that trust in its purposes, as well as confidence in its practices, can only occur in an enabling environment that respects the rights of all stakeholders.[69]

A recognition of the responsibility of the state to protect the welfare of its citizens, and the place of other forms of established or unestablished authority if the state is unwilling or unable to provide this, is central to understandings of 'auxiliary' and the identity that such a relationship entails. International law and conventions are clear that the state has the primary responsibility to respond and protect its citizens in situations of natural disasters and other emergencies occurring on its territory.[70] Together with the functional aspects of an auxiliary role (e.g. the provision of emergency goods and services) comes a role as auxiliary in *governance* of the response – a responsibility to manage and protect the meaning of 'humanitarian' in response in situations of crisis and complex emergency to which the UNV reports and IFRC governance guidelines refer. This requires recognition of the 'meaning' of governance in the contexts argued in my book, and the limitations of the humanitarian role identified with it.

A study on the transferability of international norms across cultures provides examples of how norms of governance can be translated and re-appropriated to contexts which do not accord to the political or social constructions normally understood by them.[71] In her study on governance norms in Tajiki-stan, Karolina Kluczewska observes that 'governance refers to an inclusive decision-making and coordination efforts [*sic*] between state and non-state actors with the aim of producing and distributing efficiently good-quality public goods and services'.[72] Within the discourse of development aid, she observes that good governance most often refers to promoting accountability, efficiency, transparency, the rule of law and participation. The permissibility of humanitarian actors to translate certain norms of practice and governance more suited to – or better understood in – the contexts in which they are situated is significant to understandings in my study. However, together with this is recognition of the modest role governance in the space promotes, which centre around cooperation, rather than the regulation of laws which are the responsibility of state. This is voiced by interviewees quoted by Kluczewska in her study: 'Good governance should be about a [real] cooperation of the government with communities', and where the role of an NGO is 'to support the state by bringing it closer to the people'.[73]

According to the United Nations report, governance comprises the mechanisms, processes and institutions through which citizens and groups articulate their interests, exercise their legal rights, meet their obligations and mediate their differences. This expresses a multi-faceted role that combines elements of regulation and representation and requires an agreement of transparent, collaborative partnerships.[74] Academic studies on volunteering as well as institutional reports are united in the opinion that collaboration, alliances and multi-stakeholder partnerships are essential for the voluntary sector to succeed.[75] The voluntary sector is multi-faceted, and it can be organised and managed formally within structured civil society organisations (CSOs), as well as within governments and the private sector. It can also be run informally: millions of volunteers within informal structures and groups, outside of formally recognised institutions.[76] Formal volunteering usually requires volunteers to work to organisational agendas, where the terms and conditions of volunteering are laid out within policies and structures for volunteering, and their work and contribution are measured against the targets set for the organisation using organisational indicators.[77] The range of formal volunteering is wide and includes employee volunteering in the private sector, volunteering within CSOs as well as participation in government volunteer schemes. This is the volunteering most described and analysed in studies on the topic, especially international formal volunteering for development, which is highly developed with strong systems and procedures in place to ensure volunteer ability, safety, and impact wherever they are placed. There is less data available – descriptive or analytical – regarding the scale, scope and nature of informal volunteering, especially in relation to issues of governance. The evidence suggests that those who start volunteering informally in their communities learn new skills of organising, participating and raising awareness and that this learning enables some to go on to enter new and more formal spaces to represent the community to ask for their voices to be heard and their rights respected.[78] Within both types of volunteering, a vast range of people volunteer. While they are often seen as 'tools' or instruments to improve service delivery, fill gaps and meet urgent unmet needs, many are able to articulate their needs and their rights, and 'can engage in governance activities as people with their own views, perspectives and autonomy'.[79] I argue that mutual recognition of the autonomy of voluntary service together with the communal spirit of its engagement are essential elements in building trust in its discourse.

The debates in MSF France and Switzerland presented earlier urge a 'rehumanising' of identities within the organisation and re-direction towards the spirit of its original charter.[80] This requires striking a balance between the important duty of care – of 'risk management' in corporate terminology – but maintaining the proximity of a social bond, with the access to trust and participation associated with it, as discussed earlier. This balance of a 'voluntary obligation' to care, and to take care, cements the collective identity of the organisation and its members,[81] and translates in my study as a shared responsibility between the community of stakeholders in an emergency: the affected populations and the other primary actors in the environment, together with the collection of secondary and tertiary stakeholders, described in chapter 1. These debates on security and risk management amongst two of the leading sections of MSF frame similar arguments over identity, access and participation running throughout this book which see that an unbalanced relationship with established and unestablished power risks the humanitarian identities tumbling into irrelevance with the primary stakeholders – the communities directly affected by the crisis.

Securing a clear, unambiguous identity of voluntary service is critical to understanding the nature of the space for cooperation in the humanitarian niche. For this, I return to the comparison between the nature of the 'amateur' and the 'professional' – between the social and the institutional – since an awareness of the tensions resting here are at the heart of debates presented in this book. The study of MSF raises the concern that the 'spirit' and motivation that drove the collective ethos of the organisation is being lost through a change of direction towards the management of risk and reputation borrowed from the private sector, which 'are increasingly influencing employment relationships and institutional responsibilities in the aid sector'.[82] I argue that these influences extend beyond the institutional relationships to encompass the whole stakeholder community, many of whom see this as an increasingly alien approach, reliant on institutional hierarchies and mechanisms that are irrelevant and unrepresentative.[83] In the words of one senior professional in the humanitarian sector, 'the essential DNA of our humanitarian identity is being removed'.[84]

The multiple spaces inhabited by volunteers described earlier, with their agency for activism and regulation, are where the risks of instrumentalisation and mistrust are most pronounced. Therefore, critical to arguments for spaces of prosocial discourse is recognition of the limits of purpose and practice that define the boundaries of the humanitarian niche to protect trust in the identities within them. The closing section of this chapter turns to philosophical discussions around the nature of an indispensable relationship with the state. It considers why an ethical and moral political identity that positions an auxiliary relationship to state or established authority is inescapable. By exploring its relationship with the communities it serves and the boundaries of trust and cooperation within them, it considers the place such expressions of voluntary service that is auxiliary to the state can comfortably fit the tensions and contradictions presented earlier and provide stability within the swirl of forces in the humanitarian arena.

The Precarious Nature of the State: Searching for a Stable Space

The essence of the state is ethical life [85]

Amongst the critical debates on utilitarianism and rights-based liberalism, Charles Taylor observed that a loss of confidence and trust in elected representatives to state authority led to contemporary representative institutions in Western societies beginning to be portrayed as a sham, and that established authority was seen to be 'masquerading as consensus', leading to a substantial proportion of the population becoming alienated from them.[86] As a remedy, Taylor discusses Georg Hegel's arguments on the contrasting notions of morality ('Moralität'), which he sees as a notion of individual action, with ethics ('Sittlichkeit') and the latter's related notion of 'community'. Taylor remarks that amongst Hegel's conditions on how to legitimise an independent, ethical community is that 'it must be co-terminous with the minimum self-sufficient human reality, the state. The public life which expresses at least some of our important norms must be that of a state'.[87] Reflecting arguments from Hegel, Taylor observes that the public life of the state is of crucial importance because the norms and ideas it expresses are not 'just' human inventions, but that the state expresses the idea – the 'Volksgeist' – whose ideas are expressed in their common institutions.

For Hegel, the state is the politically organised community in which individuals are not means to an end, but rather a community in which – like a living organism, where one part of the body is integral to the other – the distinction between 'means' and 'ends' are overcome.[88] It is in consideration of this philosophical shift (in Hegel's words, from 'Man' to 'Geist' and from 'Moralität' to 'Sittlichkeit') in which the individual parts of the community form a necessary and coherent whole to support the state that I position a call for the humanitarian system's more confident engagement with its political identity, and that allows for participation in its discourse. Within the spaces of this discourse, all engaged should see themselves as a holistic part of this social order in something like the way that a hand is part of a body, performing particularly needed functions within the whole. I argue that this allegorical construct is useful in forming fresh understandings of a protected humanitarian niche within the humanitarian system, with limited but indispensable functions as an auxiliary to public humanitarian services. This corresponds to respondents in Kluczewska's study, who see one of the roles of NGOs and civil society is to bring the state and stakeholders closer to the communities they serve, thereby constructing a functional place with a shared identity within the larger arena, in which my book argues voluntary service plays a critical part.

Studies of humanitarian space mentioned in the opening section of this chapter conclude that humanitarianism has lost its place along the complex of expanded humanitarian pathways which form a junction-less crossroads of identities, each melding into another. I have argued that it is this loss of difference that has put the humanitarian sector at risk, with identities, meanings and values lost in the melting-pot of the contemporary humanitarian arena. In order to resurrect its particular character and rescue its independence, this book suggests that members of this 'niche' be conceptualised as one of a 'quasi-partial community', inter-acting within structures of some public services of the state (Ministries of Health, Social Welfare etc.) and broader civil society but, through the autonomy of its voluntary representation, is able to remain apart from them. This indicates the need to forge a frame that addresses the tensions emerging in a protected space which is inclusive of a broad array of principles and ideals, yet with manageable and achievable expectations. Ambitious yet pragmatic, this niche requires to be realistic and uncompromising in its core goal of bringing protection and relief of suffering to populations in need, and the restoration of a minimum level of dignity.

The studies reviewed in chapter 1 and the opening section of this chapter have shown that a sense of mistrust and alienation with authority is a growing phenomenon in many of our societies, and there is a need for reconstruction of a common purpose acting within a responsible, popularly and publicly endorsed framework. My analysis of this growing disconnection signals that principled, independent humanitarianism needs to separate itself from the narratives of a universal orthodoxy, and to accept a more dynamic frame which is shaped and interpreted by the *context* of the environment in which it works. Arguments presented in this chapter have shown how a revised concept of voluntary service and the nature of the space in which its volunteers perform might remedy this disconnection. Central to this is my urge for voluntary service to be considered as an essential element of the partial communities, occupying a protected niche, that is formed and operating according to *context*. In his work looking at social contracts, the eighteenth-century philosopher Jean-Jacques Rousseau talked about a de-centralised federation of communities as being the surest basis of communal provision.[89] A highly de-centralised federation of communities may pose a threat to authority that would run counter to the collaborative partnerships my book promotes. My arguments do not call for a federal structure, but for an auxiliary structure which is needs-based and not imposed, with popular ownership and a popular identity; a structure which does not set the partial communities against one another but unites them together as a whole.

Scholarship presented in the collected studies by Michael Sandel[90] perceives a deep dissatisfaction with the utilitarian and libertarian models of society, with the former seen especially as an instrument for the furtherance or adjustment of interests. Because so much of the discourse from the Global North dominates IR scholarship, and political commentary and the media frame their debates through these political theories, there has been a failure to give credence to alternative viewpoints and approaches.[91] Through this restrictive focus, expectations have been severely harnessed; disabled by a failure to understand the unexpected outcomes and un-prepared for the realities of the 'messiness' of humanity.[92] This points towards the need for better recognition of the capacities, authority and legitimacy of national structures, and the role of local auxiliaries to them. It indicates a need to re-admit alternative structures of communal interest to the social fabric of civil society that work independently but in authority with established or non-established power, and which endorse the interests and responsibilities of the state to provide welfare to its populations. This paradigm suggests a modification of the 'significant differentiation' espoused by Taylor when he states that 'one of the greatest needs of the modern democratic polity is to recover a sense of significant differentiation so that its partial communities – be they geographical or cultural, or occupational – can become again important centres of concern and activity for their members in a way which connects them to the whole'.[93]

This chapter has introduced the importance that a sense of shared political identity features in exploring the positive role voluntary service might play within a distinct framework that is auxiliary to legitimated public authority in the humanitarian field. It has suggested that the fundamental essence of life which most closely rationalises a universal human need is the desire for dignity. The protection of dignity and respect within the community has been identified as being the paramount element in promoting trust and enhancing social cohesion within this distinct humanitarian space, guarded by clearly defined and achievable competencies. Proposals for a protected, well-defined humanitarian space within the minimalist end of the humanitarian spectrum is nothing new.[94] However, my arguments in this chapter provide reconsideration of the context inside which humanitarians act in environments of emergency, and their role as voluntary auxiliaries to the provision of essential services to communities at risk. This recognises the political identity that informs the meaning and function of the humanitarian system.

Questions remain as to how such a notion of voluntary service will function as an independent auxiliary within contested environments of an abusive state or manage the tensions of a hostile civil society. There are examples of these tensions within the historical and contemporary archives of the international Red Cross and Red Crescent Movement (the official position taken by the ICRC during its visits to Nazi concentration-camps in the Second World War is a well-documented example), and these are considered along with an analysis of the risks of co-optation, presented in chapter 5. The following chapters explore deeper understandings of the varied discourse around the central themes: voluntary service, public auxiliary, community, trust and reciprocity. Chapter 4 begins with studies of organisational and institutional theory and cognitive psychology, which indicate the centrality of trust as an important concept in influencing organisational behaviour.

Chapter 4

The Social Identity of the Niche

Common meanings are the basis of community.[1]

To gain an understanding of the prosocial space voluntary service might occupy in environments of humanitarian crisis and its role in building trust, chapter 4 begins with consideration of its framing within the phenomenon of community and a search for common meanings. It is within this social space and its iterations of communal needs that this book argues voluntary service draws its identity and its strength. This chapter studies the 'humanitarian community', with a focus on understandings of its existence in a distinct ethical and functional space. Studies of organisational and institutional theory and cognitive psychology indicate the centrality of trust as an important concept in influencing institutional behaviours – accepting decisions, obeying rules. People are influenced strongly by their judgements about the motives of leaders and authority. The abject failure to bring security and restore dignity to embattled communities in Syria and other countries today is not a failure of the humanitarian system, but a failure of international politics, and the most critically injured organ in this dysfunctional international body is what lies at the heart of political and civic access: the organ of trust. Steps to regain access to a shared discourse must begin with rebuilding trust and locating a common identity where trusted representation can be protected. The chapter begins by reviewing interpretations of trust and the place of voluntary service as an identity for trusted representation.

VOLUNTARY SERVICE AS A REMEDY
FOR DAMAGED SOCIAL ORDER

According to scholars of cognitive psychology, people are cognitively lazy and prefer to do the least amount of processing of their experiences as possible.[2] Trustworthiness is a complex cognitive task, requiring consideration of deep issues of 'intent'. In personal judgements and cognitive calculations, it would be reasonable, therefore, to assume that our minds prefer to process 'simpler' surface issues, such as bias, or neutrality. However, tests performed by Tom Tyler indicated that even when authorities (in his study, these were the police and judges) were acting in a biased way, people interviewed evaluated these authorities to be fair.[3] He concluded that people in the western societies he was studying are willing to forgive – or ignore – biases if authorities were seen to be motivated to act in a benevolent manner.[4] Tom Tyler and Peter Degoey remark that it is the trustworthiness of the intention that shaped reactions rather than evidence of bias, and their studies indicate that attributions of trustworthiness are central to the willingness to accept decisions in the areas examined.[5] An aspect of this research which is central to my arguments is that amongst the assessments conducted was analysis of the degree to which authorities treated respondents with dignity and respect which engage deeper consideration around the cognitive processes of intent, and how far this led to a perceived willingness to be unbiased. Understandings of 'respect' in the studies are equated with status recognition and social capital, seen as core to forming patterns in the social fabric of community. This leads to examination of how social fabric is constructed and categorised, and the prime importance it plays in reinforcing and protecting trust. Its relevance to my examination of voluntary service relates to questions about how can easily fabricated and uniquely fragile notions of trust and trustworthiness be secured and protected inside the humanitarian space? Might the varying levels of trust and social inclusion across societies – most notably those affected by emergency and conflict who are the subjects of my study – require consideration of multiple humanitarian spaces, or at the very least space for variations, in this protected place?

Issues of trustworthiness relate to the social relationship with authority, expressed through varying degrees of closeness (e.g. family trust being stronger than communal trust, and certain 'we-group' trust being stronger than family trust), and the differing social status of this relationship.[6] Identifying the nature of this relationship with authority and its status within the community of stakeholders is key to the arguments presented in this chapter. Securing trust in this relationship requires a balance that makes comfortable the competing identities between being auxiliary to public authority (the state) but able to challenge it if the strictly defined parameters of its humanitarian identity are at risk of being broken. The nature of trust and accompanying perceptions of trustworthiness in its identity takes a singular form not linked to partisan ties of 'kinship' or 'gangs' described earlier. Its association rests with affinity and recognition – even if at times with some discomfort – of a pluralist, communal identity. Its legitimacy rests on the permissibility to hold a mirror for reflection and recognition of this shared identity and construct a common discourse from the tensions embodied within it.

An article by Louise Amoore and Alexandra Hall studies the dynamics of power and resistance by engaging in discussion around Giorgio Agamben's figure of 'Homo Sacer', who occupies the ambiguous position between political inclusion and exclusion.[7] The authors compare this with the figure of the 'clown-fool' as a way of approaching contemporary practices of sovereignty and resistance. Their analysis of modern protest-movements by groups such as the Clandestine Insurgent Rebel Clown Army (CIRCA) is compared with representation of the medieval 'Fool' as being always present as a figure of resistance within the exercise of power: 'standing not inside or outside the gates but looking through, he dwells within the court but is not of its making'.[8] This allegory is a useful way to compare the place and identity of the humanitarian niche in my study, which represents a similar threshold of space where the identities within it are able to transit across the frontiers of politics and society.[9] However, there are significant differences in my own approach. Most significantly is the *sureness* of the humanitarian identities existing in an *unexceptional* space. This is distinct from Agamben's 'Homo Sacer' whose anonymity and lack of demand creates a state of exception that needs to be controlled.[10] In contrast, the niche has a very clear identity which it is rigorous to protect. A stronger comparison is with the concept of the 'sage fool' who – like Shakespeare's Fool in King Lear – occupies the singular position of being allowed to hold a mirror to power that enables a view across its boundaries and review the narratives which saw those outside as exceptions. The significance here lies in recognition of the un-exceptionality of voluntary and spontaneous expressions of a humanitarian response amongst communities affected by crisis, and the universality of its purpose – which is survival and the protection of lives. The singularity of the niche rests in its lack of anonymity and its legitimated place to assist and question. Its inclusivity rests on permissibility to hold a mirror before all stakeholders so they can see a view of themselves and craft a shared identity.

Trust in Voluntary Service: Its Social Relationship with Authority

In his study of collective intentionality and group agency, Raimo Tuomela emphasises cooperation as key to the coherence of a collective construction of the social world.[11] He sees this as an expression of joint intentions and shared beliefs that lead to collective reasoning and action, and the generation of trust. His arguments reflect two approaches, one of the group-agency or 'we-mode' approach which he argues is especially useful with respect to large, typically hierarchical groups, such as corporations and states, where theorising about individuals and their intentions is impractical. The other is the 'I-mode' approach, where autonomous action and individualistic status recognition play a more important role. Both approaches are conceptually different and with empirically testable functional differences, especially in situations of collective dilemmas.[12] His study highlights the tensions between the two approaches which stem from conceptual differences over 'external' (we-mode) and 'internal' (I-mode) authority and autonomy. Tuomela argues that the 'we-mode' involves an intrinsic disposition to cooperate, whereas 'I-mode' cooperation is always contingent on the situational states of the agents involved. He observes that the 'we-mode' is associated with stronger cooperation and functions more efficiently since human social action depends on a common cooperative core.[13] These indications for cooperation support a joint-agency approach which must be built on the foundations of trust and shared intention that are core to my arguments presented here. Accordingly, this book urges the need for a hybrid approach that engages both and which constructs a place where the fundamental needs of societies in distress can be met in a least-contested space. Critical to cooperation within this space is the understanding of a shared ethos grounded in the cultural-social norms of the community and formed from historically situated principles of common humanity. I argue that this hybrid approach can be realised through the concept of a single niche, able to represent a multiple of spaces, whose collective actions are protected by the external authority and efficiency of the we-mode and are performed with the internal legitimacy and autonomy of the I-mode.

Tyler and Degoey observe that people's orientations towards authorities change once they have established a social bond with them, meaning that incorporation into the social fabric of public life increases the likelihood of a more considered (cognitive) interpretation of the intent of authority and its auxiliary structures.[14] The opportunities for misguided or manipulated orientations are evident, so risks from such instrumentalisation must be limited. One means of mitigating these risks is to gain a clear understanding of the characteristics of trust. Amongst the most salient characteristics guiding assumptions of trust and trustworthiness are 'competence' and 'intention', and tests have indicated that intention is more dominant than competence.[15] In other words, 'good faith' is considered more critical to an assumption of trust than 'efficiency'. This indicates that to have the surest platform of public and popular trust the niche must build on both, combining a display of identified skills and competencies, governed by proof and experience of good faith.

The importance of a relational conception of trustworthiness, that draws upon estimations of intent, suggests that feelings of trust are more social in nature than materialist or consequentialist conceptions of trust based on competency and efficiency, thus highlighting the importance of social relationships, and most especially the notions of respect and dignity. Studies show that these findings are especially salient in times of crisis and conflict, when resources are low and people rely on support from the social fabric of their communities to cope.[16] In such situations, all parties share a mutual dependence on 'goodwill', linked to trust.

As the studies in Kramer and Tyler suggest, this is a long-term process, involving the construction of social fabric and social bonding, and so has more agency at local level than at international level.[17] Academic studies and agency evaluations of the international humanitarian response to refugees from the conflict in Syria indicate that material resources in the external environment of refugee camps cannot compensate for the lack of social identity.[18] Without sustenance of the pre-existing social fabric – together with the status, respect and dignity constructed by it – refugees no longer turn to social networks for support,[19] relying instead on the provision of external resources for relief and protection. By contrast, ethnographic accounts of the population under internal siege in Sarajevo[20] and personal experiences of local responses in other situations of civil conflict presented in chapters 7 and 8 provide evidence of the importance such social networks have for communities coping in crisis. People care about fair treatment and dignity because they derive a sense of identity from such treatment, thus enhancing self-worth. Any sign to undermine self-worth is considered unfair. Therefore, critical to my arguments for identifying, constructing and protecting the humanitarian niche is its ability to maintain, support and legitimise acts and intentions of good will, enhancing self-worth and dignity.

Many of the studies in institutional theory propose that the viability of institutional arrangements is largely determined by the degree to which they are perceived to be legitimate. Walter Powell and Paul DiMaggio suggest that an institution is considered legitimate to the extent that its structure and procedures follow the dictates of prevailing rules and norms.[21] Therefore, according to institutionalists, conformity with some set of rules or norms leads to legitimation.[22] The opening to this chapter suggests that an understanding of voluntary service begins with consideration of its framing within the phenomenon of community and a search for common meanings. I argue that it is within the expression of communal needs in this social space and by sustaining norms and expectations of the community, that voluntary service draws its identity and its strength. It is pertinent, then, to ask how far an institution acquires legitimacy based on perceptions about the trustworthiness of auxiliaries supporting it, and how far is the degree to which the humanitarian niche (and auxiliaries to public service within it) behaves in accordance with a given set of beliefs or norms an important source of trust? In other words, how does a positive judgement of a public auxiliary reflect positive judgements on the authority of institutions and state, and how do people's judgements about this authority link to their judgements about the auxiliaries supporting it? To mitigate the evident risks of manipulation and misrepresentation in this transaction, it is necessary to consider whether – and how far – the identities of voluntary service framed within the boundaries of the humanitarian niche can remain part of the broader humanitarian arena, seen neither as legitimising or de-legitimising authority nor as a partisan of those outside of authority, but able to represent and challenge each with equal trust. This requires recognition of a political identity in the niche that legitimates its political and social participation in the humanitarian discourse.

Legitimacy in this formulation resides on creating a balanced narrative between two competing but potentially complementary frames: that of the right for an independent auxiliary both to support and to challenge authority. Evidence from the surveys in cognitive psychology presented earlier suggests that public or state legitimacy increases proportionately to the degree of dignity and respect shown to the community by its auxiliaries. This presents clear opportunities arising from an inclusive and balanced discourse between these places of authority and the communities they serve. In order to resolve the tensions inherent in such a balance, there is a need to consider a more cooperative, more creative – and ultimately more positive – role for a constructive challenge to authority: a need to 'rehumanise' the narratives. This means locating a shared history in which a legitimate identity to question and challenge is also shared. The study by Amoore and Hall refers to the work by Enid Welsford which presents a comprehensive history of the 'fool' across cultures and outlines a common genealogy which stretches from Europe to the Islamic world.[23] This gives evidence of a demand for popular access to a dissonant identity, able to question authority and raise a constructive challenge if it sees it deviating from the accepted norms of the community. This troubled but functional relationship with authority lies at the heart of tensions in the contemporary humanitarian discourse. Finding a space where the tensions of dissonance and consensus can co-exist is where my arguments in this book seek to find a solution.

Constructive Anarchy

When profiling the community as central to the embodiment of voluntary service, it is important to distinguish between the differing approaches to understandings of community, and the relationships between the community and the individual within it. For the purposes of framing the analysis, I present here consideration of the differences between 'communitarianism' and 'communism', and their relationships to authority. An initial examination of these two sociological approaches is pertinent, since my arguments earlier examine an identity able to mount a constructive challenge to authorities when these latter risk over-riding the norms that provide protection to the community in the humanitarian sphere.

The Oxford Companion of Philosophy refers to the anarcho-communist approach of Peter Kropotkin who saw the individual as a 'social being' who can develop only in a communist-type society which precludes authoritarian rule and the special interests of dominant groups.[24] For him, the commune is the basic social unit and communal needs are balanced with individual needs. As an independent counterbalance to authority, my notion of voluntary service functioning in a protected space resembles the place of the anarcho-communism of Kropotkin, in which the individual develops within the established norms of an egalitarian community, but which is ready to challenge a dominant, centralised authority. However, it is distinct from Kropotkin's notion of anarchism through its auxiliary links to state authority. As a holistic part of the socio-political structure, working interdependently with it, it can provide both support and challenge. One of the main differences relates to the position my notion of auxiliary voluntary service occupies within the established social fabric. Instead of trying to justify existing structures of society, anarchists challenge structures and demand justification prior to accepting them. The expression of voluntary service presented here accepts established structures but is ready to present constructive challenges to variations on accepted norms within the limitations of its capacity and competencies. In contrast, anarchism must be considered a negative construction since it cannot accept any structure from the state, which it sees as an instrument of oppression, therefore can never be auxiliary to public authority.

This alternative approach might be expressed in a frame of 'co-opted anarchism' which accepts the need for a publicly legitimated social fabric but is cognizant of the 'messiness of humanity' and so recognises that differences in environment and context may give rise to variant legitimate responses to protect communities. This argues for a clear distinction which distances 'independent voluntary service' from the anarchist emphasis on the freedom of the individual, 'seen for the most part capable of rationally governing themselves in a peaceful, co-operative and productive manner', but which is threatening to established authority.[25] Its re-framing also bears close relationship to 'communitarianism', which insists that the community rather than individuals or the state should be at the centre of our analysis of a value-system, emphasising the social nature of life – its relationships, identity and institutions – but forming an inherent auxiliary part of the social order: autonomous but interdependent.[26] Integral to my discussion is the communitarian consideration of a commitment to collective values,[27] such as trust and trustworthiness, and more particularly a recognition of the intersubjectivity of these values which urges a need for mutual respect and application of common principles to engage a sense of worth and communal prosperity. This engages building a commitment to public good, and my arguments place voluntary service as one of these range of public goods.

Scholars of social psychology have tried to identify the cognitive determinants forming inter-group behaviour, and predominant amongst them are those which are seen to strengthen social influence and cohesion, such as perceived similarity of members; mutual attraction between members; mutual esteem; emotional empathy; altruism and cooperation, and attitudinal conformity.[28] Although these are indicators of an inter-group rather than an inter-personal phenomenon, John Turner observes that the main necessary condition is the perception of the 'we-group' ties between individuals.[29] One of the primary challenges experienced amongst humanitarian agencies operating in emergency and crisis environments is the competition for identity and influence between individual groups, many of whom share a common humanitarian goal, but where several of the inter-group determinants described earlier are problematic – notably attitudinal conformity, where the perception of differing mandates between the life-saving 'minimalist' approach of actors in the emergency response and the rights-based 'maximalist' approach of others in the arena can be especially divisive.

The question here is how to create attitudinal and behavioural conformity within this broad arena of humanitarian actors? Turner's solution would be to postulate a distinct form of social influence (what he calls 'Referent Informational Influence') which defines a distinct social category, with the adoption of clearly identified norms that can be assigned to others in a group.[30] This is a proposal which relates closely to my own arguments for a popularly endorsed and protected niche of humanitarians, acting as independent auxiliaries to legitimate authority – forming a distinct but cooperative 'social category', sharing common goals, and with recognised social influence. Arguments in this book position voluntary service as a primary vehicle of social influence, which can play a uniquely important role in the socialising process leading to positive changes in self-concept and which re-aligns and reinforces positive attitudes towards membership of that group.

The opportunities offered by the socialising identities of groups are well understood in studies on the topic. Rupert Brown states that 'one of the major consequences of becoming a member of a group is a change in the way we see ourselves'.[31] Within the distinct social categorisations of the humanitarian niche, and its auxiliary constructions of voluntary service, the processes of positive socialisation point towards a strengthening of self-esteem, leading to positive changes in the way the community sees itself. But the process is dynamic, unstructured and messy. Foucault's philosophical discussions on 'discontinuity' during the 1970s, and the ideas of rupture with periods of unilateral interpretations of history are relevant to the arguments in this regard.[32] As Clare O'Farrell observes, 'The aim of Foucault's history is to show that our present is not the result of some inevitable historical necessity. It is instead the result of innumerable and very concrete human practices, and as such, can be changed by other practices'.[33] In other words, if thoughts and values have changed, it is not through some historical necessity, but through far more haphazard channels of human activity.

The paradoxes and tensions presented earlier show the need to acknowledge and recognise the variant contexts in which its practices are performed and enable a place to question and challenge traditional frames of reference. They endorse Foucault's philosophical position that there are multiple interpretations of knowledge and practice that, once accepted and understood, might offer positive opportunities for the 'messiness of humanity'. This calls for an approach able to unite and make meaningful the apparent contradictions in this epistemological cauldron: one which recognises the limits of meanings and functions that identities in the niche are capable to protect.

IDENTITY AND PRACTICE: A CAPABILITY APPROACH

Volunteerism is an important component of effective governance and successful social and economic development.[34]

I have argued that central to the construction of a collective identity is location of a clearly defined space ('niche') that harbours understandings of voluntary action as an auxiliary support to the provision of certain public services, but where there is the capability of autonomous practice. This chapter began with examinations of voluntary service considered within the frame of a 'phenomenon of community', and a search for common meanings. Taylor observed that common meanings extend beyond intersubjective interpretations of language and reach towards identifying a world with common reference-points, in which there is a shared purpose that gives rise to legitimated common actions, with shared meanings.[35] This section considers the identities of an auxiliary voluntary service that might best anchor shared meanings and practices within these shifting tensions.

Abstract philosophical discussions on the human need for social cohesion and cooperation date from the earliest records of classical debates by Aristotle, Socrates and Plato.[36] All of these philosophical traditions call for ethical primacy in public service (expressed by Hegel as 'Sittlichkeit'). However, scholars have agreed that abstract philosophical ethics are not enough.

Without a shared 'meaning', a community will lose confidence and trust in the state and its elected representatives.[37] To feel truly represented, the state and auxiliaries to it must display ownership of this deeper sense of meaning for the community. Good or satisfactory outcomes are not enough: what is required is a trust in purpose as well as competence in practice.[38] The capability to build trust and to display competency is core to the identity of the niche. The following discussions consider how this identity can be framed and, within the space of this auxiliary niche, what might be the expression of this common meaning. The arguments consider what is expected from this formulation of humanitarian space and where sit the boundaries to protect its ethical efficiency and intent. They explore how members of the niche are rendered capable of meeting the expectations of the community. This begins by positioning the arguments presented so far in this book with Martha Nussbaum's formulation of the Capability Approach which calls to refine understandings of 'entitlement' that dominate many rights-based discussions. This is an approach that shifts the debates away from notions of contestation towards notions of cooperation through which my constructions of identity in the niche are framed.

Voluntary Service: Rendering It Capable

The opening to this chapter has indicated the tensions that the complexity of identities and context present and has considered opportunities for construction of a prosocial place in which positive exchanges can interact and inter-relate. Chapter 2 has presented the sense of obligation to the community that voluntary service entails, in the sense of a spontaneous and un-coerced social commitment to ensure the community's survival and protection. Henry Radice considers spontaneous acts of rescue as the touchstone to help navigate the complex identities along the humanitarian spectrum, since 'they allow us to reason from a concrete, visceral act that is recognisably humanitarian, without having to pin down *ex ante* the boundaries of what humanitarianism is, and thus what humanitarian rescue might look like'.[39] Craig Calhoun considers that the social solidarity that makes social commitments compelling is shaped by forms of integration, informed by shared culture and 'built out of networks of directly interpersonal social relations, such as those basic to local community'.[40] In order to harness the potential for voluntary service to act as a catalyst for prosocial action, it is necessary to engage an ethical community approach that complements the differing identities and contexts in which they are situated.

Amongst the propositions Taylor offers is that this community must not be a 'partial one'. As observed in chapter 3, he sees that it must not be a private institution or exclusive community, but it must acknowledge the need for co-existence along shared borders of the state. In other words, an ethical community cannot exclude itself, in its principles and its practices, from representing or supporting public services of the authorities in whose hands their welfare depends: 'The public life which expresses *at least some of* our important norms must be that of a state'.[41] This book argues that voluntary service which is an auxiliary to certain (humanitarian) functions of the state forms the basis for expression of these common norms. However, a critical condition is that its auxiliary status as representative of the humanitarian interests of the community permits it to challenge when its ethical preconditions are not met.

At a national level, voluntary service is often associated with service-delivery within community-based, not-for-profit, help groups. However, the growing formalisation of this phenomenon within international institutional contexts places it as a significant driver in global platforms.[42] The UNV report celebrating the International Year of the Volunteer highlights how volunteerism can promote peace and development in certain contexts, and provides a range of examples how people, as individuals and in groups, are pooling their energies to enable community engagement in the different spaces of national and global governance.[43] Of special relevance to my study are the opportunities for building on participation, responsiveness and accountability, seen as key pillars in the UN report and which this book considers core to formulating the collective humanitarian identity of the niche. This foregrounds competencies and expectations, situated not as a partial community which is the expression of many of the rights-based actors in the larger arena, but being an inclusive auxiliary to emergency public services in the humanitarian arena, giving expression to its unique, complementary role.[44]

Humanitarian service in environments of complex emergencies call for efficient outcomes. However, as mentioned earlier, efficient outcomes are not enough to ensure stability and trust in the community it serves. The demand for shared and 'meaningful' action suggests that whilst attention to outcome is paramount, its purpose must reflect the importance of process and engagement. This defines the purpose of the action as not a consequentialist end, nor a utilitarian means to an end, but a balanced expression of both. It is in consideration of the complex identity of purpose and practice in the niche, and the paradox of its auxiliary role as being part of the state, but apart from it, that my study turns to Martha Nussbaum's interpretations of the Capability Approach.

Nussbaum situates her philosophical interpretation of the Capability Approach as being outcome-oriented rather than procedural: an approach which prioritises a stable outcome (human survival with dignity) as the goal for human welfare, and which then seeks procedures to achieve the results as nearly as possible. She sees the procedures as flexible, since it is 'likely that procedures will change over time and may also vary with the circumstances and history of different nations'.[45] This is a formulation that aligns with the spatial-temporal concept of the humanitarian niche presented in my book and sees variant practices (or 'procedures' in Nussbaum's terminology) anchored by a stable purpose, occurring in an unstable space. The practices may vary according to context but are grounded with a stable meaning in the community by the fixity of their purpose.

'Purpose' is contingent on the political and social environment wherein it is expressed, as are the practices that support it. Hence, the need for the widest level of solidarity in the niche and the strongest sense of social belonging: a common identity that binds the community of its stakeholders together more strongly than rights-based entitlements expressed through power and politics. Calhoun considers that such solidarity can be at least partially chosen through collective participation in the public sphere that does not replace the nation state but is complementary to it.[46] Accepting the premise of this argument, then I argue that the identity of a voluntary auxiliary to public services in the humanitarian sphere attends to ways in which solidarity is most strongly achieved outside of political organization. These are understandings that go beyond the efficiency and performance of good deeds, towards ones that embody notions of cooperation and prosocial action, which Paul Dekker and Loek Halman see form 'the breeding-ground for social capital and public discourse'.[47] What, then, might be the expression of this hybrid identity?

The studies examined in chapters 2 and 3, and the analysis of these arguments presented in this chapter, express a mix of motivations that drive a path towards voluntary service. Therefore, it is not surprising there are multiple identities of volunteers working within it. Motivations and identities encompass the individual and the collective with corresponding variances that range from the purely idealistic to the materialist considerations of social capital and status. There is a consensus, however – at least amongst scholarship from the Global North that dominates contemporary accounts in academia and in organisational policy – that the closest to a universal desire is for respect and dignity: a recognition of one's place in community. This is iterated in the studies examined in the current chapter as a form of hierarchy of drives, with collective good intention and competent performance ('we-mode') taking precedence over individualistic motivations of status and authority ('I-mode'). The analysis presented there recognises the need for recognition of multiple drives that encompass the hybrid identities of the individual I-mode and the collective we-mode: a recognition of identities that accommodate the variances of practice, but which coalesce around the narrative of a common purpose. Constructivist scholarship sees narrative as the organising principle of our psychology and that a common criterion of narrative is having a stated goal or endpoint that indicates where our narrative is guiding us.[48] Whilst many of the aims in the larger humanitarian arena might be more or less contested, a pattern of shared historical and cultural narratives reflects a stable goal of protecting life and dignity – narratives of purpose which are common to the niche and those outside.

The theoretical arguments for social cohesion and opportunities for pro-social cooperation presented earlier centre round discussions of community participation, and it is within this sense of community that my study positions voluntary service as being part of its social contract with authority, and a core element of its social fabric. In her book 'Frontiers of Justice', Nussbaum highlights the primacy of dignity as an essential element in the construction of the human social contract, which she sees as a progression from the early theoretical studies on natural law by Hugo Grotius, and formally defined by John Locke, which state that we have a natural dignity and that each of us is in need of fellowship to achieve and share this dignity. She observes that to enable a productive common life, the main job should be 'to ensure that we all have the opportunity to live in accordance with human dignity'.[49] In this regard, Nussbaum considers human dignity as a form of entitlement, and that those entitlements can only be achieved through cooperation, which, in turn, entail a duty of reciprocity. It is here where Nussbaum finds primacy for outcome over procedure in her formation of the Capability Approach to render it philosophically stable. Citing elements of Grotian natural law theory of the origin of political society, which 'join together out of positive sentiments of benevolence and positive moral duties of reciprocity that derive from a mutual recognition of human dignity', Nussbaum stresses the importance of a just 'outcome'.[50] She observes that Grotius argues explicitly that we must not attempt to derive our principles from an idea of mutual advantage alone, believing that 'a society based upon sociability and respect rather than upon mutual advantage can remain stable over time'. Therefore, an account of basic entitlements is not a procedural issue but rather one of basic justice that 'involves an intuitive idea of human dignity'.[51]

The belief that social stability based on mutual dignity and respect, rather than on notions of mutual advantage, lies at the heart of the identity for the niche. Any sense of 'entitlement' formed by the philosophical essence of the niche emphasises capabilities and is reciprocal in the sense of being a transaction of *mutual participation*, rather than *mutual advantage*.[52] The identity of the niche can be conceived, therefore, as a space promoting social stability grounded in mutual dignity and respect, rather than on the concept of power that mutual advantage embodies. Considering the focus of cooperation and capabilities across the broad base of stakeholders which the arguments in my book encompass, the Capability Approach has the advantage of dealing with great asymmetries in power. Unlike contract theory, which takes the nation state as the basic unit, the Capability Approach recognises broader, more complex interdependencies at micro (community and state) and macro (international and transnational, corporations, markets, NGOs etc.) level.[53] With its emphasis on a continuum of needs and capabilities (able-human; impaired-human; non-human)[54], it rejects the idea that only those who are powerful enough or 'able' enough can be part of the social contract, and so can extend reciprocity to those with greater inequities.[55] The deciding factor is less one of power, but of capabilities and of enabling equal access ('entitlement' in Nussbaum's interpretation of the approach) to these capabilities. Nussbaum's formulation of the Capability Approach acknowledges the temporality of human 'being', displaying differing capabilities at different times. This means engaging with asymmetrical relations: an acceptance of hierarchies amidst 'islands of equality'.[56] According to Martha Nussbaum, asymmetrical relations can still contain reciprocity and 'truly human functioning'.[57] My arguments for the auxiliary role of the niche can be understood as a way of connecting asymmetries in times of humanitarian crisis, as a means of realising a purpose, rather than simply an instrument of power, or a tool for endorsing certain institutional practices.

Identity as Representation of the Common Community

One of the complexities facing policymakers and practitioners is the question of how this paradox of power and cooperation can best be represented in their aspirations for forming neutral spaces in the humanitarian arena. What sort of compromises need to be made that will enable equal access to the basic capabilities critical to human dignity outlined earlier? From a philosophical perspective, this chapter has presented ideas that an ethical approach must be an inclusive approach and not seen as the expression of a 'partial community' (see Taylor, earlier). Its moral and ethical stability depends on combining broad stakeholder considerations that are complementary rather than confrontational, endorsing its identity as an auxiliary, rather than an adversary. In order to enable a space where cooperative action can be nurtured, the discourse must reject prescriptions of 'best practice' or 'good governance' which form much of the contemporary institutional processes and which assume that, without these, no notion of prosocial action can occur. Practices vary according to context, and even the understandings of dignity and what it means to be human have been shown to be historically contingent, as the events of mass atrocity and genocide have shown.[58] Nussbaum observes that what is compatible with human dignity might vary from society to society, and from age to age.[59] Therefore, 'representation' must, for all practical purposes, be accepted as being representative of the context in which it actually exists, and subject to the contingencies of its time. This may appear problematic, but stability, which I argue is essential for giving strength to a common identity in the space, is realised through a constancy of purpose, made less contingent by the shared history and meanings in the narratives around a common humanitarian goal.

Integral to an exploration of identities and trust within the niche is consideration of how these represent the community it serves and are representative of its stakeholders. Equally important is to consider whether, or how far, a popular apportionment of trust and judgement of trustworthiness in the niche transfers to public institutions to which its humanitarian services are auxiliary (e.g. Ministries of Health or Social Welfare). In her study of ethical predicaments for humanitarian action, Jennifer Rubenstein raises the question of representation and considers how associations of NGO auxiliary action with the state and its public authorities can be viewed as a positive or negative construction in the provision of public welfare.[60] Jennifer Wolch observes that constructions of public opinion are often linked to the identities of the partnerships, and their actions and practices are seen to be part of a 'shadow state', where the political economy of commerce and state influence the way the voluntary sector delivers services and use resources.[61] This corroborates the findings in Social Identity Theory presented in this chapter that – at least in the socio-political contexts of the case studies presented – trust is influenced by perceptions of intent and purpose. That is to say, as long as the intention is worthy and trusted, and the actor displays autonomous practice, free from what Rubenstein refers to as 'institutional biases', then an organisation's choice of action is not prone to a negative construct in public opinion.[62]

Key to cooperative interaction in the niche is stability of its purpose and trust in its intention. Humanitarian actors in the niche must not be seen as 'second best' actors who are there from a misplaced sense of duty, or as a symbolic presence for institutional reasons (e.g. in search of funding, publicity and political representation).[63] Its practices must show confidence in its autonomous auxiliary role, and this might require a certain amount of compromise. What cannot be compromised is its humanitarian purpose. Actors in the niche must retain the fixity of purpose which – even if practices may be temporal and unstable – will ensure the best opportunities for trust in its representation.[64]

Arguments in this chapter have sought new pathways to navigate the tensions and contradictions arising from the complex nature of identities in the humanitarian arena that expose it to manipulation and where the meanings of 'humanitarian' risk being confiscated by the political and economic forces of state and the market. In his study on political violence, Jeffrey Murer refers to the illegitimacy of war and violence when it is waged in the name of 'humanity'.[65] By usurping a universal concept for its own political ends and 'denying the enemy the quality of being human',[66] Murer sees in this a denial of both their social and political character, thus rendering them outlawed from all participation as legitimate members of society and state. By denying them their humanity, they inhabit the state of exception described by Agamben which 'is the illusion of normality that staves off any form of political resistance'.[67] To protect the identities in the humanitarian niche, arguments presented earlier call for normalising the narratives around humanitarian identities that do not situate a humanitarian response as a state of exception, but rather as the expression of a human response to situations at the extremes of normality. Recognition of the political and social identities of this expression means that the members of the niche are not outlawed but seen instead as an integral part of the legitimate socio-political space and housed as part of the 'normal condition'.[68] To ensure the broadest engagement of trust in the niche and the legitimate representation for all its stakeholders, the identities within it must occupy a place that represents 'real life' as experienced at the extremes. The balance of identity in this space is critical. The niche must be careful not to represent an 'illusion of normality'[69] but to be a real and unimagined place which recognises the complexities and tensions of 'real life' in this re-humanised and disenchanted, space. This means there must be a place for a challenge from the maverick, who – like the medieval fool – can hold up a mirror to its stakeholders in the niche that allows them to reflect and question. Murer remarks that 'it is also through an understanding of the complexity of identity that alternate futures can be realized'.[70] How to recognise and house this complexity of identity in the niche is the topic of the penultimate chapter in my book. Chapter 5 turns to examining some of the risks and opportunities that these complexities present.

Chapter 5

Risks and Opportunities

In the preface to his book *The Dark Sides of Virtue*, David Kennedy writes that humanitarianism has evolved from the impulse to do good.[1] He goes on to observe that 'all of us who have felt a humanitarian impulse also know the satisfaction which comes from affiliating with others who share our intuitions about justice . . . coming together to exercise power on behalf of our commitments, or simply to affirm our commitments to ourselves'.[2] This collection of 'impulse', justice' and 'power' encapsulates the tensions that converge in the humanitarian space, exposed to the risks from careless, universalised assumptions described in chapter 1 and the 'impulsive' urge for justice and human welfare associated with a humanitarian identity. As Kennedy's preface remarks, perceptions of justice and welfare are open to interpretation: 'bombing Belgrade to save Kosovo can seem like a humanitarian triumph or a catastrophe, depending on where you sit'.[3] These are contingent interpretations that have been echoed in the contemporary narratives on the wars in Syria and Yemen. Humanitarians, notably in the modern environments, have always been aware of the need to balance idealism with pragmatism. Following the world wars of the twentieth century, divergent views and strategies on confronting the realities of war have converged to try and bridge the gap between the (peaceful) humanitarian aspirations associated with the regulation of war according to international law, and the political freedom associated with war.[4] Added to this complexity are the conflicts of social (re)structuring that often accompanies conflict and natural disasters, made evident in the case studies in chapter 7. Kennedy considers that this new relationship with the 'modern law of force' has meant humanitarians adapting to a pragmatic approach in dealing with complex emergencies, in which they consider and act strategically about power in the search for a more inclusive, less manipulated, access. As he remarks, 'It is here that we can most readily

apprehend the advantages – but also the dark sides – of humanitarian pragmatism',[5] complex environments of politics and power where the moral emotion
of compassion itself is seen as a risk.[6]

As indicated in 'Introduction', this book is not about the humanitarian
as an activist in a rights-based arena, and this chapter is not an account of
humanitarian dilemmas or the sensational humanitarian blunders, which are
well-documented in scholarship and the popular media. Rather it offers a philosophical reflection on the roots of the dilemmas that challenge the humanitarian identity and identifies the need to create a new platform for their resolution.

It complements studies by Alex de Waal, Tony Vaux and Fiona Terry
which identified the paradox that prescriptions of humanitarian action are
too often influenced by motives and emotions far removed from a concern
for humanity.[7] I share David Kennedy's primary concern that the ensuing
ideological and institutional directions mean that the broad humanitarian
sector promises more than can be delivered and, with this belief, presents
an institutional arrogance that risks more to the crafting of a shared humanitarian identity than the simple disappointment of unmet expectations. With
this challenge in mind, this chapter considers the risks to mutual trust such a
hubristic approach to capabilities and power might bring. It examines some of
the risks and opportunities emerging from the influences of two broad categories of power introduced in chapter 1: those of established and unestablished
power. It considers the nature of power in the social world presented by Pierre
Bourdieu that he sees being distributed within the multiple dimensions of this
space according to the set of properties active within it: properties of power
that consist of economic, cultural, social and symbolic 'capital'.[8] This book
sees political authority resting in the dimensions of a discursive space managed by established and unestablished power but where the capital values of
a shared humanitarian identity demand management in a different dimension,
where the properties of 'humanitarian capital' hold legitimated autonomy.
The challenges and the opportunities rest on how trust is built in this relationship with power. Towards this end, discussions of normative power in this
new dimension emphasise levelled understandings of the separate identities
as being 'equally capable'. This suggests ideas of partnership that shifts the
emphasis away from hierarchies of power, leading to a change in the discourse about the nature of the relationship: one that positions them as being
equally able and mutually supportive.

HUMANITARIAN CAPITAL: TRUSTED
PROPERTY IN SOCIAL SPACE

The preceding chapters have indicated the importance that good intent (purpose) and efficiency (practice) play in the construction of a trusted social

identity, one which positions humanitarians in an advantageous place, combining symbolic and material power that the elements of established and unestablished power are eager to manage.[9] Bourdieu sees the spaces as being interactive according to the properties of power or capital presented earlier. His arguments on the relative 'values' of power in the social field make clear that humanitarian capital is more than just symbolic, and that trusted identities in the niche would be fundamental to transmitting and transferring legitimacy to and from public authorities. The risks here from instrumentalist approaches are evident and to mitigate these, the humanitarian niche must define clear boundaries that set limits to its humanitarian identity as a social actor so that it does not become a way of pursuing power by other means: clear red lines must be set and the authority to resist must be legitimated. Recognising the limits of the humanitarian role in environments of crisis that define an unambiguous place for its auxiliary relationship is critical to my arguments for the legitimacy of its role and representation amongst the broader stakeholder community.

It is in consideration of 'humanitarianism' as an expression of cultural power that this book sees both its greatest threat to trust in its identity and its widest avenue to influence opportunities for change. As indicated earlier, the greatest exposure to risk is from the persistence of its identification with an exclusive dominant narrative which is increasingly challenged and tested. The influences of these narratives are multifaceted, and some have an explicit relationship with power. For example, historians see that the mobilisation of national sentiment for a humanitarian cause often went hand-in-hand with the role of a disaster abroad in promoting bellicosity as well as patriotism at home. In an examination of the transnational response to the Napoleonic Wars in Europe from 1805 to 1815, Norbert Götz observes that British relief to Germany enabled ex-patriots from German states that were not allies of the United Kingdom, such as the Kingdom of Saxony, to direct a share of British funding to benefit enemy territories.[10] Studies have commented on the instrumental role of the German Red Cross in the lead-up to the Second World War and the considerable anguish of ICRC's position at this time.[11] In this context, the humanitarian actor on the field is called on to play an important role: 'As the relay between donor and victim, he looks to embody the militant spirit of the new charitable organisations by refusing to remain silent, so awakening an individual and collective conscience'.[12] The association of economic, cultural and social power has been expressed in scholarship as being a form of 'disaster capitalism' that uses fear and desperation caused by catastrophe as an opportunity for the elements of power to engage in the restructuring of social and political space in their favour, and with policies seen by many to be a continuation of war.[13] Examples of the instrumental rhetoric linked to this are presented in the case studies on the tsunami response in Sri Lanka, and the conflict in Syria, examined in chapter 7.

Much has been written about the misuse of aid and the misdirection of policy in the humanitarian aid and development sectors.[14] Academic studies have made particular critique of the institutionalisation of the sectors and have cautioned their growing professionalisation.[15] Chapter 3 in this book has presented the urge for economic gain as one of the elements driving the 'civilizing missions' of imperial and colonial powers in the eighteenth and nineteenth centuries. In the contemporary period, criticism of the misuse of authority and resources featured prominently in evaluations of the humanitarian responses following the Indian Ocean tsunami in 2004, the earthquakes in Haiti, 2010 and more recently following the wars in Syria and Yemen. Studies of empirical data have shown the enormous growth in the outreach and resources available to the humanitarian sector. The ALNAP report on *The State of the Humanitarian System* records an increase of 27 per cent in the number of field personnel from its last report in 2013, with expenditure of $16 billion within the UN system alone in 2017.[16] Empirical evidence on the misuse of resources is available, but statistics are often contested and, as so often with statistical data, are translated according to specific agendas and messages.[17] Nevertheless, whatever the scale or the motivations, evidence has been enough to provoke a widespread political response, evidenced by growth in the enforcement of sanctions and international instruments to counter the threat of terrorism over the last twenty years.[18] Whilst these are not aimed specifically at the humanitarian sector, the prohibitions in these instruments are framed very broadly, and have included payments intended to purchase or manage the delivery of relief supplies.[19] Multilateral organisations such as the Financial Action Task Force (FATF) recognise that donation under the guise of charitable aid is one component of the broader issue of terrorism financing.[20] Recent measures have included legislation proposed by national governments to criminalise access to areas seen as a threat to their internal security.[21]

In his essay on the ideology of humanism and the complex debates linking humanitarianism with human rights, Costas Douzinas presents a rigorous analysis of the comparative position taken by universalists and relativists, whose approaches he sees as prominent expressions of postmodern humanism.[22] Historically, the unfixed concept of 'humanity' has been interpreted differently, from the Classical meritocracies of the Ancient Greeks and Romans, to understandings of the early modern humanism of Renaissance and Christian theology, presented in chapter 3. Douzinas sees the construction of modern rights-based arguments as being a very particular order of language and law, 'with scant regard for ontologically solid categories, like those of man, human nature or dignity'.[23] Thereby, the 'humanity' of humanitarianism has been co-opted by the rhetoric and the symbolic capital of 'human rights' and re-ascribed with values that exceed its original construction. This calls

for a return to the essentialism of humanity as opposed to the mystical constructs which he sees as the 'accident of European intellectual and political
history'.[24] This book challenges the assumption in the dominant narratives
that the latter reading of history is transferable without question across a universal humanitarian landscape and argues that this assumption presents a significant obstacle to engaging the broadest levels of trust. Yet recognition of
the shared histories presented in chapter 3 suggests that access to a common
narrative can easily be regained once a more inclusive discourse is located:
one that is more proximate and respectful to the community of stakeholders
it represents. Douzinas sees that the risks of alienation will persist until there
is a re-engineering of the current narratives that leads to a radical separation
of the assumed identities they share. It is his opinion that 'the dishonesty
of pity and a sense of superiority unite the humanitarians': a sense of pity
engineered by campaigns supporting the superiority of the Global North that
'increases distantiation from its targets and breeds disdain'.[25] Similarly, my
study sees contemporary humanitarian expressions mirroring the dishonesty
of the earlier 'civilizing missions', and until this troubling identity is replaced
with ones that are more honest and proximate, then access to a more universal
discourse will be denied.

Chapters 3 and 4 have indicated the mix of purpose and motivation influencing humanitarian action in the larger arena, and the introduction to this
chapter has given historical evidence of the mobilisation of national sentiment
on one hand, and a sense of cosmopolitan humanitarianism on the other.[26]
These have flavoured discussions around the humanitarian-development
nexus in the second half of the twentieth century, and developed into the
narratives of the 'new humanitarians' and the securitisation of aid which followed the collapse of the Soviet Union.[27] The growing convergence between
humanitarian narratives and governmental politics has added to the confusion
and a blurring of the respective boundaries, which my arguments in this book
are attempting to address. Studies surrounding the disciplinary approaches of
Discourse Analysis make evident the risks from an instrumentally governed
discourse.[28] Nussbaum remarks that 'narratives play a significant part in the
conditioning and regulating of our moral sensibilities, or lack thereof'.[29] What
is less evident is the level of risk from 'ungoverned' narratives. That is to say,
from an unknowable response in the informal humanitarian discourse when
calls from the formal humanitarian system for transnational action to protect
and improve humanity are presented as having a universal moral sense.[30]

Safeguarding a Balanced Reflection

The ICRC is always conscious of the risk of association with politics and
power. In *A Memory of Solferino*, Henry Dunant makes clear the need for

a space on the battlefield where professionals in the medical services can volunteer their services, free from association with the warring parties.[31] This feeling is transferred across working relationships. Archival records show ICRC's awareness of the need for an identity which shows independence from the Swiss Confederation: 'The ICRC has always been very protective of its independence vis-a-vis the Swiss Confederation. This latter, for its part, has always respected this independence'.[32] But as its main financial and institutional backer it recognises the need for a close and mutually respectful relationship. Furthermore, its relationship is seen as a neutral bulwark against the growing influence of world powers 'who might in some manner be in competition with ICRC' and prejudice its actions.[33]

The studies on Social Identity Theory presented in chapter 4 observe that people's orientation towards authorities change once they have established a social bond, meaning that incorporation into the social fabric of public life increases the likelihood of a more considered interpretation of the intent of authority and its auxiliary structures. In their review of spontaneous responses by self-organising 'emergent' volunteers, who gather together to bring assistance in situations of disaster and emergency, John Twigg and Irina Mosel observe that social capital and 'its associated features of trust, norms of behaviour and mutual obligation' have been linked with this phenomenon of emergence.[34] They remark that the motivation appears to be a product of *shared values* and *a culture of responsibility* to one's community and society.[35] This finding is important and highlights the vulnerability – and instability – inherent in the interpretations of intent and purpose and the precariousness of trust in the humanitarian identity when values are not shared. Unless there is a protected space anchoring a stable, shared humanitarian identity in the niche, then the values that inform intent and activate practices will be contingent.

A shared identity is made precarious by the multiplicity of purposes and practices – of means and ends – that make up the complex identities in the larger humanitarian arena. This shared identity is further threatened by loose and assumed associations with negative images and questionable values of a sector seen to be profiting from crises, many constructed by public attention to the privileged position in society that the humanitarian is seen to occupy.[36] Media articles on the sybaritic lifestyle of the international aid community appear regularly in the national and international press at times of high-profile humanitarian emergency,[37] and are seen to influence the narratives presented in the case studies, in chapter 7. Many of these are not born out of facts but from the identity narratives surrounding them. However, eye-witness accounts from the field confirm the construction of exclusive identities. Images of the White Landcruiser as a symbol of the international humanitarian appear in academic articles as well as the media.[38] Academic studies, anecdotal account and casual debate refer to terms such as 'disaster tourists' and 'voluntour-ists'.[39] This is not a new phenomenon, arising from modern social media net-works and the tabloid press. In her study of the work of the British National Society for the Sick and Wounded in War during the Franco-Prussian War from 1870 to 1871, Rebecca Gill refers to news reports from the Daily News in 1870 that related tales of imposture and voyeurism, and that 'for the credit of the badge, something should be done to purge it of these ruffians, and also to prevent its adoption by every dilettante sightseer'.[40] There is an awareness of the negative images that even the best intentions can bring when presented within cultures or environments who do not share similar histories. In a note written following a meeting of the ICRC plenary session in 1952, ICRC Presi-dent Max Huber acknowledges the historical, religious and cultural associa-tions that ICRC holds, and notes the need for ICRC to carve an identity that is distanced as far as possible from association with the tensions emerging in the post-imperial and post-colonial climate following the end of the Second World War.[41] In his report following a tour of the Middle East, South Asia and the Far East in 1955, a member of the ICRC Assembly, Rodolfo Olgiati, cautions how specificities of their origins may flavour the relationships with interlocutors in the region, and urges the need for ICRC to explore the ratio-nal, moral and spiritual foundations of the Red Cross to identify aspirations shared by all people.[42] This is a reminder that it is often the assumption of exclusion such 'exceptional' identities cast to those outside which form these negative associations, and can lead to rejection, or more serious threats to their security. Whilst most scholarship and policy-oriented evaluations have focused an explanation for violence against aid-workers on arguments that associate attacks with factors related to the political and strategic instrumen-talisation of aid, studies have urged an examination of factors other than these global, contextual dynamics, such as individual behaviour and organisational actions that can lead to resentment and anger.[43] Exception may become a virtue in certain environments, but the risks from intended, unintended, or simply ignorant association that distances its identity from the communities it serves will only close-down access to them. Trust and relevance require a balanced representation in the humanitarian discourse.

This chapter has brought attention to the risks that a hostile manipulation of social influence can play in designing the social fabric of the community, pro-voking negative attitudinal effects which risk damaging opportunities for the positive socialising processes of the humanitarian niche that I argue for here. Examples of this provided by social psychologists include instances when a negative (e.g. fear) is used to enhance membership (e.g. 'hazing' in the U.S. Army)[44] or recent examples of the performative violence displayed by Islamic State in Syria and Iraq. What is less well-examined is how a negative bal-ance might be created by badly judged, or instrumentally (mis)constructed, assumptions that the humanitarian 'good' is seen as 'good' by everyone. Recent studies conducted by the Harvard Humanitarian Initiative have provided evidence of the disconnect between the assumptions in the humanitarian identity and the perceptions of it by those it seeks to help or who can do it harm.[45] Their study acknowledges the restricted access the sector is facing but rather than focusing on physical barriers, it considers ways to re-connect the stakeholders by reflecting on how its principles and practices are perceived by communities affected by crisis. There has been a significant volume of work done in recent years looking at how principles are understood, misunderstood or strategically manipulated.[46]

Debates around the core humanitarian principles of neutrality, impartiality and independence have been considered in depth in the policy evaluations and academic studies mentioned earlier, as well as in a wealth of literature on the humanitarian sector. These discussions are not repeated in any detail here but instead the study explores some of the opportunities that a redirection of the narratives might present. This includes the core principles guiding humanitarian action, but more specifically on re-understandings of voluntary service and a universal identity that is the focus of questions in this book. The arguments presented here and in chapter 4 urge a process of reflection on the assumptions dominating the humanitarian space by viewing mirror images of our own identities, therefore it is useful to consider how mirrored understandings of *partiality* and *interdependence* might easily reflect more common meanings of the core principles of impartiality, and independence. The definition of impartiality contains two components: that humanitarian assistance is given in proportion to need, and that no discrimination must be made on the basis of nationality, race, gender, religious belief, class or political opinions.[47] Following extensive surveys on the application of humanitarian principles conducted by the Humanitarian Exchange and Research Centre (HERE), its study on local humanitarian actors and the principle of impartiality remarks that the application of this principle is no easy thing, especially in war-torn countries like Iraq where sectarian divisions have been among the causes of the war and local organisations are rooted in their historical, cultural and religious constituencies.[48] The report goes on to say:

> Applying the other component of the principle of impartiality, in proportion to need, is equally if not more challenging. It is a misunderstanding that a humanitarian organisation needs to deliver its services on all sides of the conflict. The determining aspect is 'most in need' and this can imply a single presence in an area controlled by one of the parties to the conflict. In such instances, other parties are likely to challenge an organisation's neutrality, which, in turn, requires this organisation to demonstrate its negotiations skills in illustrating how it is keeping with the principle of impartiality.[49]

This indicates the multiple challenges to even the most apparently universal humanitarian demand: that its assistance is given based on need and without discrimination. Similar contestations often arise in application of two of the other core principles for humanitarian action, neutrality and independence, and – as shown in the review of internal Movement documents in the next chapter – the challenges come from places where the mirror might be expected to cast a more shared reflection. As made evident in the archival records mentioned earlier, whilst the ICRC was aware of the need for an independent identity from the Swiss government, its members were aware of the need for a relationship that protected it from any potential challenge to its identity and its independence from world powers outside.[50] This does not suggest the principles are wrong, or that there must be an allowance for flexible interpretation. On the contrary, the thrust of the arguments in this book indicate that to build and maintain trust, there needs to be a stability in humanitarian principles: their purpose must not be contingent. The risks emerge when the humanitarian narratives give an illusion of being universally representative but where the discourse is only a distant reflection of the complex reality of interests and identities on the ground. The discursive strength in the humanitarian niche will be determined by how successfully it is able to give a more honest reflection of this narrative – one that can engage both consensus and dissension to reach a more universal humanitarian discourse.

Managing the Messiness of Humanity

In her book *Social Constructionism*, Vivien Burr refers to Theodore Sarbin who sees narrative as the organising principle of our psychology, present in many facets of our daily life, and that a common criterion of narrative is having a 'stated goal' or end point that indicates where the narrative is leading.[51] Whilst many of the goals in the humanitarian arena might be contested to differing degrees, the stable narratives, historically and culturally, are to do with protection of life and dignity. To ensure the best opportunities for their incorporation into a shared discourse, these narratives must not be 'private matters', specific only to the niche, but must include the narratives of all stakeholders who share the constancy of the humanitarian discussion.[52] However, to render the extensions in these narratives more fixed and to maintain the boundaries of relevance and protection in the humanitarian niche, these need to reach beyond a simple inter-relationship and engage with an agency that acts as auxiliary to the narrative and can help guide and challenge the discussions: a voluntary agency that is part of the structure but apart from it. This is a managed inter-relationship with all stakeholders and should include potential spoilers or 'enemies' (what Burr calls 'social ghosts' in the narrative),[53] especially where an agency for positive constructions in the humanitarian narrative might be linked to their influence. This idea of engagement with a narrative that is 'malign but constructive' relates to the positive role the wise fool or the constructive anarchist can play to bring harmony from dissonance, suggested in the opening to this chapter.

ICRC has a well-documented history of successes in engaging with the potentially dissonant and makes special cause to ensure a presence, if not proximity, with the widest possible range of interlocutors. Some recent experiences show this strategy of engagement may have limited outreach,[54] but this may not be because these organisations are less trusted. It could indicate instead that the interlocutors themselves have less outreach in a more fractured social network, or the reasons could be the expression of symbolic or performative violence discussed earlier. What is clear is that the increasing distance has meant restricted access to a shared humanitarian narrative, and the importance of a balanced engagement with all stakeholders in the discourse.

This book has stressed the importance of maintaining a cross-disciplinary approach to interpret and understand the dynamism ('messiness') of cooperative engagement between stakeholders in the environment of crisis – the location of a middle ground between the 'institutional orderliness' of a 'system' and the disorder of outside society. Richard Scott sees that institutions are social structures that have attained a high degree of resilience and operate at multiple levels of jurisdiction, from the world system to localised, interpersonal relationships.[55] Imbalances in these relationships, and disregard for mutual recognition and respect, present evident risks in these institutionalised hierarchies – whether at a macro-level (international, transnational) or at a micro-level (national, local). Scott sees three pillars of institutions: (i) the 'normative pillar', which defines goals and objectives and identifies the appropriate ways to pursue them; (ii) the 'regulatory pillar', which legitimates laws and rules; and (iii) the 'cultural-cognitive pillar', which preconditions a deep understanding of traditions.[56] The humanitarian niche that I present rests on the normative pillar, seen by Scott as holding a deeper moral base for asserting legitimacy. The surrounding narratives must include identities supported by all three pillars that encompass ties of kinship and authority, and other expressions of social identity presented in chapter 4. This will result in locating a stable, inclusive discourse that recognises the hierarchies and the imbalances of power inherent in them but occupies a space where these are not the determining factor. Instead, it offers a respectful and interdependent narrative that 'orders' the spoken rules of pillar (ii) and the unspoken rules of pillar (iii), so occupying the middle ground that is able to craft an ordered narrative from a disordered environment.

To locate the best place for management of this middle ground, we return to consideration of political identity in the niche and the risk from the binary approaches cautioned in chapter 1. The niche needs to be distinct from the duality of social structure – of 'system' and 'society' – that is prominent in much of social science. It needs to encompass both idealist (humanitarian) and materialist (political) features of society and highlight their interdependence.[57] Systematic approaches in social science distinguish between the system and its environment, often emphasising the importance of maintaining boundaries between them. Those within the system see the environment outside as being less 'ordered' and so less valued by those inside.[58] This dualist approach makes difficult any cooperative interaction in the niche. To avoid de-stabilising the space, my book argues that those within the system (state and certain stakeholders) need to recognise the complementary strengths of those outside who might be fringe members of the stakeholder community. The space in the niche must provide the authority to rethink boundaries that characterises an interactive 'system', one that is aware how its behaviour affects the behaviour of others, as well as a 'society' that takes account of the action of others based on legal or moral obligations that embrace the legitimate interests of others – the position of a 'humanitarian all-man's land' sitting between the power-politics of a system and the moral orientation of society.

The opportunities to determine and legitimise this middle ground arise from regarding the common humanitarian purpose in the niche as a 'floating signifier': that is to say, one which is not automatically linked to any particular 'signified' or meaning,[59] other than that of the common humanitarian identity. This is a hybrid signification that helps to govern and define, but not to regulate the space, and is able to manage both the regulated structure of its institutional association and the dynamic and goal-oriented nature of an organisation, encompassing both idealist and materialist features of social life. Their identity is linked to the normative pillar, which, as indicated earlier, is seen by Scott as holding the deepest moral base for asserting legitimacy. It would enable an easier reconciliation of the tensions identified in chapter 3, being part of a system that is inter-active but instrumental, and with notions of society which express moral obligations that are more personal, and which embrace the legitimate interests of others.[60] These are structures that form the social capital identified by Bourdieu as an essential factor of power in social networks.[61]

Analyses of the studies presented in chapter 4 have indicated that public opinion is considered as the most valuable element in securing and sustaining social capital. But it is also the hardest to restore once damaged. Faith in the charity sector has been questioned as a result of recent scandals and researchers increasingly question the motivation behind some in the sector.[62] The discourse surrounding them is flavoured accordingly. Recent scholarship has presented new ways of studying the sector through the lenses of anthropology and sociology, engaging in wider debates about their identification with politics.[63] Hilhorst sees defining the work of NGOs as a highly normative process, since it rests on a moral claim of 'doing good' and where the reputation and legitimacy of the organisation rests on crafting and sustaining this identity.[64] The varied interpretations and contested meanings of 'doing good' is one source of tension, and exposure to risk comes from the pressure to gain and maintain this moral reputation. Managing this means the need to operate with a certain restraint. Competent management of the risk is paramount, since faith in its moral compass is critical for popular legitimation, and its external legitimation is critical if it is to have trust and status.[65] I have remarked earlier in the book that competent performance is not enough: there must be a balance of beneficial impact and good intent. The notion that 'being humanitarian' and 'doing good' are inevitably the same is one deeply embedded in the discourse of the Global North,[66] but as the study by the Harvard Humanitarian Initiative shows, this is not universally the case. It sees that dismissive assumptions in the sector which do not mirror the perceptions or lived realities of stakeholders have created a confused and competing logic in the role of international humanitarian response.[67] The assumption of 'good motivation' as the primary driver of humanitarian action may also be open to challenge. Esther van Leeuwen and Suzanne Täuber observe that acts of cooperation may be driven in part by strategic 'in-group-serving' motives which stem from the need for independence and positive distinctiveness, and can be viewed as 'prosocial behaviour' but below the surface is a challenge to authority or an attempt to maintain social dominance.[68]

Reputation and trust are fragile. Amongst studies on the fragility of trust, Roderick Kramer refers to the work of Paul Slovic whose research found that trust is easier to destroy than to create due to various cognitive factors. He observed that negative events that destroy trust are more 'visible' than positive events that build trust, and that negative events impact judgement more strongly than positive events of a similar magnitude.[69] Voluntary organisations are particularly affected by the fragility of trust given the prominent role volunteering plays in the formation of social capital: 'As participatory organizations they facilitate social connections and co-operation, and by virtue of repeated interactions they engender trust among members'.[70] But the relationship between trust and social capital is highly conditional, 'dependent on the structure of civil society and the legitimacy of the political system . . . mediated through processes like social inclusion and participation'.[71]

The fragility of the pillars supporting the humanitarian identity and the need for strong and transparent buttresses of interaction and cooperation is evident. The mix of motivations and interests that combine nationalism, patriotism and the politics of identity look to call for a more complex alloy than the 'simplicity' of a shared humanitarian identity. Nevertheless, I argue that reducing this fragility lies, paradoxically, in a return to simpler, less alloyed identities. In the humanitarian niche, it is the simplicity of its fixed, existential purpose that provides it with the strength to unite. However, the aforementioned discussions have indicated the risk of hierarchies such an approach might entail. The solution this book proposes is an approach involving a discourse that recognises hierarchies of power but where these hierarchies are not the important factor. Instead, the emphasis is on *capabilities* rather than capacities or entitlements. The complexities in promoting such a discourse cannot be under-estimated. Nevertheless, confidence that a common identity can be found amongst the medley of interests finds its universal expression in an extract from the Minutes of a meeting of the Red Cross Council of Delegates during debates on the formulation of its Fundamental Principles: 'At all times and in all parts of the world, the Red Cross has only one single meaning: that is to fight against suffering and death, and to ensure the dignity of all people, without distinction'.[72]

In this chapter, I have presented consideration of the risks of association in a complex and contested space surrounding the search for this common meaning and have suggested directions along a path towards a more coherent, trusted partnership. Chapter 6 looks in greater depth at the origin and evolution of two principles of the Red Cross and Red Crescent Movement referred to in the aforementioned context: Voluntary Service and Universality. Using evidence from the Red Cross archives, it underlines the complexity of the debates and the need to find a simple, common language, which led to the proclamation of the seven Fundamental Principles in Vienna in 1965. Chapter 7 then turns to providing evidence of these complexities on the field, looking at the discourse and narratives presented in the public media and in the institutional and organisational narratives during the humanitarian responses to the Indian Ocean tsunami, in 2004, and the conflict in Syria which began in 2011.

Chapter 6

The Spirit of Humanity

Chapter 2 presented an account of how the idea of mitigating human suffering occasioned by war and disaster evolved from ancient Classical expressions of communal responsibilities and later Renaissance, Reformation and Enlightenment theories of freedom, dignity and justice. These transformed into the humanitarian expressions we are familiar with today. With the international legal recognition for rights of protection and relief which followed the founding of the ICRC in 1863, and the growth of the charity sector following the First and Second World Wars, came increasing professionalism of the humanitarian aid and development sectors. This gave rise to the emergence of minimum standards and codes of conduct to guide their action in the 1990s.[1] Whilst these were mainly aimed at improving accountability, security and project quality for the benefit of its stakeholders, project advice at a technical level was frequently accompanied by messages with a focus on 'best practice' and 'good governance' that reflected discourses dominated by the interests of actors who sit in government, international organisations and third sector society in the Global North.[2]

The practical idealism of the amateur that formed the humanitarian drive over the previous century was being replaced by a more assertive assurance of the professional, together with the strictures and prescriptions that an accompanying bureaucracy entails.[3] The policy narratives and reporting from the field shifted tone accordingly. What had begun with a search for tools for the humanitarian sector to address the challenges following perceived failures of humanitarian responses in Rwanda and the Balkans in the 1990s began to resemble a set of rules to govern and prescribe its performance.[4] This chapter explores the sentiments and motives which formed and framed performance of humanitarian action in the years preceding these changes in the 1990s.

Taking the foundation of the ICRC and the genesis of the Red Cross and Red Crescent Movement as the starting-point of modern humanitarianism, and considering its Fundamental Principles to be the essence of contemporary humanitarian values, an understanding of the modern humanitarian identity can be gained from examination of documents in the ICRC and IFRC archives covering the period leading to the proclamation of these principles at the 20th International Conference in Vienna in 1965.[5] Until now, academic scholarship and policy studies have concentrated attention on the principles of impartiality, neutrality and independence which frame much of the contemporary debate about access, security and independent ethical action. Whilst all related action is framed by the essential principle of humanity, two of the Fundamental Principles that are less examined – but which this study considers key to a re-formulation of least contested understandings of humanitarian action – are Voluntary Service and Universality. The focus of examination here is not restricted to the institutional and organisational narratives of the Movement, towards which commentaries on the Fundamental Principles normally focus, but are to be considered as an expression of a broader understanding of the *universality of suffering* and its agency to drive a spontaneous, mutually shared humanitarian response. Looking at institutional and organisational perspectives presented by ICRC and the League of Red Cross Societies (hereafter referred as 'the League'),[6] together with the perspective of a national Red Cross society through a series of essays presented by the Japanese Red Cross Society in the approach to the Vienna Conference, the examination encompasses discussions within the Movement that acknowledge changing contexts and the need for stable identities to navigate the new humanitarian environment. The study culminates in a review of the internal reappraisal of the role of the ICRC which took place in the 1970s, looking at its interaction with members of the Movement and all stakeholders in the social and political environments in which they work. The opening section charts the history of the proclamation of the Red Cross principles of Voluntary Service and Universality, and how interpretations of the Movement's Fundamental Principles have influenced the identity of its humanitarian expression.

THE EVOLUTION OF FUNDAMENTAL HUMANITARIAN PRINCIPLES

A principle is simply a rule, based upon judgement and experience, which is adopted by a community to guide its conduct.[7]

There is a common understanding that the modern humanitarian expression, especially in times of war, dates from the founding of the ICRC in 1863,[8] symbolised by the voluntary provision of 'neutral' care to those injured in war, whose rights and protection as non-combatants were legally codified in the first Geneva Convention of 1864. As early as 1875, Gustave Moynier, one of the founders of the Red Cross Movement and a long-term President of the ICRC, spoke of four core elements that would frame membership of the Movement. These were 'foresight', meaning that advance preparations should be made in peacetime, to provide assistance should war break out; 'solidarity', whereby the member societies undertake to establish mutual ties and to help each other; 'centralisation', which implies that there is only one Red Cross society in each country, but whose activities extend throughout the entire national territory, and 'mutuality', in the sense that care is given to all the wounded and the sick irrespective of their nationality.[9] These were incorporated into the statutes of the ICRC in 1921. After the Second World War, the League supplemented these with a further thirteen principles and six rules of application, approved by its Board of Governors in the Oxford Declaration of 1946.[10]

The first systematic analysis of the principles was presented in 1955 in the book written by Jean Pictet (English translation, 1956), in which he listed seventeen principles divided into two categories: (1) the Fundamental Principles, which express and inspire the reason for the Movement's existence, and (2) the 'organic' principles, which concern the Movement's structure and how it works.[11] These were framed by the over-arching principal of 'Humanity' which Pictet articulates in his book as 'the Red Cross fights against suffering and death. It demands that man shall be treated humanely under all circumstances'.[12] In his later commentaries, he describes this as the essence of the Red Cross doctrine 'from which all the other principles flow' and which 'enables the institution to define its tasks, to outline the field for its intervention and mark its limits'.[13]

Pictet's study provided the basis for the formulation of the seven Fundamental Principles of the Movement adopted in 1965 at the 20th International Conference of the Red Cross in Vienna, and which remain the framework for Red Cross and Red Crescent action today.[14] The values underlying the Movement's Fundamental Principles are founded on respect for the human being, and in the opinion of the Movement 'that is why they can be universally recognized and accepted'.[15] It is towards this elemental nature of humanitarian principles that Pictet directs us in the epigraph given in the beginning of this chapter. Distancing us from dogma and ideology, it calls for the simple recognition of the need for affected populations to survive, and to be enabled to lead a life with dignity and respect. It is this universal, human dimension towards which the debates leading up to the formal proclamation of the Fundamental Principles in 1965 focus most clearly, and to the voluntary 'spirit' of service to human suffering that they appeal.

The Debates

Notable amongst the correspondence within the Red Cross Movement over this period are the discussions around notions of 'spirit'. In the language of moral philosophy this often translates as 'motives': emotional, empathic connections which take dominance over prescriptive rules.[16] In the civilisations of ancient Greece and Rome, Cynics and Stoics encouraged the notion of a universal human community based upon the equal worth of each human being. Classical ideas about belonging to a universal human order were taken up by a number of Enlightenment philosophers, most notably Immanuel Kant.[17] According to Kant, the truly 'moral' actions are those which are followed for their own sake (duty) and not for motives of prudence (job).[18] Translated into the context of this study, this means that the most moral and legitimate humanitarian actions are those which are done to accomplish the principles of humanitarian duty: that is to say, reaching a principled end, even if the means to that end may be contested. By this interpretation, humanitarian ends can be interpreted as a 'duty', framed by stable motives and driven by a united spirit of service, in which the actions to accomplish this are less fixed. The dynamics of this approach are expressed in a number of ways in the documentation present in the archives and are linked to the notion of volunteering as a concept of 'free will', referred to in the Red Cross correspondence as being *disinterested*, and without the desire for material gain. As noted in chapter 2, there are several concepts on voluntary service and interpretations of the word 'volunteer', and these variations are recognised within the RCRC Movement. Early Movement handbooks on the concept of voluntary service observe that common to these is the readiness to help all in need.[19]

The reluctance of some in the Movement to 'codify' its doctrine provides evidence of the desire to retain the spontaneity and dynamism that marked the spirit of its birth at Solferino in 1859, as well as an awareness of the risks that a prescriptive identity could bring. For example, minutes of the meeting from a plenary session of the Standing Commission[20] in June 1959 to discuss the approach to codify the Red Cross Principles note that the then ICRC President Leopold Boissier remarked: 'To codify is to limit. There is a Red Cross spirit, and as Carl Burkhardt observed, *where the spirit is there is liberty* and it is this which should guide and inspire the Red Cross'.[21]

This reflected the opinion of the joint ICRC-League of Red Cross Societies Working Group set up by the Movement to review and formulate the Red Cross principles which found in its meeting three months earlier (March 1959) that these were rooted in the *character* of the Red Cross, which 'as a voluntary institution, animated by the spirit of service, focuses solely on the humanitarian interest of people'.[22]

The Working Group asked itself the fundamental question: what is meant by a principle:

> Everyone talks of principles and yet in essence no-one has formulated what a principle means. It is often confused with descriptions, goals or rules. The original meaning of a principle is lost. A principle is certainly found in the formulation of pure ideas, and to reach this formulation there is certainly a variety of means of proceeding, but in all cases the impetus which must be displayed to achieve the goal <u>can only be good will</u>, whether for work, or whether for reflection or meditation on things always outside of personal interest. In fact, nothing is invented; rather one discovers things which already exist and which are relevant. Therefore, it appears to me that <u>a principle is the very foundation and departing-point of a general idea, first observed by a few, then it becomes accepted as a possibility, until finally it becomes clear and evident, first for an elite and thereafter by the majority of people who are deliberating a [related] problem.</u>[23]

This presents an unambiguous statement on the understanding of the 'nature' of the Red Cross Principles during the process of their official formulation, with the voluntary spirit of 'good will' as key to understanding its creative, least-prescriptive, personality. It should be noted that although the Working Group was tasked to formulate the principles specific to the Movement (what became known as the 'Fundamental Principles' in the final declaration), de Rueda goes on to state that the motivations (spirit) behind the drive are not exclusive: 'The Red Cross partakes of some principles over which it cannot claim any monopoly, but its unique character makes it appear to own certain elements of these principles'.[24] References to the 'spirit' of the Movement and calls for the recognition of its 'unique character' feature prominently in the documentation reviewed in the archives and the concept is used to formulate the neutral personality of the work of the Red Cross Movement. Formal replies and handwritten notes in the margins of correspondence indicate the centrality the concepts of *spirit* and *service* hold for the ICRC, which stress the primacy of the notion of humanitarian *service* in directing understandings of humanitarian *action*.[25]

A review of replies from the Movement's National Societies who responded to the draft wording for the Principles proposed by the Working Group and sent by the Standing Commission under joint signature by ICRC and the League which were collected in summary August 1960 provides a useful chart of the evolution in formal proclamation of the Fundamental Principles.[26] The comments coalesce around two concepts: (i) the voluntary spirit of the founding doctrine and its emerging principles that question how prescriptive the original motives behind the humanitarian identity are to be considered and (ii) given the differing social and political environments, how each society might have the capability to share in a mutually supportive and universally accepted space for its humanitarian action. Some of the key tensions evident in the debates – and across the broader humanitarian literature – are those emerging from interpretations of mutuality and the auxiliary nature of this support. Gustave Moynier, in one of the earliest presentations on the foundation of the Red Cross, gives clarity to an understanding of complementary humanitarian *service* and *reciprocity* in cases where access in whatever form is not possible by national Red Cross societies of their own states:

> The societies of warring parties cannot always, despite the desire to do so, bring relief to their wounded or sick ill who have been captured by the enemy, but they compensate this disadvantage by bringing care, with equal dedication, to all those who fall into their hands, without discrimination. The result is a true and touching mutuality; an exchange of services which assure proper treatment for everyone wounded, regardless of the [national Red Cross] society who would normally have taken care of them.[27]

Understandings in the arguments which follow indicate the dynamic character of this mutual assistance, informed by principles that are both 'fundamental' and 'organic'. The former are seen to be 'fundamental motives' unaffected by circumstances and do not vary, and the latter relate to the organisational structure of the institution and the way it works, which take account of the context and conditions which prevail.[28] Common to all is the primacy of an understanding of 'voluntary' which signifies uncoerced service that is freely given, and a spontaneous, meaningful act of care. The following section examines the Movement debates around Voluntary Service and Universality more closely.

VOLUNTARY SERVICE

> *Voluntary and disinterested character*: The Red Cross is a voluntary organisation, with strictly humanitarian interests. Animated by the spirit of service, it derives no commercial profits from its activities (proposed text, 1959).

> *Voluntary Service*: The Red Cross is a voluntary relief organization not prompted in any manner by desire for gain (approved text, 1965).

Of the ten written replies provided in the summary document,[29] all except one (from the Polish Red Cross, who commented only on the question of neutrality) made reference to the importance the voluntary concept has in identifying, guiding and protecting the work of the Movement. This is voiced variously in terms of the Red Cross 'spirit', as an act of 'free will', and as 'service' to humanity.[30] The main points of contention in these responses relate to notions of whether Voluntary Service is paid or unpaid and is concerned with practical considerations regarding recruitment and retention of staff and volunteers (Swedish Red Cross; Netherlands Red Cross), support at an institutional level (American Red Cross; Canadian Red Cross, Netherlands Red Cross, Swedish Red Cross, Finnish Red Cross) as well as philosophical considerations (Japanese Red Cross; Canadian Red Cross, Red Cross of the German Democratic Republic).

In its response, the British Red Cross states:

> The Red Cross is a voluntary organisation prepared at all times to carry out its national and international tasks. The service of its members must be given from disinterested motives. Payment must never be made a condition for receiving Red Cross help. . . . The Red Cross, owing to its primary object in war and to the nature of its work at all times, must be prepared for immediate and very varied action in times of emergency.[31]

Significant here is the requirement that its members must be prepared and well-resourced to carry out its work, and that the motivations are not driven by profit or personal gain. The strictures placed against payment are that this must never be made a condition to receive help, but do not imply that the service should be unremunerated or un-resourced. Indeed, the urge to 'be prepared for immediate and very varied action in times of emergency' indicates the need for a range of well-resourced professional and technical capacities to be able to respond.

In a lengthy submission, supported by the Norwegian and Danish Red Cross Societies, the Swedish Red Cross is of the opinion that the proposed wording of the Principle of Voluntary Service is too prescriptive:

> It is stated, after mentioning the voluntary character of the organisation, and the spirit of service as its animating force, that the Red Cross does not derive any commercial profit from its activities. It is probably meant that the private Red Cross member shall not either derive any profits from his activities. However highly this would be desirable, it has in Sweden, where samaritans[32] often are recruited from people with low income, been found impossible to apply such a rule strictly, if one wants to keep the activity going.[33]

Concern about the prescriptive nature of this is echoed by the American Red Cross:

> Might it not be well to have the second sentence beginning: 'it derives no commercial profits . . .' read: 'Its members derive no commercial profit from Red Cross activities'. Our reason for suggesting this change is that we understand many Red Cross Societies do derive commercial profits from some of their activities. This would be true in the case of a number of Societies which have

been given or bequeathed business enterprises of one kind or another. We would hesitate to see any language which condemned this kind of financial support, since it would seem to us that each Society must determine as best it can how it can raise funds to finance its activities.[34]

It should be noted that the cautions against prescriptive wording do not apply only to the principles of Voluntary Service and the strictures against remuneration. There are strongly worded comments related to the proposed wording about independence. For example, the American Red Cross remarks that the proposed statement 'Red Cross action is entirely independent and free from any influence' is too sweeping:

> We wonder whether this also may be stated in terms somewhat too broad and too sweeping. National Societies, for example, operate in accordance with the laws of their countries and under definite limitations imposed by these laws. Red Cross Societies are not sovereign powers which this language might lead one to believe. Also, of course, Red Cross Societies should be 'influenced' by many, many types of humanitarian consideration. We do not take issue with what is meant here, only with the wording, which we feel may mislead those who are unacquainted with the Red Cross.[35]

The Canadian Red Cross remarks that 'we have always considered that the international and universal character of Red Cross to be fundamental',[36] but questions an approach that divides the Principles into two categories: 'fundamental' and 'organic':

> We feel that the Working Group has gone a long way towards condensing and consolidating basic Red Cross philosophy, but there are a few points with which we are not in agreement. We have always questioned the desirability of dividing the Principles into two categories, mainly because there can be disagreement about which Principles are 'fundamental' and which 'organic'.[37]

The Canadian Red Cross suggests that there should be one set of principles 'applicable to all Red Cross bodies' and a set of rules for National Societies, that together guide Red Cross doctrine: 'the latter to be comprised of some of the draft "Organic Principles" combined with an expanded text of the draft "Rules of Action"'. Its submission goes on to propose some alternative wording, supporting less instructive injunctions towards the National Societies. Notably, these remove the words 'independence' and 'neutrality' from the statement on the Principle of 'Impartiality':

> We have deleted 'Independence' because each National Society must work within the restrictions imposed by its country's laws. . . . We have deleted 'Neutrality', although we should like to see it included if some way can be found to do so within the bounds of strict accuracy.[38]

The comment is careful to note that 'even Mr Pictet concludes his excellent chapter on this subject by the statement: 'National Red Cross Societies, as can be seen, are not and ought not to be neutral'.

The importance of the philosophy underlying notions of voluntary service is made in the response from the Japanese Red Cross. Whilst strongly supporting the principle, it cautions on the tensions that arise from culturally misunderstood – or politically misconstrued – notions of 'free service':[39]

> What we have to be careful in the principle of 'Free Service' is that, because the relief is free, it is apt to become a favour and give an impression of contempt to the relieved or become an incomplete relief. The Red Cross should not make a difference between paid and non-paid relief, which is not always easy to do.[40]

This urges not to make a qualitative difference between paid and unpaid service, but to consider questions of competency and intent. These are often linked directly to the philosophical debate about the difference between the amateur and professional (which were prominent at the time of these discussions during the period of the Cold War, pitting the Communist ideologies of the USSR against the Liberal identities of the USA and its Allies), where the former is not necessarily seen as being less skilled, but where the spirit of engagement is different. One where values of the intent and the spirit of engagement took precedence over outcome.[41] It provides the important but distinct relationship between 'purpose' and 'practice' and indicates a requirement for careful formulations of their co-existence which acknowledge the intent and agency of each.[42] The significance of the distinction is made in the response from the Red Cross of the German Democratic Republic, who consider that volunteering is linked inherently with a spontaneous, freely given 'spirit' to act, which is an engagement that is different from one made with financial or other forms of incentive. It suggests that a voluntary spirit will combine a willingness to act and so, in both a philosophical and practical sense, will be more efficient:

> When there is a <u>willingness</u> to serve, this presupposes a 'spirit' of service. Therefore, [by combining the two] we are one step ahead and so lessen the distance between a motive [*disposition*] of spirit and an act of help.[43]

The response from the Netherlands Red Cross confirms the risks that confused interpretations of the identity and purpose of the Red Cross Movement might present:

> The use of the term 'Red Cross' brings us to the essentiality of our observations, namely that the words 'Red Cross' are sometimes used to indicate either the organisation or the activities. On the one side more or less statically, relating to the structure, the duties and competencies of the various organs and on the other side more dynamically, related to the method of working.[44]

This offers an indication of the recognition amongst members of the Red Cross Movement of the complex, hybrid nature of its identity and the need to separate, but engage equally with, the philosophical concept of the Red Cross purpose and the practical character of its humanitarian action. The tensions in this duality are summed up by the Netherlands Red Cross as follows:

> This difficulty, which is caused by the use of the term 'Red Cross' both for the organisation and for the activity, becomes most obvious in the case of the principle 'humanity'. In our opinion one cannot describe the structure of an organisation and the delimitation of its duties and competencies as humane. We think humanity is a quality which can merely be provided by actions and it should therefore be a basis for the Red Cross work.[45]

This understanding of a close but distinct relationship between the motive (purpose) and action (practice) underpins the arguments presented in this book which frame opportunities for confident access through a more inclusive, less divided and least contested discourse. With this in mind, my examination turns to considerations of universality. While not regarded as one of the core principles outside of the Movement, its associations have been a source of contestation: 'The Red Cross's principle of "universality" is sometimes impugned as a veil for neo-colonial power and a prolongation of religious missionary activity in a new form'.[46] Discussions within the Movement itself displayed a variety of interpretations, with opinions as to the significance of its identity ranging from understandings in relation to a sense of meaning for the Movement and a more practicable identity in relation to its function. A reconciliation of the tensions between purpose and practice might be reached through consideration of humanitarian action as 'praxis'. Interpretations of praxis have evolved from Classical understandings in Ancient Greece, where it was characterised by certain ontological assumptions concerning human action, and its construction under the European enlightenment and the expressions by Marx and other social thinkers in the nineteenth and twentieth centuries.[47] Contemporary interpretations of praxis have been presented by Friedrich Kratochwil which offer a harmonisation of these divided debates. His study urges a re-direction of analysis back towards a philosophical consideration of its meaning in society, yet which broadens the debate towards an understanding of its place in the practice of communication in evolutionary science.[48] Kratochwil is of the opinion that knowledge of the social world is acquired through participation in an existing historical society: 'It is through "commerce and conversation" that we develop the competencies for social life'.[49] Kratochwil observes that cooperation is not simply a human phenomenon, 'but is deeply rooted in and dependent upon certain biological capacities for communication'.[50] He provides examples of non-human cooperation, referring to studies by the biologist Karl von Frisch who demonstrated how bees communicate with other bees about food sup-plies[51] and studies on wolves who learn to act together to execute certain moves as part of a larger activity or plan. This situates understandings of praxis – of purpose and practice – in a broader, social construction that can-not be reduced to individually held beliefs, nor the recognition of a collective mind: 'the critical element in collective intentionality is a sense of doing (wanting, believing, etc.) something together, and the individual intentional-ity derived from the collective intentionality that they share'.[52]

Considerations of collective intentionality direct examination in this chapter towards these shared understandings of a philosophical and practical approach to a universal social identity within the Movement debates. A focus on the Working Group's responses to the Fundamental Principle of Univer-sality indicates how a universal approach with a shared understanding of the motives (duties) and actions (jobs) of the Red Cross Movement are central to a common identity: one that has a stable goal and able to function within the variances of the contexts and environments in which its members operate. A narrative common to almost all submissions – and one iterated by Pictet's study which frames the basis of the final drafts – is the need for a straightfor-ward doctrine that recognises the differences, yet which provides a platform for unity and a shared expression of meaningful, achievable action.

UNIVERSALITY

Universal and egalitarian character: The Red Cross is an international and universal organisation in which all the National Societies enjoy equal rights and recognise their duty to help one another (proposed text, 1959).

Universality: The Red Cross is a world-wide institution in which all Soci-eties have equal status and share equal responsibilities and duties in help-ing each other (approved text, 1965).

The principle of Universality complements the Red Cross principle of Unity,[53] which states that there can be only one Red Cross Society in any one country which must be open to all and must perform its humanitarian work throughout its territory.[54] Although – in the context of the Fundamental Principles of the Red Cross – the latter principle is seen to apply specifically to the Movement, together they urge a unified platform from which the universal humanitarian purpose can most coherently be performed. The Swedish Red Cross expresses this in its submission to the Standing Commission, as follows:

Besides the above four fundamental rules which must govern, justify and con-dition the whole Red Cross movement and any Red Cross action,[55] whether undertaken by individuals (nursing personnel, first-aid workers etc.), or by national or international organisations, there are many other rules which have been worked out for the organisations which carry out the Red Cross activities and for their actions. Among the most important may be mentioned that, for giving full effect to the Red Cross idea – the Red Cross should be a universal organisation and that in each State there should be a Red Cross Society, and only one Society, extending its activities to the whole territory. The Societies should recognise their duty to help one another.[56]

Understandings of universality comprise recognition of equal status between its members. It suggests the existence of mutual capacities for cooperation. However, the reality is that there are hierarchies within the humanitarian sector, just as in all aspects of social and political life. Equal access to the capabilities to achieve this directs answers to the central questions in this book. With understandings of voluntary service as a shared, universal expression of mutual good-will and cooperation, it suggests that the auxiliary character which humanitarian action in emergency environments present can offer opportunities for all stakeholders to be rendered capable, at the very least, of equal representation. Arguments presented in the opening sections to this chapter position legitimate humanitarian actions as those done to accomplish a sense of humanitarian duty, framed by stable motives and by a united spirit of service. Whilst several of the debates focus on Universality in the frame of its particular identity within membership of the Movement, the focus of discussion centres on agreement over the universality of a common obligation to unite in a spirit of service and cooperation that is accessible to all. The corollary to this call for access is the need for autonomy and the freedom to act in what is considered a common humanitarian interest – an interest that may not be shared in common with the structures of authority present in the environments of complex emergency.

The tensions are made explicit in the discussions around careful considerations of the Movement's interpretations of universality, where the strength of its approach comes not from a demand to replace authority but to act as a supplement when requested, or as a substitute when no other suitable options for the provision of humanitarian assistance are available. The Movement discussions around universality search to mitigate the tensions by distinguishing interpretations of universality as an expression of equal capability to access urgent humanitarian needs, while acknowledging the different capacities and hierarchies surrounding the nature of this access: the expression of mutual responsibilities that are complementary rather than exclusive and which are open to all. There is acknowledgement through the debates that a recognition of state responsibility, or the responsibility of others with sovereign authority in a state, will be the means to engender trust as well as promoting a sense of social responsibility. This is expressed in a collection of documents during a review of the role of ICRC in the modern world[57] where one participant stated his position on the criteria for its humanitarian action:

> In my opinion, there are only three criteria which are truly important:
>
> 1. What is in the interest of the victims, as against the interest of 'politics' or public opinion?
> 2. Once an action is launched, or even as it is being planned, one must on each occasion pose the question: 'Is there really no other authority which would do as well, if not better, than the ICRC?'
> 3. Is there truly no other acceptable intermediary who has the same capacity to act?[58]

The notion that modesty is a strength in the quest to gain trust and access recurs regularly in the discussions between members of the Movement, as well as in formal documentation from minutes of meetings. This acknowledges the acceptance of boundaries and limits to Movement authority in the scope and parameters of its action. Pictet makes the distinction between the principles which determine the Movement's meaning and its function, interpreted in my study as the distinction between purpose and practice. In his study of the Red Cross principles,[59] Pictet takes care to distinguish the organic nature of the Red Cross identity that defines its meaning, from the functional features linked to identification of its effective/efficient performance and the regulatory parameters defined by the Geneva Conventions. Considerable discussion in the Red Cross files centres around acknowledging the human (natural) influences that have led to the formulation of its moral and ethical principles for action, 'that have grown out of the experiences of human suffering' and so form a common experience and a universal appeal.[60] The shared history of survival in crises form the common backdrop, seen as the common narrative uniting a collective human experience, and to which one returns to give meaning to the principles for humanitarian action. Reflecting on the tensions within the context of defining the principles, the Standing Commission urges attention to the primary sources which gave rise to their common formulation, when faced with the uncertainties of life ahead.[61] There is, nevertheless, a realistic acknowledgement that both practices and purposes are contingent. Whilst recognising the strength generating from a stable history and a narrative of shared experiences, de Rueda cautions against adopting a static position, which remains immovable as times and contexts change. The Red Cross must be given the necessary 'life' to gain the authority it requires and the space to act in whatever context it finds itself.[62] The report of the meeting concludes with the observation shared by all participants that 'the current goal of the Commission is to formulate a declaration in the simplest manner possible, which can be adopted by everyone, even if each country gives words a slightly different meaning'.[63] The importance of the message here is one which understands a sense of *universality*, rather than one that is *universal*. That is to say, the fundamental spirit to respond to human suffering is one that can be universally understood, but there are no universal prescriptions to translate into templates for humanitarian action. It is its organic vitality, able to adopt and adapt, which generates strength and stability in the humanitarian identity.

The distinction is expressed in the RCRC Movement documentation which distinguishes between principles seen as those formulated to organise and manage the institution and those which are fundamental to identifying its meaning. This blend of the philosophical and practical approach is evident in the discussions in the Red Cross archives. These can be usefully considered through examination of a collection of essays presented by the Japanese Red Cross from 1961 to 1963, in preparation for the Vienna Conference of 1965. In these, the General Director for International Affairs, Masutaro Inoue, focuses on the 1955 study by Jean Pictet (using the English translation, 1956), with special attention to the distinction made between the organisational and institutional nature of the Red Cross principles. Throughout the three studies, emphasis is placed on the universal theme of a disinterested service common to all. Whilst Essay One focuses on the nature of the Fundamental Principles, Essay Two considers more specifically the organic principles of the Red Cross:

> The Fundamental Principles of the Red Cross are those principles which are fundamental among various principles that have to be observed when the Red Cross engages in actual operations after the establishment of its organization. However, for the organization to start working, the organization itself ought to be established beforehand. And to establish an institution, some principles should exist. These principles are called Organic Principles.[64]

The essay continues to define its view on how a member national Red Cross society is organised:

> All the organisations are composed of three elements: Object, Subject and Function. a) As for the <u>Object</u>, the Red Cross Organization is a pure relief organization and it has only one object, that is, 'to mitigate the suffering of human being'.[65] . . . b) The <u>Subject</u> is composed of people of goodwill [. . . . .] c) The <u>Function</u> is dynamic.[66] For relief work means to take measures appropriate to a given circumstance within a given period of time, and circumstances are always changing.[67]

In the first essay, goodwill is identified by the Japanese Red Cross through expression of voluntary service 'which is an assembly of popular good will'.[68] Essay Two expands on identification of the subject:

Principles necessary to form the Subject: 1 <u>Voluntary Service</u> (Volontariat): Relief works require sacrifices (time, labour, money),[69] therefore, the members should be recruited among volunteers.[70] However, the institution is a place where all the works are being carried out on the basis of the Red Cross principles. Therefore, the persons who have any inconvenience in carrying out work based on the Red Cross principles, or those who have no intention to do so are not qualified to participate in the institution.[71] 2. <u>Auxiliarity</u>. It goes without saying that the highest authority responsible for the relief of people is the State;[72] therefore, it is also the responsibility of the State to organize, in peace time, auxiliary organ [sic] which has enough strength and reliability to operate.[73]

Throughout the three studies, emphasis is placed on the universal theme of a disinterested service common to all, driven by the overriding humanitarian objective to bring relief of suffering to those most in need. The essential driving force to accomplish this is defined by a spirit of disinterested selflessness, identified in the essays and in Pictet's study as meaning 'the organisation does not aim at its own existence . . . it makes no distinction between friend and foe'.[74] Emphasis is placed on the fact that the spirit of voluntary service is freely chosen and is wholly committed. Questions of remuneration are, to this extent, unimportant. Understandings of universality engage with notions of equality of the human being when faced with situations of extreme vulnerability and is not a political or hierarchical ascription. It refers to access to equal capabilities to survive, the only distinction which can be made is according to proportion of need.[75]

The concluding section considers the strengths and limitations some of the Movement narratives foresee around the evolving auxiliary but autonomous role. It expands on discussions around meaning and function – between fundamental and organic – raised in the debates on the Red Cross identity. It connects understandings of voluntary service and universality across a broader stakeholder discourse.

Evolving Identities: Articulations of Strength in a Political Environment

The ICRC had always been aware of the need to recognise the strengths in diversity that a diverse and pluralist approach would bring, and the risk that an essentialist codification of rules and principles might entail. 'Multitudinism' features as one of the organic principles in Pictet's study and he states that 'The ranks of a National Red Cross Society must be open to all the citizens of a country concerned'.[76] Whilst the focus is on inclusiveness and non-discrimination, Pictet emphasises the value of a multitudinal approach as an expression of purpose as well as of practice: 'while it is important that the Red Cross ranks are open to all, the main point is that it should bestow its benefits without distinction to all who need them. We are concerned there with the Movement's ultimate purpose and not merely the means of achieving it'.[77] This is relevant to understandings of humanitarian identities as 'praxis' in my book and which are discussed at greater length in chapter 8.

An inclusive approach is an important feature in the debates but there is a recognition of risks from a careless assimilation. In a review of activities in the Middle East and Asia written in 1952, Huber notes the need for ICRC to carve an identity that is distanced as far as possible from association with tensions emerging in the post-imperial and post-colonial climate following the end of the Second World War. But he also cautions against going too far in an opposite direction that fabricates a cultural assimilation which could lead to mistrust and suspicion on all sides. He expresses the need for a careful balance so that the spirit of the humanitarian ethic can survive and flourish. Without this, he writes, 'it would be as sterile as a flower cut from its roots; it would be beautiful but would inescapably die'.[78] In his report following a tour of Asian countries three years later, Olgiati observes the need to 'pay attention to ensuring unity between doctrine and action; between ideal and reality'[79] since 'the Red Cross sees itself as an expression implicit amongst almost all peoples'[80] and must ensure that it is worthily represented in this regard.[81]

Together with evidence from the debates presented earlier, these urge that the messages surrounding principle and practice must be straightforward, meaningful and be universally relevant. In a comprehensive study on the role of the Red Cross (the 'Tansley Report'),[82] the authors felt that the Movement's principles were not being readily transmitted, and suggested that they be restated in 'a language and in a form which can be easily understood'.[83] The Fundamental Principles that were finally approved at the meeting of the Council of Delegates in Prague in 1961, then formally proclaimed at the International Conference in Vienna in 1965, were seen by the Movement to have achieved this aim as best possible. Conclusions from a meeting held by the Movement in Bucharest in 1977 to discuss the findings of the Tansley report stated:

> Its fundamental principles are the most valuable asset of the Red Cross, they constitute a binding force, a set of guidelines, a programme of action, the source and expression of an ideal, and a guarantee of universality. There is no need to re-formulate them; the main thing is to live up to them and make them known and respected.[84]

The evolution of the Red Cross doctrine since 1863, with a period of ten years of formal consultation within the Movement, resulted in the seven Fundamental Principles that form the Red Cross and Red Crescent identity today, four of which – humanity, impartiality, independence and neutrality – have been accepted as the universal expression of the humanitarian identity world-wide. As questions raised between partners in the Movement sixty years ago indicate, the concern then and now relates to how accessible the humanitarian message remains with its stakeholders. This chapter suggests that within the humanitarian sector, there is a perceived need to retain the spontaneity that drove the voluntary spirit and framed the principles which emerged after the Battle of Solferino in 1859. It must ensure that the humanitarian purpose and its practices remain relevant and capable of addressing the complexity of needs in the environments of emergency in which it acts. This includes forging a trusted identity that provides competent representation of the community of stakeholders it serves.

In his book on the Fundamental Principles of the Red Cross which framed the basis for the discussions presented earlier and the proclamation of the Principles in 1965, Pictet echoes the sentiments expressed a few years earlier by Max Huber: 'If the Red Cross were to lose its human touch, if it were to lose its voluntary character and become tied up with red tape, it would be like a flower that has been plucked and soon withers and dies'.[85] He recognised that protection of the human dynamism and the spirit of service which marked the nascence of the Red Cross Movement on the battlefields of Solferino was essential to an identity that brought trust and justice to the purpose and practice of humanitarian action – the very 'genome' of its moral character. Kant's rights-based approach to justice asserts that humanity cannot be based on utilitarian empirical considerations, since moral duty results from freedom of choice based on reason: 'basing morality on interests and preferences destroys its dignity'.[86] In his 1952 report, Huber echoes this philosophical caution:

> I will set aside all efforts to justify the Red Cross on the grounds of its 'utility'; this character of its work is adequately displayed by the concrete actions of the Red Cross, but the introduction of a utilitarian function to the fundamental doctrine of the Red Cross would destroy its essential spirit. For the defining characteristic of the Red Cross is its <u>disinterested</u> action. Otherwise it is [all just] a good example of collective social egotism, unless it involves voluntary cooperation, representing a genuine sacrifice.[87]

Maturing Commentaries: Simplicity of Purpose, Practice and Expectation

It is clear from examination of the documentation provided in this chapter that the Red Cross principles are seen to provide two functions: one that is regulatory and organisational, and the other giving meaning and direction. The Movement debates on understandings of purpose and practice provide evidence of the tensions within the humanitarian identity and the space in which it functions: the complexities of being part of a system, yet apart from it. The consolidation of trust in the stakeholder community and access to a common discourse requires a strong identity. The Japanese Red Cross essays frame the organisational principles as a means of gaining strength and the Fundamental Principles as a means of using strength.[88] In these, strength for universal recognition of the Movement is created through the confident assimilation of the Subject (summarised as good will and voluntary service) and the Object (humanity), and where the identities coalesce around expressions of mutuality. That is to say, shared and complementary support that recognises difference. It is here that a principle of universality is linked to a mutual spirit of service which combine to generate complementary practices of effective action. The sense reflects philosophical understandings of 'praxis' referred earlier in the chapter which – in Kratochwil's interpretation[89] – is more than an abstract theory but is linked to evolutionary practices of sharing and communication. Cooperation is reliant on intent as much as efficiency and gains its trust from expressions of both; for a universal approach to succeed there must be a synthesis of differences, not the search for sameness.

The reappraisals of its role and practice conducted by ICRC in the late 1960s and early 1970s[90] acknowledge the distinct roles and characteristics required to make the humanitarian purpose succeed. The Movement in general, and ICRC in particular, is consistent in stressing that the responsibility to care and protect populations in need rests with the state, and that an obligation to provide similar care and protection rests with any group exercising an equivalence of sovereignty amongst populations in need.[91] The Movement debates around formulation of the Fundamental Principles presented in the first section of the chapter and the internal debates within ICRC, together with the essays from the Japanese Red Cross presented in the second section, acknowledge the need for humanitarians to engage with their political identity. Notes from one of the Working Groups studying the role of the ICRC in its contemporary environment remark that there had been a 'loss of innocence' after declaration of the Geneva Conventions, 1949, which, through its formally mandated role as guardian of these international conventions, had placed the identity of ICRC firmly within the regulatory framework of global politics.[92]

The growth in the number of national Red Cross and Red Crescent societies in the fifty years following the First World War extended the Movement identity into being an important feature of the social life of communities, with obligations to the societies they belong to:

The national societies, who are government auxiliaries, have become important elements in social life, on which government should be able to rely. In the same way, whether we like it or not, ICRC has become an organ of the international community who, when certain circumstances align, <u>must</u> act.[93]

The expansion in membership of the Movement and the increasing activities and role of the ICRC after the First and Second World Wars (as well as its regulatory role as guardian of the Geneva Conventions, the archived documents make reference to increasing calls for humanitarian engagement in global crises in, for example, Congo, Cuba, Korea and Hungary)[94] gave impetus to the breadth and depth of the studies examined in this chapter. There may have been strategic reasons behind the Japanese Red Cross position and the considerable efforts it made to endorse details of Pictet's analysis on the Fundamental Principles which, they felt, had been omitted in the drafts for the final declaration (the government of Japan had been putting pressure on the Japanese Red Cross to organise and manage the re-patriation of ethnic Korean residents of Japan who left North Korea between the years of 1955 and 1967).[95] However, the passion for endorsing an identity that can be universally acceptable to all stakeholders is unanimous in all the discussions examined. In his study, Pictet writes of the Red Cross principles that 'they inspire the institution, characterise it and determine its aims'. At an organisational level, they 'take account of the material and spiritual realities of the life in society in which it undertakes its work', and 'with disinterestedness the Red Cross finds the first and the most important of its organic principles'.[96] The prominence given to the principles of Universality and Voluntary Service is made evident in two diagrams attached to the collection of essays presented by the Japanese Red Cross. In one, Universality is seen as the base supporting the institutional structure, and in the other, Voluntary Service is presented as the door to open its institutional and organisational access. Despite some calls for the Movement identity to expand beyond its core normative goal of bringing relief from suffering to those left unassisted in times of crisis,[97] there is recognition that the Movement's strength comes from recognising limits to its authority and that responsibility must not be devolved from the structures entrusted by their communities to protect them – limits and responsibilities made clear by Resolutions 10 and 12 from the Toronto International Conference which restate the role of the Movement as an auxiliary to the provision of public humanitarian services.[98]

The challenges of a universal approach are evident. The documentation in the archives shows ICRC concern about codification of the Red Cross principles. Robust representations were made for an autonomous and independent place within the movement space to enable ICRC to perform its role as guardian of the Geneva Conventions. Influenced by Movement disagreements at the International Conferences in Toronto and New Delhi, there were strong demands for solidarity in promoting unity of purpose and practice. There had to be a united spirit of humanity since, as the President of the British Red Cross stated in a plenary session of the New Delhi conference, 'Universality without unity of purpose is useless'.[99] Humanitarian space is a social space, and humanitarian society, like any other, needs solidarity, unity and cooperation to succeed. This raises questions of how a repositioned humanitarian identity will be any different from the calls for access to the socio-political discourse already demanded by civil society. How will the community of stakeholders be able to trust an identity that claims to be a part of politics but remaining apart from it without the instrumental conjuring of identities presented in chapter 3? How can a new discourse address the tensions between auxiliary and independence; between conformity and challenge? The resolution proposed is greater recognition of a common identity and shared histories which provide access to the discourse for humanitarians working on the frontiers of state and society. Pictet re-iterates the call for unity and universality when he reminds us that the Red Cross ideal demands that each of its bodies should not be simply a group of unconnected elements, but a real working community 'all of whose members are striving towards a higher purpose common to them all'.[100] The case studies in chapter 7 examine the extent to which these elements connect to provide a united purpose for the community of stakeholders in a humanitarian crisis.

Chapter 7

Case Studies

The previous chapter has considered two of the Fundamental Principles of the Red Cross and Red Crescent Movement that are less widely examined in the scholarship of humanitarian action – those of Voluntary Service and Universality. Seen as principles with specific relevance to the Movement, I suggest that recognition of their common relevance across the broader humanitarian arena can open a more cooperative discourse within the community of stakeholders. This chapter examines whether expressions of voluntary service and the universality of a shared purpose lead to understandings of a common identity amongst them. Using a straightforward count of the frequency selected words appear in the texts examined reveals where the focus of discussion in each constituent narrative has importance. The presence and, as significantly, the absence of certain words or terms which my study sees as having salience in opening access to a common discourse within the humanitarian arena makes evident how far discussions take place within silos of disconnected identities. Certain key words are prominent (see tables) but, as the following analysis displays, each serve a particular internal or external socio-political narrative which remain distant from representations of a shared discourse. The words or terms may be identical, but their interpretation in the contexts where they occur are often very different.

This chapter examines expressions of a common identity and understandings of partnership presented across stakeholder narratives in two humanitarian responses to a situation of complex emergency.[1] The first study explores whether and how far expressions of voluntary service and universality share a common identity and focuses its analysis on the Indian Ocean tsunami which struck Sri Lanka in December 2004. A second, shorter, study on the conflict in Syria turns towards the varied interpretations of 'partnership' in these environments and searches to find whether the varied and contested constructions of a shared identity in humanitarian response present opportunities for participation in a space of shared discourse. Using eleven search terms, the analysis in the first study looks for discussions with relevance to understandings of voluntary service and universality which I argue present opportunities for construction of a prosocial discourse that promote common expressions of trusted interaction within the humanitarian arena. These are: *volunt(ary/eer)*; *service*; *humanitarian*; *donor(s)*; *auxiliary; stakeholder(s); trust*; *access(ibility)*; *purpose; practice* and *communit(y/ies)*. These words have been selected according to their relevance to the concepts of community trust and representation that feature in the key arguments in my book and which feature as core to a prosocial discourse in the literature reviewed. The second study, focusing on the conflict in Syria that started in 2011, uses six search terms: three directing towards cooperative engagement (*partnership; support; dialogue*) and three towards contested engagement (*opposition; challenge; rebel*). Whilst the humanitarian response took place in a similar situation of complex emergency, the sociopolitical boundaries in Syria differed from Sri Lanka in several ways. In Syria, the strict government control over public narratives meant there was greater restriction to the permissible discussion. In consideration of the securitised nature of the discourse, and the reduced access for participation within it, the words or terms in this section are searching for evidence of the varied constructions of partnership within the shared situations of complex emergency.

The concluding section of the chapter makes a short review of some of the key outcomes of the analysis in these documents. It introduces comparison with reaction to humanitarian responses following Cyclone Nargis which struck the south-east of Myanmar on 2–3 May 2008. As a humanitarian response to a natural disaster that occurred in a situation of ongoing civil violence, this was another environment of complex emergency. Whilst analysis in this book examines influences across the broad humanitarian sector, as indicated in chapter 1, the lens of study is purposely focused on the national rather than the global environment of humanitarian practice. Consequently, the case studies in this chapter give predominance to the national and regional media that influenced discourse in the environment, with a shorter comparative study on the discourse surrounding the international institutional and organisational narratives. By examining notions of voluntary service as a common identity amongst stakeholders in the humanitarian discourse, the case studies search to identify shared and contested understandings of humanitarian action in the contexts of a complex emergency. At the core of this debate are the contradictions perceived to be inherent in notions of volunteers acting as an independent auxiliary to public services, and the tensions related to associations with power and influence. The analysis informs arguments in the concluding chapters on whether and why access to the discourse has changed, and what opportunities might arise from a reappraisal of the humanitarian identities that emerge in the contemporary narratives.

1. INDIAN OCEAN TSUNAMI, SRI LANKA, 2004

On 26 December 2004, a massive earthquake off the west coast of Northern Sumatra generated a series of tsunamis that killed people in 14 countries around the Indian Ocean. The countries most affected were Indonesia, Sri Lanka, the Maldives, India and Thailand, where over 227,000 people lost their lives and some 1.7 million were displaced. In response to the disaster more than 90 governments and millions of individuals and private companies worldwide donated some $13 billion to emergency relief and reconstruction. Thirty-five countries provided military or civil defence assets and around 300 relief groups converged on Aceh and Sri Lanka in the first month.[2] Analysts were unanimous that this was too many: 'the local communities had their own organisations, and authorities were too often shunted aside and not consulted'.[3] In the case of Sri Lanka, enforced by a growing negative public opinion on the purpose and practices of the expanding humanitarian aid and development network, perceptions of neutrality and impartiality became increasingly contested. This created an environment which grew more hostile through manipulation – wittingly and unwittingly – of the notion of 'humanitarian space'.[4]

The problems that arose from overconfident assumptions of the nature of this space in Sri Lanka emphasised the need to recognise the force of influences informing the humanitarian identities within it. Dorothea Hilhorst and Bram Jansen approach the question of humanitarian space in the form of an inclusive 'arena' wherein a broad range of principles and influences – political and apolitical – are working together and negotiate the outcomes of aid.[5] According to this framework, 'the realities and outcomes of aid depend on how actors along and around the aid chain – donor representatives, headquarters, field staff, aid recipients and surrounding actors – interpret the context, the needs, their own role and each other'. By recognising these complex relationships and the need to navigate the interactions, humanitarian actors are seen to inhabit a complex socio-political place where trust is contingent on the context and the stakeholders they engage with and are seen to represent. The following studies of common terms in the humanitarian discourse give evidence of how contingent these can be.

National and Regional Media Narratives

The first study in this section examines the discourse in the 'Spotlight' section in *The Sunday Leader*, and in the 'News' section of *The Sunday Island*, two of the Sri Lankan weekly newspapers based in the capital, Colombo. These are written in English and were widely read by the large number of English speakers in the national population living in the predominantly Sinhala populated areas of the country, as well as by foreign and ex-patriot workers. The second study examines articles in the 'Features' section of *TamilNet*, an English-language online newswire service founded in 1997 aimed at providing news with a Tamil perspective on issues concerning Tamils in Sri Lanka.[6] All of these were a frequent source of opinion and comment amongst the UN, Red Cross and Red Crescent and NGO community. The period of analysis covers the six months following the tsunami, from 01 January to 30 June 2005. This includes the period of transition from humanitarian relief to recovery and when, in the case of Sri Lanka, the focus of political rhetoric around issues of national sovereignty and local authority was at its sharpest.[7]

The Sunday Island; The Sunday Leader

As table 7.1A indicates, the four most frequent of the search terms in the Sri Lanka context are *communit(y/ies)*, *donor(s)*, *humanitarian service(s)* and *voluntary/volunteer(s)*. The analysis finds significant correlation with associations of service to community that expresses national engagement and local agency.[8] Articles in the first days following the tsunami highlight the role that local communities played in first emergency response, with a significant number of narratives expressing pride in a community response and local coping capacities. A passage in *The Sunday Leader* is typical of these:

> The people of this country worked untiringly over the last one week to ensure that people in the areas where the tsunami unleashed its terror would receive help as fast as possible. Getting essential items together and sending it to these

Table 7.1A. Indian Ocean Tsunami – Sri Lanka 2004–2005

Search term	Sunday Island 'News' (68,985 words)	Sunday Leader 'Spotlight' (41,718 words)	TamilNet 'Features' (38,714 words)	IFRC Quarterly Reports (32,649 words)	TEC Synthesis Report (50,412 words)	Total
Community(ies)	69	26	40	142	103	**380**
Donor(s)	37	19	51	29	158	**294**
Humanitarian	29	17	14	58	144	**262**
Service(s)	47	28	17	27	55	**174**
Voluntary/Volunteer(s)	30	21	3	95	9	**158**
Access(ible)	15	6	4	4	32	**61**
Practice	1	1	3	6	33	**44**
Purpose	12	13	4	1	2	**32**
(en)Trust(ed)	4	0	3	1	8	**16**
Stakeholder(s)	6	2	0	6	1	**15**
Auxiliary	0	0	0	0	0	**0**

Table 7.1B. Syria 2012–2013

	Syria Times 'Opinion' (22,354 words)	Syria Times 'Commentary' (28,147 words)	Gulf Times 'Opinion' (22,020 words)	OCHA-IASC Report (27,650 words)	IFRC Operations Updates (22,781 words)	Total
Humanitarian	3	3	13	257	31	**307**
Service(s)	2	2	9	16	86	**115**
Voluntary/Volunteer(s)	1	0	0	7	99	**107**
Community(ies)	2	6	13	53	24	**98**
Access(ible)	0	0	0	42	52	**94**
Donor(s)	0	0	1	21	22	**44**
Practice	1	6	1	9	3	**20**
Purpose	3	4	0	1	0	**8**
(en)Trust(ed)[9]	0	0	0	6	0	**6**
Stakeholder(s)	0	0	0	0	0	**0**

areas was the order of the day, with several organisations and countless individuals providing immediate relief while the international community pledged and presented large amounts of aid and financial assistance to the government.[10]

The Sunday Island presents the opportunities for community cohesion and political reconciliation:

> The government has also assured them that areas held by the LTTE wouldn't be neglected in the distribution of urgently needed relief supplies. Premier Mahinda Rajapakse said strict instructions had been issued to relevant authorities to distribute the relief equally. The premier, speaking to the Sunday Island, on his way to tsunami ravaged Batticaloa from Trincomalee, stressed that the government wouldn't discriminate.[11]

Articles in *The Sunday Leader* referring to the health centres that were established in the immediate aftermath of the crisis recognise the state and commercial sector support to those affected by the disaster, but the tensions are already being made manifest:

> Medical aid for these centres is provided by private sector supporters as well as through various government institutions. . . . While their clearing operations and medical camps are well planned and provide necessary services to people in dire need, their biggest constraint is that they are not well fortified in the area of relief supplies.[12]

As international aid was mobilised, media narratives became increasingly focused on the international response and donor resources. By the end of

January 2005, expressions of national and local community agency remain prominent but the discourse shifts towards questioning the impact and efficiency of the service provided by the state and by the international humanitarian community. From this point on, notions of *service* in many of the articles are presented as an obligation to the community which is not being fulfilled by the state structures responsible to provide them, or the international structures mobilised to support them:

> The Civil Aviation Authority (CAA) as well as Sri Lankan [Airways] insists that the relevant authorities are being regularly reminded of the awaiting packages [of humanitarian aid] to no avail. What it does to the donors to watch piles of relief lying at the international airport on television is nobody's concern with the Social Services Ministry falling way behind in its duty to dispatch the goods to affected people.[13]

Articles in *The Sunday Leader* are especially critical of the Presidential task forces[14] that were established following the tsunami to manage the humanitarian response:

> Even after the appointment of different task forces, the relief is not reaching the people, particularly those in the north and east. Aid is sent and often there is no needs-based evaluation.[15]
>
> Trained to take charge of emergency situations and treat victims of natural disasters, these doctors were not facilitated, nor were they sent to places where their services were vital.[16]

In articles during the first days following the tsunami, terms engaging the word *humanitarian* are generally positioned to indicate a positive engagement ('humanitarian relief; 'humanitarian assistance') and pride in the spontaneous expression of goodwill and cooperation. An undertone of political narrative dominates association with many of these, with a focus on the national political discourse related to the forthcoming elections or with a national security discourse related to the conflict in the north of the island and the risks to sovereignty posed by the call for an independent Tamil homeland and the military-political dynamic led by the LTTE.[17] As the recovery and reconstruction phase progresses, there are increasing narratives surrounding geopolitical implications of international aid and development interventions.[18] These narratives engage a corresponding increase in references to trust or mistrust at a national political level and at an external institutional level:

> Given Sri Lanka's appalling track record as far as corruption issues are concerned there is little trust as far as government and other officials are concerned that the large amount of foreign aid pledged will indeed be utilised in the correct

manner. Suspicion extends also to expatriate workers based in the island who are not completely trusted to ensure that aid in such massive quantities will be distributed equally and in a transparent manner.[19]

Positive uses of the word *voluntary/volunteer* are predominantly linked to the local response. Articles in the first days following the tsunami highlight the role that local communities played in first emergency response, with a significant number of narratives expressing pride in a community response and local coping capacities. As international aid was mobilised, media narratives became increasingly focused on the international response and donor resources. Notions of spontaneity, impact and efficiency feature as a significant part of these positive associations. Negative narratives in these contexts are associated with political or demographic rhetoric, linked to the forthcoming elections or the conflict in the north of the island. Volunteer association with the international response is positive in articles published during the emergency phase but become increasingly hostile as the focus of narratives moves towards recovery and reconstruction. As with the term *humanitarian*, there are frequent associations (positive and negative) with the concept of stakeholder interests in the articles. Linkages to abuse of authority[20] and misuse of funds feature as a component in these narratives. The use of the word *donor* is predominantly associated with an external agency, such as 'international', 'overseas' and 'foreign'. 'Local' or 'national' are not linked as a donor in any of the articles examined.

Both publications raise questions regarding the equitable and transparent provision of emergency aid and resources for reconstruction, and urge close consultation with communities for a fair distribution. The articles show contestation over the mechanisms to achieve this, though there is a call for an approach that unites the capacities of all communities in Sri Lanka. When linked to narratives about the emergency phase and expressions of community response in the local environment, the discourse around *purpose* and *practice* is predominantly positive. Pragmatic expressions of impact and efficiency are often twinned with empathic notions of compassion. As the operating environment shifts from emergency to recovery the articles begin to focus on agency and accountability, with escalating rhetoric on the political implications of the stakeholder response to the tsunami. The narratives become increasingly securitised, focusing on the political and economic influences of responses in the humanitarian environment, with calls for transparency as to the purpose of its delivery and the practice of its distribution. With growing international donor support to calls for a joint mechanism of delivery, and the government proposal for the Post-Tsunami Operating Management Structure (P-TOMS), the articles in *The Sunday Leader* and *The Sunday Island* present rising concern over a loss of central (state) control over the humanitarian response:

> Trincomalee harbour and the adjacent coastal areas, regarded for centuries as a strategic prize, and of particular concern to Sri Lanka and India owing to the recent LTTE build-up, were affected by the tsunami. However, they have not been exempted from the ambit of the P-TOMS.[21]

The securitised discourse is not confined to LTTE-controlled areas in the north and east but extends towards political movements in other areas of the country. In response to the highly publicised efforts of the Janatha Vimukthi Peramuna (JVP)[22] on bringing relief to communities in its strongholds in the southeast, *The Sunday Leader* remarks that 'relief packages themselves have become a part of the JVP's propaganda'. Following widespread support to the community-led initiatives during the first response to the disaster, all narratives urge a more centralised control over the relief and recovery process once the emergency phase is over. A unity of purpose that foregrounds intent and efficiency frames much of the discourse around support for centralised, state-led action.

TamilNet, 'Features', January–June 2005

The two most frequently used of the eleven search terms in the *TamilNet* articles are *Donor* and *Communit(y/ies)*. The frequency of the pairings of each is significant and may reflect the material and political significance that the overseas Tamil community played in fund-raising and mobilising material (in-kind) support and public awareness of the impact of the disaster on the north-east of the country.[23] The linkage with an international donor response to the exclusion of any reference to an explicit national or local donor response is evident ('international donor' occurs fourteen times, with no results showing for 'local' or 'national' donor). All other references refer implicitly or explicitly to foreign donors, with no mention of a national or local donor response. This contrasts with associations of *community* in the local disaster response and its framing as an important force for strength and social stability amidst the crisis, where there are frequent calls for the fullest involvement of the affected local community. The dominant expression of both words in the context is highly political. References to the international donor community are predominantly calling for recognition of the capability of the Tamil population in general, and of the Tamil National Alliance (TNA) in particular, the largest Tamil political party at the time, to assess the needs and implement recovery programmes.

Service(s) is the third most frequently used of the search terms. Most of these are nominative or descriptive (civil service; health services; social services; financial services, agricultural services etc.). The ontology of its expression throughout is linked either directly or indirectly to a sense of social engagement and organisational efficiency ('the rendering of effective and efficient services') but with a distinct political message, linked to opposition in the northeast of the country for a centralised, government-controlled system for recovery and reconstruction:

> The TNA also stated that centralization of the relief and reconstruction efforts and the formulation of plans at the center without consultation with the affected people and without local participation would not produce effective and efficient results in dealing with the calamity. On the other hand, in LTTE controlled territory, such coping mechanisms have been in place during the period of the conflict to address humanitarian needs. These efficient, tried and tested mechanisms have had the fullest involvement of the affected local community.[24]

A recognition of the Tamil community's capacity to cope without centralised control is recurrent in the narratives, linked to freedom of choice and a voluntary spirit which this study argues is an important element of a common identity and service to the community (examined later in this chapter, and in chapter 8):

> There should be no interference with the free wish of individuals or institutions to be of service to whomever they desire to help.[25]

The failure to provide public services or the inability for communities to access these is used as a means of apportioning political blame:

> The biggest hazard we face in such situations is community health. The Sri Lankan government's public health service system has shown that it is not capable of handling emergencies like this.[26]

Like *service*, the use of the word *humanitarian* is predominantly nominative or descriptive (humanitarian needs; humanitarian operations; humanitarian issues etc.) and is most frequently linked with expressions of positive social engagement:

> President Kumaratunga has taken a courageous move which has threatened her government, however, for humanitarian reasons, it was the right move.[27]

The counterpoise between the positive instrumental use of the word humanitarian is turned, when politically expedient, to a negative instrumental criticism of central governmental policy, casting doubts on motives, purpose and practice:

> The Tamil people and the LTTE have lost hope entirely with the government of Sri Lanka when it comes to humanitarian aid . . . the Tamil people and the

LTTE have strong doubts of the president's sincerity of purpose when it comes to delivery.[28]

As with the articles in *The Sunday Leader* and *The Sunday Island*, positive associations with *Voluntary/eer/s* are linked to motivation and community identity:

> Mr. S. M Izzadeen, a member of the local monitoring mission for the Batticaloa district told TamilNet Thursday that although Tamils and Muslims are coordinating relief and rescue work in many parts of Amparai and Batticaloa, more volunteers in the remoter areas of the southeast coast are urgently required.[29]
>
> We have easy access to areas of North East; most of our volunteers and staff are from North East, so we can help.[30]

Institutional and Organisational Documentation

The second section of studies on the Indian Ocean tsunami response in Sri Lanka examines institutional and organisational documentation (practitioner, policymaker and donors) covering humanitarian action in the same environment over the same period. First, a selection of the quarterly reports by the IFRC on its activities and those of the member RCRC National Societies who were working under its umbrella at that time. These number three reports, covering the period from 26 December 2004 to 30 June 2005. Second, the joint evaluation by the Tsunami Evaluation Coalition (TEC) of the international response to the Indian Ocean tsunami, an international initiative where participating agencies collaborated on evaluations of the tsunami response.[31] The TEC synthesis report covers a period of the first eight months of the response and has two main aims: to improve the quality of natural disaster response policy and practice, and to account to both donor and populations in the affected country.[32]

IFRC Quarterly Reports

The most frequently used term is *communit(y/ies)*. Most of these are nominative or descriptive (tsunami-affected communities; local communities; affected communities; community needs; community health etc.). Association is predominantly linked to the programmatic framework of the Movement's identity, its organisational focus of working with the Red Cross/Crescent National Societies and developing their local capacities: *community-based* presents 40 results (community-based disaster management networks; community-based preparedness; community-based health programmes etc.). The local community focus is dominant in these reports.

The second most frequent of the search terms is *voluntary/eer/s*. These are uniformly positive and non-politicised, linked to the Movement identity, and most often associated with motivation and acknowledgement of local capacities. The search shows significant pairing with training and capacity building, linked to developing volunteer capabilities to provide service to the community ('volunteer training' presents eighty-one results).

In accordance with the operational reporting focus of the reports, most uses of the word *humanitarian(s)*, *donor(s)* and *service* are linked directly to the Movement's programme framework.[33] There is one direct link with understandings of 'service' as a social role:

> SLRCS's[34] credibility as a social service organization will be vital to the successful implementation and achievement of objectives.[35]

Stakeholder(s) in the report refer to coordination, communication and advocacy for humanitarian principles across a broad range of institutional partners, state and civil society:

> Coordination with UNDP and other stakeholders on development of a community-based public warning system is ongoing.[36]
>
> CBDP[37] proposals reviewed following consultations with different stakeholders and after inauguration of the government's disaster risk management roadmap.[38]

Among uses of the word *practice*, 4 refer to directions of 'good' or 'best' practice:

> A key role of a regional delegation is to ensure good practice and success stories at country level are shared and used more widely.[39]
>
> These activities are underpinned by their coordinating nature and promoting a uniformity of approach and best practice.[40]
>
> There have been discussions to create a regional disaster management group in which national societies in the region could share knowledge, lessons and best practices.[41]
>
> The distribution to all national societies of capacity building fact sheets highlighting good organizational development practice by Sri Lanka under the tsunami operation is another example of a coordinating tool provided by the regional delegation.[42]

Tsunami Evaluation Coalition: Synthesis report

The report of the Tsunami Evaluation Coalition[43] has two main aims: to improve the quality of natural disaster response policy and practice, and to account to both donor and people affected by the disaster. The introduction to the TEC report states:

> Good practices illustrate how local and national ownership of aid programmes can be supported through patient, discerning and context-sensitive approaches.[44]

Like the IFRC report, given the focus of evaluation on accountability and impact in the humanitarian response to the tsunami, most of the search terms in the TEC report are of an operational definition and so are mainly nominative or descriptive. The two most frequently used of the search terms are *donor(s)* and *humanitarian*, followed by *communit(y/ies)*, with the narratives centring round analysis of objectives, evaluation of their achievement, and the relationship these terms have in enabling an effective and accountable response to the disaster. 'Representation', 'consensus' and 'consultation' feature regularly in relation to donor and community references, highlighting the significance the report gives to ownership and accountability 'which addresses the degree to which the international response recognised and supported national and local ownership of the response, during both the relief and recovery phases'.[45] Community access to information and the need for aid agencies and authorities to facilitate such access is a prominent feature in the report and notes that a lack of information to affected populations about relief and reconstruction plans greatly limits their capacity to proceed with their own relief and rehabilitation projects:

> The international humanitarian community needs a fundamental reorientation from supplying aid to supporting and facilitating communities' own relief and recovery priorities.[46]

The report states there is a need to develop an aid principle based on the right 'to seek, receive and impart information':[47]

> This would establish freedom of information regarding all disaster response efforts, including international activities. It would imply a responsibility to inform affected people in an accessible language – not just about performance.[48]

References to *humanitarian* are made less contingent but are often linked to definitions of standards and approaches defined by the formal humanitarian and development sectors:

> Recovery and support to preparedness are embedded in the objectives of humanitarian actors, for example, in the GHD principles, the Sphere standards and the Red Cross Code of Conduct.[49]

S*ervice(s)* refers to public services, such as health facilities and municipal water services (twenty-two results). Other references are to military services, meteorological services and consular services. Among the uses of the term *practice(s)*, thirty-three present a direct pairing or linkage to 'good' or best' practice. Whilst these are associated mainly with reference to the institutional and organisational guidelines mentioned earlier, it is significant that the criticisms for failures in coordination, impact and accountability are levelled at agencies in the international aid and development sectors, rather than at local or national structures, who may not be aware of such prescriptions, or feel any need to adhere to them:

> The failure of agencies to meet their formal commitments to, for example, Sphere or the GHD principles, suggest that the various quality initiatives are not having a sufficient impact.[50]

The report is careful to acknowledge local capacities:[51]

> Some of the best practice noted in the TEC Capacities Report was observed when the definition of affected communities was broadened to include entire geographical units, such as the district in Sri Lanka, so that inequities were not heightened and conflicts not exacerbated.[52]
>
> Good practices illustrate how local and national ownership of aid programmes can be supported through patient, discerning and context-sensitive approaches.[53]

2. CONFLICT IN SYRIA, 2011

The Syrian uprising which began in March 2011 emerged in the wider regional context of the Arab Spring that started in Tunisia at the end of 2010. During the first months of the uprising the movement was explicitly non-violent, but the situation became militarised in autumn 2011 with the creation of the Free Syria Army, comprising mostly Sunni defectors from the Syrian government army. February 2012 marked a severe worsening of the crisis in terms of the levels of violence, numbers affected and extent of needs. In the summer of 2012, factions within the armed resistance to the government increasingly embraced Islamic extremism, and foreign jihadist fighters arrived to reframe Syria's political and economic conflict as a sectarian-oriented fight.[54] Exact figures of casualties and loss of life at the period during which this study focuses remain difficult to confirm. According to the IFRC Operations Update, up to July 2012, it was estimated that more than 20,000 persons had lost their lives and some 2.5 million people inside Syria needed support. The UN Inter Agency Standing Commission report indicates that by March 2014, there were an estimated 150,000 people killed in the conflict with 6.52 million people displaced inside Syria, and 2.58 million Syrian people living as refugees in Lebanon, Jordan, Turkey, Iraq and Egypt.[55]

The widespread conflict which became increasingly divided into competing territories meant physical access was a very significant issue for humanitarian response. As well as questions of physical access, like the Sri Lanka Case Study the Syria study raises questions around the nature of discourse surrounding the equitable and accountable provision of emergency aid, and how closely this reflected access for discussion with affected communities. Given the centralised control of the national media, the official (public) narratives were undivided, but access to participation the discourse was restricted.[56] Both the state control over the national printed media and the historical suspicion of stakeholder identities, give evidence of an even more overtly securitised discourse than Sri Lanka. Therefore, it is not surprising that the narratives present less reference to stakeholder or broader partnerships, though as will be seen, this assumption is countered by frequent references to dialogue and support. It is towards this apparent contradiction in the discourse that the case study on the conflict in Syria turns its examination: What expression of partnership can counter suspicions of motivation?

The analysis in this section examines public narratives in the national media presented in the *Syria Times*, an English language online publication that is supported with funding from the UN but is under the authority of the Syrian Ministry of Information, and provides evidence of the nature of discourse channelled to the public by state authority. The study of a regional narrative over a similar six-month period is made with the *Opinion* section of *Gulf Times*, an English language publication based in Qatar, which, like *TamilNet*, was in opposition to the state and its sponsors in the conflict. From an international perspective, the analysis includes a review of the institutional narratives provided in IFRC Operations Updates and an external study commissioned by the UN on the background to the conflict and the humanitarian environment surrounding it over a similar period.[57] As was the case in response to the Indian Ocean tsunami in Sri Lanka, these are set in a situation of complex emergency and the study shares examination of whether expressions of voluntary action and the universality of purpose can lead to understandings of a common identity.

Whilst the analysis is based on shared terms and platforms of narrative, situated in a similar environment of complex emergency, the definition of boundaries for national discourse is different to the case of the Indian Ocean tsunami. The English language media in Sri Lanka openly took a party-political bias, and publications opposing government, or factions within the government, were frequently critical of government approaches. In contrast, the supervision of national media publications in Syria under the central control of the governing Ba'ath Party allowed no space for contesting narratives.[58] This made the tensions in an intersubjective relationship more pronounced, and influenced the presentation of the regional and institutional narratives studied here. A numerical comparison of the frequency of terms related to expressions of voluntary service and universality used in the Syria narratives is presented in table 7.1B. In this section of study, my search is directed towards expression of cooperation and opportunities for prosocial interaction, and the analysis examines the frequency and contextual interpretations of the discourse around 'partnership' (tables 7.2A and 7.2B). These focus on six terms: three directing towards cooperative engagement: ('partnership'; 'support'; 'dialogue') and three towards contested engagement ('opposition'; 'challenge'; 'rebel'). The analysis of a contested discourse around interpretations of voluntary support and challenge is especially salient in a context where the Syrian Arab Red Crescent (SARC) auxiliary status was placed at the centre of the international humanitarian response.[59] A comparison is made with the frequency and interpretation of these terms in the documents studied in the tsunami response (table 7.2B).

The words or terms in tables 7.2.A and 7.2.B are searching for evidence of the varied constructions of partnership within the shared environments but differing contexts of the two case studies. 'Support' is ranked the most frequent in both tables. In Sri Lanka, the greatest prominence is in external/international documents (IFRC OU, 154 results; TEC report, 111 results), and in Sunday Island News (99 results). In the Syria study, 'Support' is

Table 7.2A. Indian Ocean Tsunami – Sri Lanka 2004–2005

	Sunday Island 'news' (68,985 words)	Sunday Leader 'Spotlight' (41,718 words)	TamilNet 'Features' (38,714 words)	IFRC Quarterly Reports (32,649 words)	TEC Synthesis Report (50,412 words)	Total
Support	99	14	26	154	111	**404**
Partner(ship)	27	8	6	61	28	**130**
Challenge	15	7	10	6	6	**44**
Opposition	19	3	19	2	0	**43**
Rebel	13	1	2	0	0	**16**
Dialogue	7	0	1	2	0	**10**

Table 7.2B. Syria 2012–2013

	Syria Times 'Opinion' (22,354 words)	Syria Times 'Commentary' (28,147 words)	Gulf Times 'Opinion' (22,020 words)	OCHA-IASC Report (27,650 words)	IFRC Operations Updates (22,781 words)	Total
Support	47	60	34	66	289	**496**
Opposition	33	55	33	55	0	**176**
Dialogue	60	55	7	5	1	**128**
Partner(ship)	1	6	3	28	57	**95**
Rebel	4	5	57	9	0	**75**
Challenge	6	11	13	18	21	**69**

evenly frequent across all narrative platforms, except in the IFRC Operations Updates where it has notable prominence (289 results). 'Partner(ship)'
is the second most frequent term in the Sri Lanka tsunami narratives, and
once again is most prominent in the IFRC document (sixty-one results).
'Partnership' is ranked fourth in the Syria study, and is specially prominent
in the international/institutional documents (85 results out of a total of 95,
most notably in the IFRC reports), but with only 10 results in the national
and regional media. 'Dialogue' is ranked 3rd in the Syria case study (128
results), and most frequently in the national media narratives (115 results). Its
prominence in these centralised and controlled public platforms is significant,
even if its interpretation is instrumental and highly conditional. In the case of
Sri Lanka, 'Dialogue' is sixth (last) most frequent across all narratives and
is most prominent in one of the national media (Sunday Island News, seven
results).

When considering the three terms which might contest ideas of partnership, across both case studies 'Opposition' is the most frequent (a total of 219
results) with most prominence in the Syria study. 'Challenge' appears a total
of 113 times, balanced evenly across the media and institutional narratives
in both studies, which provides an indication of its relevance in the discourse
across a broad platform of contexts and stakeholders, and engages both positive and negative associations. 'Rebel' is ranked fifth most frequently in both
tables but is numerically more frequent in the context of the conflict in Syria,
appearing fifty-seven times in *Gulf Times*, where it is seen as signifying a
positive challenge to the prevailing socio-political environment.

CONCLUSION: PURPOSE AND PRACTICE IN CONTEXT

The discourse presented earlier is a complex one. Many of the narratives
across the examples in the national Sri Lankan media call for a unified position regarding the assessment of needs and the fair distribution of available
resources: the core expression of the formal humanitarian system for neutral
and impartial humanitarian action that is needs based and equitably distributed, without prejudice. However, the socio-political mechanisms to achieve
this are contested. All centre around the agency of the national or local (sub-
national) community, but there are divisions over the methods to enable this.
The *Sunday Leader* is critical of the joint mechanisms[60] proposed by the
international community, which would engage the TNA, and seen as a threat
to the central authority of the Government. Conversely, articles in *TamilNet*
present a uniform narrative in support of the joint mechanisms, and its access
to vulnerable populations. Common to both are narratives about access and
trust, with contestation coalescing around identity and representation within

the constituencies they target. Narrative in the international/institutional documentation also centres round the humanitarian expression of equitable, needs-based assistance to populations affected by the crisis. They share a common focus on supporting a community-led recovery and enabling means of access to this. The differences lie in the focus of discourse around the constituencies each seek to represent.

Prevalent within the Sri Lanka media narratives is an accusation of national and international level corruption, or abuse of resources. It is noticeable that in the first month after the tsunami, the primary focus was on positive reports about the voluntary responses by local communities during the initial emergency response and the constructive engagement of international resources with national capacities. By mid-January, by which time emergency response was seen to begin its transition to recovery and rehabilitation, there was a change in tone reflecting an increasingly contesting narrative. This assumed an aggressive political rhetoric with hostile language directed towards perceptions of political corruption within national offices and abuse of national sovereignty by the international presence in the country. As with the Syria study, much of the discourse centres on contested interpretations about notions of humanitarian action, with questioned associations of motivation and purpose. Whilst instrumentation of the national political narratives is not evident in the international documentation examined, there is an engagement within its institutional discourse on the humanitarian identity which is instrumental. For example, of the six instances of the word 'practice' in the IFRC reports, four of these direct towards an institutional interpretation of 'best' or 'good' practices. In the TEC report, there are similar directions to institutional studies on 'good' humanitarian practice. As indicated earlier, these include reference to the Good Humanitarian Donorship initiative, as well as the Sphere Guidelines and the Red Cross Code of Conduct.

In the Sri Lanka study, of the forty-six results for the word *access(ible)*, all except a short section on access to information in the TEC report refer to geographical access or physical access to material or financial resources and infrastructures. In the Syria study, *access(ible)* does not appear in any of the national or regional media narratives, though is prominent in the international/ institutional reports, where all refer to the physical or financial channels for humanitarian access, including two references in the IFRC Operational Updates on access to information. *Trust* is absent from the media narratives in the Syria case study, and with only six results in the UN report.[61] 'Stakeholder' and 'Auxiliary' are absent from all of the narratives. However, despite the textual absence, notions around the concept of a space for participation of some form is evident and is significant to understanding the *nature of the* discursive space constructed in arguments for the concept of *praxis* discussed in chapter 6. In both studies, the direction of narrative is towards constructions of socio-political space. In the national and regional media narratives, the predominant expression is political, and relates to issues of sovereignty and authority. In the institutional and organisational narratives, the predominant expression is social, and relates to partnerships that endorse accountability and impact. Both foreground understandings of community as the primary vehicle for gaining access to the environment. However, the focus of community agency in all the narratives is either external, driven either by outside donors and the 'international community', or by national institutional structures that are themselves quite distant to local community structures (e.g. the P-TOMS). Ideas of mutual support are, in this sense, in opposition rather than auxiliary: that is to say, the crisis environment is seen as exceptional, where 'normal' transactions between community and state, and between state and outside, are seen to be in competition,[62] with corresponding tensions in stakeholder relationships. In these contexts, interpretations of mutuality are ones which understand mutual advantage, rather than mutual respect and equality of access which form the basis of the humanitarian relationship seen as key to partnership in the discursive space presented in the book.

It is interesting to compare experiences of how different socio-political environments and the varying approaches of stakeholders in these environments alter the narratives around a cooperative and mutually supporting space for humanitarian action in contexts of complex emergency. The experiences of the humanitarian sector during the response to Cyclone Nargis which struck Myanmar in 2008 presented a different operating environment for the humanitarian responses. The leading role played by the Association of Southeast Asian Nations (ASEAN) in planning and coordinating the humanitarian response[63] meant a much closer engagement with regional structures, with shared affinities and approaches. This reinforced an environment of trust and shared responsibility. My earlier study on the humanitarian response to Cyclone Nargis remarks that, while this was an operating environment where trust was most fragile and where the mystery of its political system ran deepest, the humanitarian response has been seen in most analyses as being a greater success, more inclusive and less donor-driven than was the case in Sri Lanka.[64]

The study on partnership in the context of the Syria conflict presents evidence of a cynical, instrumental countering of narratives around 'support' and the auxiliary identity of the 'volunteer': one that sees voluntary action as positive if in support of state authority, but negative if in support of any opposition to it. The prominence of these instrumentalised narratives indicates the importance of such an identity in the constructions of the socio-political discourse surrounding it. It should be noted that the public media narratives in both studies are aimed at a core community of national and international stakeholders, and the selections hold considerable political bias.[65] The significance of the analysis in both studies lies not in the numerical rankings but in the variation in use and prominence of the terms according to context, and according to its significance as an indicator influencing the discourse in the socio-political environment.

Is there a unified position or shared discussion in the cases studied? There are common and shared terms, but my analysis indicates the inconsistencies in interpretation of a shared identity and the absence of a common approach. However, there is a universal direction in the narratives leading towards access to (what are often instrumental constructions of) influence and authority in the social and political space of humanitarian action. A solution to the quest for access to a shared discourse directs the argument towards consideration of cooperative action as 'praxis' – as understandings of purpose and practice – presented in this book. This means understanding a concept of space that offers mutual support through a differing presentation, or an alternative re-location, of authority. This presents a new space for discourse that is aware of the anarchies and hierarchies,[66] and where the strength of its discourse rests on sociological rather than political authority.

This un-fixed but inter-active relationship is made evident in the differing prominence of shared terms in the national, regional and international narratives in both case studies. In the national and regional media, the predominant expression is political, and relates to issues of sovereignty and authority. These are not constructions of mutual advantage, but of one-sided transactions, where un-shared interpretations of support, dialogue and partnership play an essential role. In the international narratives, the predominant expression is social, with emphasis on a partnership which calls for an interpretation of mutuality as mutual respect and equality of access. It is the successful navigation of these diverging pathways which forms the precarious balance of trust and representation in construction of the humanitarian relationship presented in this book.

As I will argue in the concluding chapters, trust and legitimacy are derived and generated in a process that requires a constellation of factors to piece together a model of participation and cooperation – even if only at a temporary level of emergency response. The case studies make the recognition of contesting social and political influences in the variant contexts evident in the way trust and access is allocated, on which the basis for partnership is formed. There is need for a discursive space that recognises the authority of both, and which can participate in a discussion across the widest possible range of contexts and stakeholder interests. The opportunities for access to this discursive space and the adjustments to contemporary narratives are examined in the next chapter, where arguments look at ways to craft identities that make these differing approaches complementary. It builds on the formulation of a space in which interests across the broad community of its stakeholders can be represented and made relevant to a common humanitarian response. This means a space which is not only focused on the provision of relief and protection but is also able to offer spaces of dissension where a constructive challenge can be raised and can be considered as a cooperative interaction, rather than one of contestation. The arguments that follow explore some of the reinterpretations of the humanitarian space that are required to enable mutually supportive identities in contexts that appear to be mutually exclusive. This will mean defining boundaries and identifying the frontiers for access to a discourse that can navigate the political tensions around sovereignty and national identity, and the focus on accountable partnership. This identifies that the role of the volunteer auxiliary in environment of crisis is not a relationship in stasis. The humanitarian volunteer inhabits a liminal space on the frontiers of the socio-political space described earlier. This crafts an identity which is both a part of and apart from this space, and which offers profound significance for new associations of trust and access. A dynamic where, in situations of crisis when normal systems breakdown, the humanitarians in the niche enact identities that are assigned and approved by the community of stakeholders – arguments that are presented in the final chapter.

Chapter 8

Re-Harbouring the Humanitarians

This book has positioned the identity of a community with a common purpose as key to cooperative action in times of complex humanitarian emergencies. Chapter 1 remarks on the need for the humanitarian sector to acknowledge its political identity within this community, allowing it to participate with greater relevance and representation in the construction of a prosocial discourse. A careful formulation of what is meant by relevant representation is critical to determining the nature of the space in which the niche is seen to be able to govern, and where the humanitarian identities will be housed. As discussed in chapter 2, my arguments see that vulnerabilities in its contemporary identity are linked to its over-ambition, arrogance, and desire to be always relevant and representative of all. An over-extension of aims and an over-expectation of its capacities have led to less trust in its moral authority. This hubristic self-enchantment has entrapped humanitarians inside narrative spaces where discussions have become a series of unheard echoes within a disconnected chamber. It is from entrapment in this narrative that this book seeks ways for the humanitarian sector to navigate a reconnection with the community it represents. Reconnection requires more than refining the ways humanitarian programmes are implemented, or continuing reflection on existing typologies of the 'humanitarian grand strategy'.[1] It requires re-directing the lens to review how the contemporary humanitarian image can be reprocessed, re-translated and transferred to become relevant and representative to the community of stakeholders it serves. This means enabling broader access to the humanitarian discourse. This chapter looks at how a more modest approach – the recognition of a humbler identity – will bind together the qualities of relevance and representation that are essential to the cementing of community and its social bonds, the expression of which were prominent in all the narratives presented in the case studies.

The analyses in chapter 7 have indicated the shared prominence of some of the core terms presented in this book together with how their interpretations, or sense of meaning, vary depending on the constituencies the narratives address, and the nature of the space they construct. There are common themes of community and social identity but ones where, in the national and regional media narratives, suspicions of motivation and a lack of trust block access to cooperation. Tensions are reflected in a different way in the institutional narratives, where the space for discussion is more social than political. In both cases, these expose the apparent contradictions of being independent from authority, yet a volunteer auxiliary to it in times of crisis. The search to navigate these tensions between freedom of choice and compliance is a theme running through this book. This chapter aims to chart a path through these tensions by considering the theoretical approaches presented in the earlier chapters, together with the empirical studies conducted in chapters 6 and 7. It begins with considerations on how to define the boundaries and locate common frontiers.

POLITICAL BOUNDARIES AND SOCIAL BONDS

In order to make sense of the theoretical constructions on space and boundaries, it is useful to turn to some practical examples from experience on the field. Chapter 7 referred to the emergency response in Myanmar following the cyclone as a comparison which provided useful contrasts to the narratives which emerged following the humanitarian responses in Sri Lanka and Syria. Cyclone Nargis occurred in a country that had been economically and politically isolated by the Global North since the violent suppression by its military government of the pro-democracy uprising, twenty years earlier.[2] Concern for the humanitarian response at the time focused on problems of access. Early reports from the United Nations agencies in the country indicated they had been able to reach only 30 per cent of those in desperate need of food and warned of an outbreak of infectious disease.[3] The Inter-Agency Real-Time Evaluation observes that although there were certainly very real restrictions, local groups and some international organisations were able to access affected areas immediately after the cyclone.[4]

Concerns about physical and material access predominate most of these analyses but less attention is paid to access to a space for discussion which was critical in opening the practical avenues for the humanitarian organisations on the ground. The involvement of ASEAN was a factor that played a critical role at central level to open channels of negotiation with the government of Myanmar. Nevertheless, strict controls over participation and access for international personnel and the definition of projects at municipal level remained a serious constraint.[5] Travel restrictions and bureaucratic regulations from central government were reinforced to assure the status quo, which municipal authorities in the cyclone-affected townships were unable to circumvent. Through the Myanmar Red Cross society (MRCS), the IFRC obtained a letter from the office of the Prime Minister in the capital Nay Pyi Taw (which had been tasked by the government to manage the emergency) that authorised the broad parameters of its proposed humanitarian response.[6] Once this authorisation was presented at the municipal level, a fear of non-compliance with central regulations was replaced by pro-active cooperation and an eagerness to define and approve humanitarian projects at an operational level in the affected Townships, according to the needs identified by the local communities, among which local government officials and the military authorities were part.[7] This meant procedural restrictions to access were no longer an issue. Organisation of the humanitarian response became a representation of the local community, managing projects that were relevant to them and to the authorities responsible for monitoring them.[8] What was seen as solely a political space became a socio-political space and cooperative discourse was enabled accordingly.

In the case study on the tsunami response in Sri Lanka, there are common invocations of community in the narratives but there is no sense of a shared purpose in the confrontation with both national and international institutions or humanitarian organisations, where the emphasis is on the political rather than the social. As the international presence and its access to huge financial resources grew, the Sri Lankan government made a series of negative public comments about international humanitarian agencies, echoed by headline attacks in the national media about the intrusion of foreign agencies into the political space of the country. This created a public discourse of hostility and distrust of humanitarian organisations, notably amongst the Sinhalese population who were concerned about the transfer of resources to Tamil separatists in the north, and increased restrictions were placed by the government on visa applications and the approval of programmes.

Those of us who had been present at each of these humanitarian operations on the ground shortly after the disasters struck were almost unanimous in remarking that – counterintuitively – the response to Cyclone Nargis in Myanmar was more efficient, relevant and had greater impact on addressing the urgent needs of the populations affected: it was more 'humanitarian'. External evaluations and internal reports on the crisis have remarked on the fact that access to a cooperative and coordinated response was much better than had been the case following the Indian Ocean tsunamis four years earlier. Amongst the reasons for this was a more realistic management of expectations across the stakeholder community. The visa restrictions and other controls on access which were imposed by the government of Sri Lanka in the weeks following the tsunami had pre-existed the cyclone response in Myanmar, and confrontation with the military government had been a constant feature of IR that had permeated both the foreign and national discourse for over twenty years. There were severe restrictions on the foreign media, and Western governments and the opposition National League for Democracy attempted to sanction the regime by discouraging tourism and foreign investment. Political isolation was intensified following the 'Saffron Revolution' which occurred eight months earlier. This period of political unrest, sparked by a series of non-violent demonstrations against the military government led by Buddhist monks, had elicited a brutal response by the government and its militant civilian wing, the Union Solidarity and Development Association. The United Nations agencies, members of the Red Cross and Red Crescent Movement and NGOs who were already in the country had learned to navigate along these political and structural frontiers and were aware of the limitations an internationally driven response would face. The engagement of ASEAN as a regional facilitator provided the catalyst for access. A platform for shared ideals and mutual respect for sovereignty and non-interference was a critical difference in altering the climate of mistrust. Once access to a discussion with the military government had been secured, then the practical access to resolve operational demands in the affected townships became less contested. In the case of Syria, questions of humanitarian access and participation were contested from the earliest days of the unrest. Even before the civil disorder of March 2011 and the escalation of armed conflict in the country, the Syrian government had taken measures to control access for international humanitarian partners, when it appointed the Syrian Arab Red Crescent (SARC) as the focal point for approval of international NGOs seeking to respond to refugees and displaced populations in 2006, and the droughts in 2009. This was managed by the Syrian Arab Red Crescent headquarters in Damascus, which meant that the 14 SARC branches countrywide (including the Damascus Branch, which ran the operations centre and its ambulance service) were able, in the main, to remain apart from the political identity of this role. As Slim and Trombetta observed in their report, the SARC branches in general, and the Red Crescent volunteers in particular, were respected by the public for their effectiveness and impartiality in its countrywide response.[9]

The conflict in Bosnia and Herzegovina presents another example of the human realities of navigation along political and social boundaries. Communities who had lived together for centuries were cast into conflict following the break-up of Yugoslavia, and the politics of identity played a significant part in the fracturing of social bonds at that time.[10] However, throughout the war there was a reluctance by many to take sides. This was most marked in the urban communities, such as Sarajevo. Evidence of this was gained from personal experiences at the time, when, after some months of work in the city, I was invited to join local colleagues in the hidden bars and cafés in Sarajevo, where Croats, Serbs and Bosnian Muslims intermingled.[11] These were important places to maintain a spirit of cohesion and social resistance for a population forced to comply with political authority. An example of resistance to enforced compliance with a (politically) constructed identity and the strategies to maintain a self-ascribed identity with a wider social community is presented by Mary Kaldor, referring to David Rieff's account of Serbian soldiers who telephoned their Bosnian Muslim friends in Sarajevo after a period of shelling from their positions overlooking the city on Mount Igman, to check that they were safe.[12]

Ivana Maček's book describing life under siege in Sarajevo provides an ethnographical view on communities coping in crisis, navigating the socio-political frontiers. [13] This constructs an account of the consequences for people on the ground and observes that what happened cannot be understood through an analysis of elite negotiations, or a statistical calculation of the numbers of dead and wounded – nor by the abstract narratives employed by media and political discourse, such as 'genocide', 'ethnic cleansing' and 'crimes against humanity'.[14] Instead, Maček uses similar strategies that the Sarajevans used to cope with its destructiveness, by finding forms in their everyday lives – in artefacts, practices, ideas and phrases they use whilst living under total devastation. Maček struggled with her own orientation towards the conflict, and sorted her ideas into three different modes of experiencing war, categorising them as 'Civilian mode', which manifests itself during the outbreak of war in 'initial disbelief' at witnessing the collapse of social norms they had thought secure; 'Soldier mode', which marks a realignment under a secondary stage when there is an attempt to order and explain events, which includes selecting one side or the other, for protection and solidarity, and thereby constructing a process which makes the destruction seem necessary and acceptable, and 'Deserter mode', when delusion, distrust and disappointment sets in. This manifests an abandonment of the neat divisions between civilian and military, friend and foe, leading to abandonment of allegiance to any side, and people re-taking responsibility for their own actions. A state of normality amidst abnormality is set in place.[15]

A comparison can be made with the international response to support an estimated 850,000 refugees who had fled across the Rwandan border and settled in and around the town of Goma in July 1994, following the massacres in Rwanda. This provides a good example of a situation where access to resources and participation with the narratives were available (the media, policy, diplomatic debate as well as scholarship had been raising awareness of the impending conflict for some time).[16] Instead, the constraints were from a lack of willingness of the international political structures to respond and the failure to engage with an appropriate strategy to address the mass atrocities once they emerged. The complex dynamics which influenced the environment are documented by Kurt Mills and provides analysis of the failures in this strategy to respond.[17] In his study, he sees that humanitarian responses to the refugee crisis in Zaire (now the Democratic Republic of Congo) and Tanzania[18] were used as a substitute for any meaningful political or military response to the atrocities. Studies have shown that the resources and structures enabling an efficient emergency response were well supported but these are seen by Mills as being a palliative, placing unfair expectations on a humanitarian response to resolve a political problem which they clearly could not do.[19] Despite an unprecedented and rapid response, the capacity of the agencies present in Goma was quickly overwhelmed. Within the first month, approximately 50,000 refugees died from a combination of cholera, dysentery, dehydration and violence.[20] Nevertheless, many operational reports and practitioners on the field considered the early emergency response to be a success. The endurance and commitment shown at every level, and amongst every agency, was impressive.[21] Personal notes from the time indicate the sense of motivation, solidarity and moments of good humour.[22] Amidst the traumas of the environment, there were frequent instances of kindness, selflessness and examples of the 'mundane' which, as Maček has noted in her account of Sarajevo under siege, are an indication of humanity coping in crisis. Media reports and academic studies have indicated how quickly social infrastructures were established in the camps: roadside shops selling videos and music cassettes, together with stalls offering tea and coffee, and others offering haircuts. This social dynamic, together with the proximity of an international response that engaged the presence of volunteers from the local community and from within the refugee population itself, was significant in normalising an abnormal environment: one which – at least for those working there at the time – presented a different discourse to the state of exception that dominated many of the stakeholder narratives. The proximity of volunteers and the organisational structures that support them plays an important part in restoring a social bond, which the study by Maček sees as being an essential process in coping and regaining trust in a disordered world. The IFRC World Disaster Report, 2015 observes that, as well as being better connected to the populations they serve linguistically and culturally, the role and practice of volunteers in a community exercise a special kind of moral authority through simple, straightforward acts of voluntary kindness.[23] It is the modesty of this approach, one of spontaneous, non-judgemental welcome, which my study sees as the strength and legitimacy in the niche: one that makes communities feel they are relevant and that they 'belong'.[24]

The discussions in chapter 7 reveal the tensions that emerge from the institutional and organisational disconnections between stakeholders in the social and political spaces they represent. The common denominators in the narratives are expressions of solidarity, and of service to community. Once these discussions are positioned within a more cooperative, interdependent discourse, there are opportunities for recognition of a more universalist approach towards a shared humanitarian purpose. The internal debates within the Red Cross and Red Crescent Movement over its Fundamental Principles presented in chapter 6 indicate that the tensions are not confined to a political or securitised dynamic, but are evident within the less politicised, more social, places at the heart of the humanitarian system. Recognition of this common space means considering the theoretical and philosophical arguments that help identify this place of shared relevance and participation: one where the competing tensions of compliance and non-compliance – of accepting and not accepting – can comfortably coexist.

Within a discourse of the Global North, the identities being called for here are a secular and less exclusive version of the spirituality emphasised by Kant, Rousseau and the philosophers of the Enlightenment – a spirit of humanity that does not render one role or group of role-sets as pre-eminent or morally superior and so prescriptive of a best practice. This ambitious declaration of identity must recognise the limitations of its role, but where the humility of its profile becomes its strength to contest. The challenge of this paradox lies in limiting the function of the niche whilst increasing its relevance to the broader community of its stakeholders. How do the identities in this moral platform sit comfortably as an auxiliary to functions of power and yet retain a robust degree of confidence across other, less like-minded, inhabitants in the larger arena of aid and development? In other words, how do the identities in the niche manage the tensions between intimacy and power in this moral platform? To answer these questions, the study returns to the discussions of boundaries and the need to recognise the vulnerability of the humanitarian identity to a loss of trust, while depending upon trust for access to these contested spaces.

The Power of Humility: Stable Boundaries in an Unstable Space

In his study on contemporary expressions of ethics and human rights in a globalised world, Michael Ignatieff points out the strengths of a shared, communal moral language of what he terms 'ordinary virtues'.[25] He describes these as a common moral 'operating system' that are 'anti-theoretical' and 'anti-ideological' – that is to say distanced from institutional regulations or organisational directions – and whose common expression acts as a glue to enable communities to function in the multi-cultural environments of modern globalised societies.[26] By 'ordinary' Ignatieff means 'common-place and everyday' with all the opportunities and challenges that the creative messiness of humanity presents. These are characterised as life skills, seen as a universally achievable 'practice' rather than as an elitist expression of a moral judgement: what he describes as 'the vernacular of common identity' where, according to the subjects of his study, 'we simply felt welcome'.[27] As already mentioned, the non-judgemental spirit of this spontaneous engagement within the community is critical to legitimising a feeling of honest representation. This rejects patterns of action that are seen more in common with national or international elites than those representing the community. Instead, it presents an unambiguous moral distinction that is a 'simpler' account of what is relevant to ordinary citizens and so is made more accountable to them.[28] This relates easily to arguments presented in this book that see voluntary service as an unforced, spontaneous and easily accessible practice sharing a common purpose of bringing support to others: humble displays of humanity which open access to trust in good intentions, and where judgements of one's personal worth are not present – in Ignatieff's words, an 'individual capacity to imagine and follow-through on conduct necessary for effective social cooperation'.[29] This echoes the hybrid identities which this book suggests are best placed to construct and sustain the broad base of trust necessary to open access to the community of stakeholders in crises: the individuation of the 'I-mode' and the collective of the 'We-mode' that together actualise the space for a shared moral purpose.

Together with the central pillar of a stable purpose, core to building trust in this platform is the careful identification of its capacities to perform, and the definition of its boundaries within which efficient and effective action can occur. This means recognising limits to its purpose and practice that secure the space for an interdependent relationship, so does not stray into areas of unapproachable contestation and failed expectations. The general programmatic demarcations of the IFRC humanitarian response to Cyclone Nargis that were approved at a central level by the government in the capital Nay Pyi Taw and then left open for project definition at community level, presented in the opening section of this chapter, provide an example of the nature of trust and access being described here.

According to Ignatieff, community is the key to any moral operating system and my arguments in this book suggest this is what demarcates the boundaries of trust in the niche. The sense of community here must be broad and extend beyond simply representing the primary community (the affected population and local/national stakeholders) to include all common stakeholders (state, internal/external forces, markets, donors – the protagonists in established and unestablished power). The role and function can involve a range of practices which are constantly evaluated and adjusted according to the context, so balancing expectations and achievement. To earn trust and legitimacy there must be evidence of intent and efficiency, not defined by a regime of prescribed and regulated roles that the community must follow but ones which are 'voluntary obligations', driven by a common purpose. Correspondingly, the methods of guiding and protecting a voluntary obligation must assume an intersubjective character.[30]

Chapter 1 states that the resolution to the problem of access and identity can be found through the philosophical interpretations of *praxis* that directs the discussion towards a shared meaning that is relevant to all stakeholders in environments of crisis, and not an exceptional domain of humanitarian professionals alone. In Richard Bernstein's words, towards 'an extended and open dialogue which pre-supposes a background of inter-subjective agreement and a tacit sense of relevance':[31] a narrative made relevant by its shared history and expressions of common practice. This means that in order to define the opportunities that might emerge from a re-framed recognition of (auxiliary, humanitarian) voluntary service, there is a need to understand the phenomenon's broader ontology.

Adler and Pouliot consider this approach to converge round an ontology 'that depicts the social world as intersubjectively and collectively meaningful structures and processes'.[32] This understands that although practices are performed by individual social beings, collectively they are acted out by *communities* of practice constructed by the diffusion of a shared background knowledge across individuals in these communities. Since their actions are coordinated by common structures they can be understood as being both 'individual' and 'structural', meaning individual ideas and beliefs interacting within collective structures.[33] This accords with understandings presented in chapter 2 that common meanings extend beyond inter-subjective interpretations of language and reach towards identifying a world with common reference-points.[34] The common reference points in my study are the shared humanitarian identities in the niche, and the common structures which coordinate them are the social and political spaces their stakeholders define. The point of agreement whence its agency derives is the stability of its purpose, even if the stakeholders have differing goals.[35] Navigation within these spaces and along their frontiers requires balancing compliance to political authority with retaining the strength in its voluntary moral authority described in the opening to this chapter – the recognition of a humanitarian social contract. To consider this fully, the analysis turns to look more specifically at issues related to management and compliance that have traditionally been seen as the pillars framing legitimate representation of a trusted identity in areas of law and IR, and which together frame the basis of a social contract.

Compliance, Security and the Social Contract

Scholarship has traditionally positioned the levels of enforcement and management as the primary indicators to measure and enact compliance with a system of law and so ensure a stable platform for trusted action.[36] Studies in

Organisational Theory and Social Identity Theory presented in chapters 3 and 4 of this book have indicated that recognition of (good) intent holds primacy over force and efficiency in most of the communities that they studied. This is confirmed by Manuel Castells's observation that 'meaning' has primacy over 'function' in the stable construction of trust and legitimacy in a representation of identity.[37] *Stability* is a common denominator in academic discussions about trusted representation.[38] Scholars who have analysed the environments of modern conflicts frequently assert that the space for legitimate action and trusted representation of traditional norms in warfare and complex emergencies has been destabilised by the 'new' wars following the end of the Cold War period. In the latter, balances of power and reciprocity enabled an environment of compliance which the new asymmetries have destroyed.[39] In the same way, the laws and customs of war (The Hague and Geneva Conventions) have become highly destabilised in the asymmetrical environments of modern conflict, with corresponding instabilities in the space for institutionalised humanitarian response. Institutional practices – as institutions themselves – fall into crisis when their legitimacy collapses and the binding quality of their rules is rejected.[40] In order to re-stabilise the institutional framework for humanitarian action, a process must begin to re-legitimate its identity. This starts with a clear and agreed understanding of its common meaning and recognition of the contexts for legitimate variances in its action. Arguments presented earlier have indicated the difficulty for flexible, context-based variations within the institutionalised character of contemporary humanitarian expression. Freedom to adapt and to engage continuing relevance in the changing environments requires attention to the conceptual identities in the niche: praxis and 'the spirit' of behaviour and intent.

The debates amongst members of the Red Cross and Red Crescent Movement presented in chapter 6 have highlighted the importance that 'spirit' has played in the formulation of their Fundamental Principles. The case studies in chapter 7 have demonstrated the significance of identification with shared principles of voluntary compliance across the broader community of stakeholders in environments of crisis, and the legitimacy of an evolving social bargain. These highlight recognition of the intersubjective nature of behaviour in relation to social *mores* and the norms of prosocial interaction. The passionate debates on principles and the expression of variations on practice illustrate the constructive tensions that an interdependence of individual and collective identities can bring. This means recognising how interaction between the membership (e.g. the Red Cross and Red Crescent Movement, United Nations agencies and NGOs) and the collective (the broader community of stakeholders: state, non-state actors, market, donors and affected communities) to determine meaning and function foregrounds the social nature of action in the humanitarian space.

Recognition of the agency that this social interaction takes in forging a trusted identity is important in order to understand the potential force of new narratives around stable representation in an unstable space: an understanding that has relevance to local contexts of complex emergency and the variant needs and influences within them. It elevates the importance of representation as one of the keys to open access in a social community, formed as an alloy from a process of individuation and collective responsibility. The uncoerced and uncoercive nature of its formulation is fundamental to the legitimacy of its identity. This calls for a very intimate social bond that is representative of the common interests of all stakeholders but whose formation is seen as autonomous from the dominant expressions of established and unestablished power.

The hostility surrounding the discourse of a political identity has meant the meaning of an auxiliary function and the role of the auxiliary have been associated with the fear of conspiracy with the elements of established and unestablished power – a prejudice made evident by the absences of the term in the narratives presented in chapter 7. Most of the challenges in academic debate and in policy analysis have been directed at the humanitarian principles of neutrality, impartiality and independence. However, these challenges are also extended to identities and interpretations of voluntary service, which, unless constructed by (Western) defined norms of free-service and altruism described earlier, are viewed with suspicion by those given direction by the predominant humanitarian discourse. For trust in a humanitarian social contract with authority, there is a need to 'de-conspire' the narratives and position more pluralist identifications of auxiliary voluntary service that legitimise its meaning and function across the broadest community of stakeholders it supports. This means presentation of a less certain space for discourse that departs from the self-referring logic dominating the contemporary humanitarian narratives.

This also requires a new understanding of compliance with authority, and the reasons for participation with it in a humanitarian response. Compliance is often portrayed as a tactic in a moving strategy for power and influence. However, as the preceding chapters have indicated, accounts of the lived experience of a humanitarian crisis and historical debates on humanitarian identity reflect a discourse on the principles forged from a spirit of *humanity* as stable anchors in a shared communal response to crisis. In such instances, this discourse needs to interpret compliance as a positive force, supported by competent action to enable the community of its stakeholders to function with meaning and relevance: an identity seen less as an expression of power but as an authentic expression of a common voluntary desire to help in times of crisis. At the very least, the orientation shifts away from association with the 'military' mode, described by Maček, towards the 'civilian' or the 'deserter', where participation with power is no longer seen as a threat to the community's ability to cope. This leads to an examination of the nature of community and its participation as citizens in the emerging social bargain.

CITIZENSHIP AND COMMUNITY

Suspicion of the auxiliary has featured prominently as a constraint in the arguments presented so far. The risks of instrumentalisation and manipulation in a niche where a shared purpose is positioned to be relevant and representative across the community of its stakeholders are evident (see chapter 5) and so the construction of trust in good intent is fragile. To mitigate these risks, the boundaries discussed earlier must define the limits of purpose and function in order to guarantee the predictability necessary for stable human interaction. This relates as security of space on a platform where moral risks (e.g. those of cooperation) are rewarded and trust is returned. An examination of what kind of arrangement with authority this community needs to form is distinct from ideas of *citizenship* presented in traditional theories in humanities and the social sciences, most often associated with debates around human rights, entitlements and the political discussions of a social contract. However, it does share ideas of *communal norms* that frame a less complicated, simpler identity for legitimated access to a common moral space. This is identified with understandings of humanitarian (moral) virtue constructed in its most accessible form – an identity that all stakeholders in the community feel capable of achieving and so feel part of it if they are present, and represented by it if they are absent.

Scholars have identified trust and belief in state institutions as being critically important features of a social contract and are contingent upon functions within this relationship.[41] Recent studies have challenged conceptions on the fragility of such contracts in societies exposed to conflicts, where trust in state institutions has traditionally been seen to breakdown.[42] Rather than abandon such structures, these studies argue that belligerents – opposition or rebel groups – refashion these contracts with societies under their control, often using government strategies and frequently designed on more equal terms. This is an approach presented by Meike de Goede and Francis Nyamnjoh[43] which sees relationships not as a site of altercation but as 'a site of interaction, where convivial agency occurs'.[44] Nyamnjoh's work on conviviality urges a constructive re-engagement with the African continent by turning the lens away from the binary approaches that influence much of the aid and development discourse in the Global North, which my study is likewise seeking to discard. He argues that recognition of diversity and engaging with the strength from a sharing and convivial society will enable a new approach to the idea of universality that is different from the universalist pretensions predominant in much of the contemporary discourse. Rather than calling for a levelling of the hierarchies of power, he invites us 'to recognise the interconnections, hierarchies and gradations that spring from the messiness of lived experiences'.[45] This resembles a direction towards the formulation of the Capability Approach discussed in chapter 3 that recognises the hierarchies of power and authority but demands as a minimum equal access to participate in the discussion. The proximity to the frontiers of competition and the capability to engage with the diverse elements of community and authority who manage these frontiers is fundamental to enabling cooperation and endorsing more legitimate representation. This means the capability to cast a gaze that connects disorder to an ordered system, providing fresh engagement with the social contract of interaction and participation – one that encourages a discourse that is less binary and less exclusive; one that is more relevant and more representative.

In recent years, the discourse in policy and scholarship about resilience of the state-citizen social contract in crisis environments has shifted from assumptions of extreme vulnerability and inability to cope, which was the dominant expression of colonial and post-colonial studies, towards a recognition of the agency and capacities of affected communities.[46] This has seen a focus shifting away from regarding crisis as a state of exception to acknowledging the abilities for communities in crisis to continue and survive – as a continuation of life that is, instead, seen as an extension of the normal.[47] However, as Ayesha Siddiqi and others observe, their resilience is dependent on how far the social contract is open to change. Stability and continuation are dependent on the opportunities for 'contextually-driven turns'[48] that are ready to acknowledge shared and changing responsibilities in an altered environment; ones that recognise a shared representation of capacities to cope in the most extreme situations of normality.

The dynamic nature of this relationship makes it an ambiguous and temporal one. It resembles anthropological presentations of liminality, which mark a period of transition from one (prescribed) space of social identity to another.[49] In periods of crisis, when normality is disordered, social identities can transfer to participate in a space where prescribed identities are suspended, and unaccustomed modes of cooperation are enabled. The relationships in this space are never in stasis. Like the liminal spaces described by Arnold van Gennep and Victor Turner,[50] there is always a way in and a way out: a temporary space for some and a permanent space for others. Its stability comes from the voluntary assignment and approval of mutual trust by the stakeholders it represents. Discussion of the liminal nature of the humanitarian niche is presented in the concluding chapter. First, the analysis turns to examining the place of community in crisis and the agency of a voluntary identity as a legitimate representation of authority and community in these environments of complex emergency.

The Legitimated Responsibility of the Volunteer

As indicated earlier, situations of crisis present opportunities for contextually driven turns. There is abundant evidence that one of the surest of such turns is the increased profile of the local communities to become the primary representatives of a public capacity to respond in the early onset of an emergency. Media reporting in the immediate aftermath of a disaster, as well as real-time evaluations on the field and academic analyses, consistently indicate the primary role the local community plays in providing immediate life-saving action and early emergency support,[51] with the actual functions determined by whether/how far the state is able or willing to respond. The supportive purpose of the humanitarian role is never in doubt. At least in the earliest days of a crisis, authoritative responsibility for a shared purpose and function lies with the local.

There is much contemporary debate around the meaning of 'local', and what is understood by 'localisation'.[52] All agree that identity of the local is a shifting concept, depending on context and interpretation. At a macro-level, national authorities and NGOs are seen as local compared to international organisations and international NGOs, whilst at a micro-level, community structures are more local than centralised national hierarchies.[53] In the context of this book, the local is understood as being a voluntary representative of the common needs of stakeholders in situations of complex emergency and presenting a locus for moral order.

Michael Ignatieff's study on 'ordinary virtues' reminds us that in the middle of the eighteenth century, Adam Smith emphasised that moral order could be generated through human sympathy, where individual capacities combine to provide effective social cooperation. My arguments reflect this as an understanding of cooperation not only as a key plank in the construction of shared identity in the moral platform but also understood as a channel for robust interaction that challenges the comfortable spaces of an 'echo-chamber' which, as this book has argued, distracts the narrative and hinders access to a more inclusive, interactive and humanitarian discourse. Relevance can be regained by focusing on a shared, common identity framed by uncoerced and uncoercive service to community in times of crisis. This means understandings of service (function) as a voluntary 'spirit', legitimated by a common and stable meaning that recognises itself, and is recognised by others, as being an interactive (auxiliary) representation of a public service. This forges an intimate but relational identity that can be more confidently associated with intent and motivation. Together, this enables greater access at a physical level, but – as importantly – at an ontological and conceptual level that provides equal and trusted access to the discourse.

The definitions of trust presented in 'Introduction' emphasise the importance of interdependence in understanding the nature of the relationship, since the interests of all stakeholders rest on confidence in the reliability of each. Studies have indicated that the nature of trust changes positively as interdependence increases.[54] Therefore, the strength of an *interdependent humanitarian relationship* with stakeholders that understands the authority each one exerts is critical. Chapter 4 has considered interpretations of voluntary service that include arguments around empathy and altruism discussed in theories of management, the social sciences and biological science that endorse its cross-disciplinary relevance in academia. In areas of institutional practice and policy, prominence is given to 'the power of humanity' as the statement of collective identity, used by the IFRC since 2000.[55] The strength of this message lies not in its symbolism but as an expression generated from experienced reality, as the practical examples of communities coping in crisis presented earlier in the chapter clearly indicate. The Red Cross and Red Crescent Movement, in concert with other humanitarian actors in crises and complex emergencies, has persistently documented the strengths and opportunities emerging from the capabilities of populations in distress. Important initiatives have been generated from these shared experiences, such as the Code of Conduct and the Sphere guidelines,[56] in the wake of perceived successes and failures in international responses to crises over the last thirty years. These have been followed more recently by initiatives generated from the World Humanitarian Summit, calling for increased local participation. This mean recognising the strength and agency evolving from a modest, less arrogant – more humble – representation in the humanitarian relationship.

Interdependent Humanitarian Relations

A call for humility is seen to be increasingly relevant when faced with the struggles for identity in the environment of contemporary politics and markets, seen by many as the established and aspiring hegemonies of power and influence, and is significant in the formulation of a less complacent, more cross-disciplinary approach explored in this book. Within the disciplines of business and management, humility is generally considered a character strength that is deeply aligned with, and uniquely representative of, the interdependent nature of today's organizations and marketplaces.[57] Management studies identify that humble individuals are not self-deprecating, but rather they recognise their strengths, admit their mistakes and weaknesses and assume their role with others in a broader community.[58] In the context under study here, this translates as the courage to recognise the modesty of an identity able to call for access and with the confidence to reach mutually constructive agreement on the limits of its boundaries: the confidence to comply, combined with the strength to challenge. Calls for greater recognition of such a 'spirit' of service and the creative powers of humanity coping in crisis have been a frequent theme in modern scholarship across the disciplines.[59] As observed earlier, fully representative scholarship in the discipline of IR needs to engage in a broad inter-disciplinary approach. Bertrand Badie presents a new model of IR and power where the world order consists of dissimilar actors and unique capacities, and where discussions around cooperation and interaction replace those of contestation and competition. As well as presenting opportunities for mutual interdependence, where weakness and humility are seen as a strength, it offers a new approach to address the changed structures of IR at the start of the twenty-first century in a post bi-polar system, and an escape from the echo-chamber which excluded the voices of those not seen as part of the 'club'.[60]

In an article examining opportunities to restore the fading mantle of global negotiations for peace, Oliver Richmond has suggested that a new age of peace-making cannot be achieved without an engagement with anthropology.[61] Evidence to support this call has been supported by evaluations that document the failures to recognise the importance of cultural influences that may have led to more efficient and competent response to the Ebola crisis which afflicted regions of West Africa in 2014–2015.[62] This recognises the need to cast a lens further than theories of security and economy that tend to disengage from consideration of local communities and focus on factors at the macro-level, and instead to direct the focus towards considering the localised legitimation of identities and their meaning to communities – one that looks to a new direction that will challenge the hegemony of dominant paradigms and their methods and norms.[63] This does not mean a total rejection of the traditional theoretical approaches. It acknowledges the realities of 'real-politik' but also recognises the instrumentalist character of the narratives of humanitarianism constructed in imperialist and colonial discourse which has continued with similar expression, albeit in a differing language, in the post-colonial and post–Cold War narratives. The new discourse will display heightened awareness of the differences and sensitivities inherent in other cultures and will address the challenge of locating a distinct place to balance the merits of emergency survival and broader humanitarian advocacy in the larger arena. Directions towards this new space for cooperative engagement are identified in the concluding chapter 9.

Chapter 9

Changing the Social Order

This concluding chapter reflects on how far the arguments in the book have addressed the problem identified in chapter 1: the lost expression of meaningful, trusted representation of the broad community of stakeholders in environments of crisis and complex emergency. The question was whether a revised presentation of the narratives around the humanitarian identity, focusing on shared values of voluntary service and the common spirit to assist in times of crisis, can offer new avenues for access to an inclusive, prosocial discourse? The central theme that has emerged is that the humanitarian environment has changed but the institutional narratives surrounding it have remained static. The book began by exploring the possibility that within this environment the space for independent humanitarian responses has diminished, constrained by growing national assertiveness and international regulation at the end of the twentieth century, and the insecurity which emerged from the collapse in the old social and political order. Whilst insecurity has undoubtedly caused a loss of proximity and diminished the space for physical access, my arguments suggest that the conceptual space of discourse has not shrunk. Rather, the avenues to access the spaces for discourse in the changed environment have shifted and the traditional narratives have lost their path, locked inside a discussion that is no longer relevant or representative of the community it purports to serve. My study argues for the location of a new, more social, less exceptional space for the humanitarian identity to be defined and protected that enables trusted interaction with the broad new community of stakeholders it represents: a space of prosocial discourse. The book has aimed to add a fresh perspective on the traditional analysis of humanitarian principles, offering a new space for participation in the socio-political environment of complex emergencies at the beginning of the twenty-first century.

Bertrand Badie sees opportunities from a breakdown of the established order of the Westphalian system and the shift from a bi-polar world by acknowledging changed norms of participation and a new sense of collectivity.[1] This new engagement requires new perspectives on identities and new patterns of partnership that allow a place for support and for challenge, and where the discourse shifts from one of independence towards one of interdependence. Notions of the auxiliary and anarchist presented in the book do not herald a return to the turmoil of a pre-Westphalian system, but rather a better understanding of the historical context and messiness of interactions of the current socio-political environment and the changes required to make partnership function in the post–Cold War world.[2] The arguments complement emerging scholarship around a Quantum Approach to the study of IR, which recognises the positive agency from interference and disorganisation.[3] The new perspective links with feminist discussion around intersectionality, sharing a call to step away from notions of sameness and the constructions of coalitions of the like-minded that endorse exceptionalism and exclusion. The difference rests on what my study presents as the politics of identity, appealing to more nuanced – and temporal – coalitions capable of participating in the complex political and social spaces that many of the debates around identity politics present.[4] The acknowledged strength of diversity and partnership in the humanitarian sector at an operational level needs to be extended towards a new way of thinking that enables access to broader participation and engagement in the humanitarian discourse: a shared engagement that strengthens the place for principled humanitarian action. Platforms offering a solution must present a broader recognition of participation that is less prescriptive, recognising the multiple social and political influences that shape the environment.[5]

This niche of discursive space does not claim partisan attachment to any of the humanitarian typologies in the studies mentioned in this book but shares elements of most of them. Its common identity rests at the minimalist end of the humanitarian aid and development spectrum where the focus on survival and protection relates closely to the promotion of peace, understood as a pacificistic ethic of responsibility rather than as a pacifist opposition to war.[6] The concern for the protection of human dignity recognises the structural imbalances in society and the need for a longer-term focus on issues to address these. Just as my study does not place its identity within any of the typologies of aid, it also claims no affiliation with the 'classical' and 'resilience' paradigms presented by Hilhorst and others, discussed in chapter 8. Instead, the identity seeks a more modest position that occupies a middle ground between them. It suggests a transfer of agency not to any one, or mix, of the typologies or paradigms described earlier – nor even to any of the particular identities. Rather, it calls for a shift of agency to the *narrative* surrounding the identities which, I argue, gives access to a common discussion. This marks a transformation of discourse that re-orientates the stakeholder community towards a different, more shared, humanitarian strategy than the one directed by most contemporary humanitarian narratives. In order to test the robustness of the arguments to guide this re-direction, the opening section returns to reviewing a core theme emerging from my book: trust in representative humanitarian identities, able to navigate the social and political boundaries they inhabit.

RESETTING HUMANITARIAN RELATIONS

My book has referred to the fragility of trust. It has argued that humanitarian action is particularly vulnerable to manipulation and mistrust given its prominent role in the construction of social capital.[7] The relationship between trust and social capital is highly conditional, dependent on the structure of its society and of the political system surrounding it. This emphasises the need for careful interaction within carefully defined boundaries that are restrictive but inclusive. Understanding the nature and the extent of the boundaries of this humanitarian social space is important to the construction of avenues for trust and access in my study. Fredrik Barth's collection of essays on the nature of ethnic groups provides a useful interpretation of 'culture' and the socio-economic factors (what Barth refers to as 'ecologies') that influence this, and which relate to expressions of humanitarian identities argued here: a stable humanitarian purpose, or culture, with varied expressions of its practice.[8] Barth notes importantly that sharing a common culture is an implication or result of ethnic grouping, rather than its definition, meaning that the boundaries are set elsewhere, formed by what he refers to as 'ecological factors' and tradition.[9] These must be seen as separate factors, where the stability of 'culture' is retained despite divergent ecological practices. What is important is what is 'socially effective'. This requires the definition of boundaries that harbour an efficient form of social organisation, but which are porous, allowing the 'osmosis' of meanings and practices to keep its agency relevant and representative. In a similar way, humanitarian identities in my study can be understood as traditions and practices that are the most socially effective in the defined and limited space of humanitarian response and protection in times of crisis: a form of humanitarian social organisation. In this construction, humanitarian 'culture' is not formed by objective social norms but by certain principles which the actors themselves see as significant.[10] These become distinct boundaries within the socio-political environment. Whilst accepting the porous nature of these boundaries, the expansion of this social relationship needs to be closely managed. This implies governance of its principles and its practices rather than their regulation, which latter role needs to remain a responsibility of the political realm of power and authority.

Understanding humanitarian identity as forming a place for social organisation rather than for its professional institutionalisation is an important theme in my study. Chapter 5 has indicated the tensions that a growing professionalisation of the humanitarian sector has provoked. It suggests that gestures to the market and its dominant stakeholders have led to the sector's increasing distance from the evolving national and regional architecture of humanitarian aid, just as increasing physical insecurity has led to its loss of proximity to the populations in need of its protection. While acknowledging that this professional focus has contributed to accountability and effectiveness, my study sees the risk of the humanitarian sector losing sight of its ultimate goal – its humanitarian *telos* – that is to save lives, alleviate suffering and protect human dignity.[11] Although this directs attention towards the moral platforms the humanitarian identity occupies, my book is not a study of ethics, though it strongly urges direction of a discourse towards understandings of a 'moral sense' that Anaïs Rességuier sees emerging from a 'moral culture'[12] and which articulates some of the key concepts of purpose and practice featuring in this book. Guidelines such as Sphere and the Code of Conduct have given definition of entitlements and rights of protection in situations of crisis and articulate how these translate into practice. This has great merit when the influence of the international community was seen to be important to address failures in responsibilities to protect at the end of the Cold War.[13] However, changes in the contemporary environment marked by the re-assertion of sovereignty, the rise in social media, and the re-emergence of politics of identity require the formulation of a new expression that acknowledges a sociopolitical environment which is less homogenous and so less ready to accept external prescriptions, unless these are seen to be relevant to the communities it represents. This requires a humanitarian *sense* that extends beyond simple aid delivery, its supporting services and the application of constructed norms of entitlement, to one which translates into an inclusive and conceptual narrative able to take a more reflective, less prescriptive, approach.

The current humanitarian system is based on assumptions that seem increasingly at odds with the changing realities. This book has looked at ways to redress these assumptions, indicating that national actors want to play – and are capable of playing – their legitimate role. It adds to the current debates on localisation, subsidiarity and the emerging new paradigm of resilience but suggests a re-engagement, rather than a new engagement: one creating opportunities for cooperation, building on shared success and having access to shared capabilities. The IFRC World Disasters Report 2015, observes that the 'success of cooperation often depends on the reasons behind an engagement'.[14] My study interprets this as being more dependent on trusted expressions of intent, motive and motivation that emphasise the 'spirit' of the engagement, than the impulses of social or political capital and the material resources supporting these. It examines the identities of engagement which extend beyond the funding (donor power) and physical access (moral, social and political power) of one exceptional group and shifts the exploration towards the capabilities of a common group. This structural redesign requires a corresponding redesign of the discourse, moving from its contemporary focus on the international stakeholder community towards a common community of stakeholders that include the national and the sub-national. It contributes to the call for increased localisation but is careful not to be a simple conjuring of words that leads to a de-rogation of responsibility, or to a 'virtual' engagement which retains control but is distanced from physical or reputational danger: a dynamic which has been criticised by practitioners and academics alike for creating the sense of irrelevance and lack of representation which this book decries.[15] It recognises the external support necessary to help respond efficiently, effectively and accountably, but this support needs to be positioned within a framework that considers differences in context, focused by a transparent and commonly shared expression of purpose. In essence, my book calls for a re-positioning of relations in humanitarian responses that transform the stakeholder divide into a stakeholder relationship. This means transforming the narratives from contestation to cooperation, where the politics is around one of an *ordinary humanitarian society* instead of an *ordered humanitarian system*, with the institutional baggage and organisational constraints the latter concept entails. Access to this discourse of a well-disordered society means enabling an approach which emphasises capabilities to participate and be heard.

Trusted Interaction along the Humanitarian Frontiers

This book has identified two main understandings of the space in which new navigation is required: (1) as a conceptual space for cooperation and representation which (2) provides access to an operating environment that recognises its political identity but is protected as far as possible from the contesting influences of politics. 'Access' in this discussion is as much about the ability for actors and the community of stakeholders to participate in the narratives and to contribute to the discourse as it is around the security of physical access in these environments of crisis. The questions examined are how this model of humanitarian society is constructed and its identity defined. Critiques of the historical legacies presented in chapter 3, and the omissions of core narratives for social and political cooperation in the case studies, have indicated that these have been (and continue to be) articulated in an international space which has a presumed relevance to populations affected by crisis as well as to the greater stakeholder community. Chapter 5 has proposed an engagement with the 'politics of humanity' that is able to direct an inclusive, achievable and more accessible pathway in the new spaces for humanitarian response. The book has made evident the relationship between representation and power, observing the positive dynamic of intersubjective, interactive identities. This approach indicates a new articulation of authority in the space that recognises opportunities emerging from interdependence and creative interactions. Dylan Loh and Jaako Heiskanen see sovereign authority grounded in three distinct spaces: domestic society, the international realm and a liminal space that exists between them. This liminal border zone is capable of playing a dual role that both undermines and underlines the boundaries of power, and in which the identities are in perpetual tension. The duality in this liminal space maintains the inside/outside distinction, and it is the recognition of both which provides its essence and its strength: 'a space pregnant with unique and innovative practices'.[16] The arguments presented in my book share the recognition of a space for discourse that engages such a spirit of productive, rather than subversive, participation.[17]

Chapter 3 has referred to the dissatisfaction that stems from ideas of homogeneity emerging in a utilitarian model of society, since, according to Charles Taylor, 'societies built on this model are experienced as a spiritual desert, or as a machine. They express nothing spiritual and their regulations and discipline are felt as an intolerable imposition by those who aspire to absolute freedom'.[18] Hegel understood this dissatisfaction and made the demand for autonomy a central part of his theory, weaving the radical autonomy of Kant and Rousseau together to form his theory of differentiation.[19] This is the challenge my study sees as a product of the exclusion of ordinary virtues from the exceptional discourse of the contemporary humanitarian system – one that sees the dominance of one pattern of narratives denying anyone with differences of opinion from participation in its society. Taylor perceived a dilemma of this kind in (his) contemporary society, which he saw as having moved towards greater homogeneity and greater interdependence, 'so that partial communities lose their autonomy and to some extent their identity'.[20] The discomfort arises since great differences remain, and so in the homogenous environment these differential characteristics no longer hold meaning and value for those who have them. Since then, the dynamic is seen to have reversed in contemporary socio-political environments which see growing domestic heterogeneity and divisive sub-national politics as contesting both the authority and the efficiency of established power from within.[21] However, the sense of homogeneity has remained within the hierarchies of the humanitarian structure and their narratives remain dominant; tensions from this disconnection in the discourse persist. The resolution my study suggests is combining a hybrid approach within the niche that is homogenous in the sense of being rooted in a stable common purpose but remains 'partial' through its voluntary identity and its legitimacy to challenge. Acknowledging and including differences and decreasing the risks of minority alienation – at least within the boundaries of the humanitarian niche – gives place for a constructive challenge: the identification of a quasi-partial 'all-man's land' where continued engagement can be offered in the face of contest to its principles, seen to be more legitimate than either homogenous or partial spaces. The studies by Nyamnjoh referred in chapter 8 encapsulate this in the form of the Frontier African who inhabits and co-exists with others in the 'uncertain peripheries' of hierarchy and power.[22] This is an identity of those who operate across frontiers and see the value of 'a world where one can simultaneously belong and not belong'.[23]

The concept of this space of belonging yet not belonging – of being a part of something yet apart from it – has been a feature of anthropological scholarship since the introduction of the concept of liminal space by Arnold van Gennep in 1909.[24] Liminality (from the Latin word *limes* meaning 'threshold') was introduced as a concept to analyse traditional rites of passage across cultures and societies.[25] Bjørn Thomassen sees liminality occupying a place between structure and practice that 'implicates the existence of a boundary' and a place to facilitate the relationship between structure and practice.[26] He observes that liminal spaces as spaces of exchange are part of any culture. In the context of my book, this means that with correct identification (one that escapes from forms of social, religious and political ritual or institutional dogma), the identities being argued for the humanitarian niche can provide a known and accepted space for both auxiliary support and constructive challenge to dominant patterns of authority. In his article examining the intellectual history of the concept, Thomassen makes a distinction in his description of liminality: 'liminal experiences can be 'artificially produced' as in rituals, or they can simply happen, without anyone planning for it, as in natural disasters or the sudden disappearance of beloved persons'.[27] The distinction is important with relevance to construction of the humanitarian identities presented in my book since, taking their agency from environments of crisis that call for communal cooperation to survive and recover, its temporal spontaneity helps distance an association of the niche with the spaces of pre-determined institutions and so remain relevant to the 'ordinary' disorderliness of humanity struggling to cope.

The emphasis on an unexceptional nature of the environments of crisis, in which everyone has the capability to act, provides the opportunity for reconciling the spaces. By acknowledging the capacities of a community-led response, the agency shifts from an external, non-local expression of a need to respond, to how people in need are given access (capabilities) to respond themselves.[28] This articulates that the space for humanitarian response exists – as it always has – though not as the pre-defined place assumed by dominant practices over the past thirty years and more, but rather as an evolving space whose ownership cannot be claimed by a hegemonic narrative. To meet humanitarian needs in the modern environment involves continuous adaptation but remaining fixed to fundamental principles. This requires an approach that acknowledges a shifting environment and creates a space for constructive interaction between all its stakeholders that is different from the one they normally inhabit.[29] As argued in chapter 8, this requires recognition that the community of stakeholders is part of a complex interconnected web of social activity over which no single actor, or set of actors, has the legitimacy to dictate. There have been many calls for a reformation of the international humanitarian expression to make it more relevant to modern times, and to clarify a distinction between values and intentions where a lack of clarity has led to the closing-down of access to the shared narrative. Indeed, the wealth of study on purpose and practice suggests that humanitarian values have never been so clearly articulated. However, my argument is that these values have been articulated with reference to an international space, strongly influenced by human rights frameworks that have presumed to become a 'universal vocabulary of political legitimacy'.[30] These demote the relevance of local expressions for socio-political legitimacy, and where their exclusion leads to the absent narratives on trust and participation identified in the case studies. The re-opening of this space requires an approach that re-casts its authority towards a more modest place, legitimated by a sense of inclusion and the capability to belong.

In his book examining the narrative structures and cultural ideas that have shaped the British identity, Ali Ansari talks about 'an excess of governance' which, rooted by complacency in its authority, he attributes as one of the causes for decline in the British Empire.[31] This sense of complacency – that 'we know best' – echoes the assumptions of an international identity suited to local particularities which marked the colonial drive referred in chapter 3. As remarked in the previous chapter, the irrelevance of identity to its community leaves a discourse empty of representation and moral authority. In his review of authority, Ansari recognises the risks of an absent narrative and a need to fill any vacuum before new, contesting narratives emerge.[32] My book has argued that a careful reflection of identities and the history of their shared meanings indicates there is no gap in the humanitarian narrative, but a continuity that has been ignored in its contemporary discourse. Therefore, its moral authority remains but requires to be re-positioned in a space made more accessible and relevant to all its stakeholders. This does not mean reinforcing existing meanings. It must not entail a repeated cascade of traditional patterns re-legitimated by conjured new vocabularies,[33] but rather a wider engagement with a fresh narrative considered to be an honest reflection of the way humanitarians are seen – and see themselves – as a support to communities in crisis. This does not call for a separation from the political narrative, but for acknowledgement of its political identity, nuanced by an understanding that humanitarian engagement needs to remain part of the narrative chamber and not an unrepresentative or irrelevant echo within it. This locates a new kind of engagement with the stakeholder community, representing it with regenerated moral authority distanced from the 'hypocritical piety' that dominant expressions in current humanitarian discourse are often seen to portray.[34]

Together with a review of understandings around voluntary service, my book has considered the need to elevate recognition of the principle of universality as another means to anchor the humanitarian identities. As made evident in chapter 6, the importance of this as an identity to bond the moral and the organisational network of a shared humanitarian response, grounded in articulations of *humanity*, framed an essential part of the Red Cross Movement debates about the Fundamental Principles. A sense of universality in this discussion emphasises ideas of a common purpose. This locates a place where agreements of a shared narrative on the practices of humanitarian action can take place that are at once relevant to the needs and the context of performance – and are representative of the community it serves. In order to access this place, and to operationalise its purpose, my study suggests a need to approach understandings of voluntary service, its auxiliary character and the universal relevance of its identity in a less prescriptive way. It must not get boxed-in by narrow definitions driven by distant, less locally relevant articulations of best practice and good governance. It requires confidence in the modesty of its own articulations and to escape the risks which an 'excess of governance' entails. Instead, its legitimacy will derive from its participation in a common conversation with its stakeholders. Chapter 3 has noted the change of language in the aid community over its long history from the era of Victorian philanthropy to the narratives of contemporary rights-based humanitarianism. The tensions this inevitably raises between different cultures and their polities make participation in this discussion essential.[35]

The Red Cross and Red Crescent Movement has highlighted the importance of presenting a single, coherent image of a well-functioning humanitarian network, where the diversity and complementarity of each component of the Movement is seen as important.[36] This includes recognising the unique mandate given to ICRC under the Geneva Conventions, the responsibility of the IFRC as the Secretariat representing its global membership, and the (statutory) relationship that each national society has as an auxiliary to public humanitarian services in its own country.[37] Without trust in the complementary nature of the network, good coordination and effective, united response become difficult, with responsibility then devolving onto the individual organisation within states (e.g. NGOs and community-based organisations) rather than the collective, with a corresponding weakening in the legitimacy of collective representation and a reduction in mutual trust.

Legitimising the Auxiliary Role

Jean-Jacques Rousseau observes that mutual trust entails reciprocity and the agreement to follow common principles and socially contracted norms, rather than prescribed regulations, and so is contingent.[38] Evidence from evaluations and surveys amongst practitioners referred to in this book acknowledge the prominence that context has in shaping humanitarian access in the operating environment. The regional consultations held in preparation for the Red Cross Movement *Council of Delegates*, 2015 noted that 'context matters' and reference to this recurred frequently as a topic in defining the role for Movement partners in crises to address the challenge to independent access and acceptance.[39] The operational context is seen to be a key driver of the identification and allocation of responsibilities, building on complementary strengths of each component in the environments.[40] This demotes the prescriptions for a standardised 'best practice', placing them in a perspective that sees best practices shaped variously, according to context, rather than confining their definition to any single theoretical box. The platform for legitimation of this diversity rests on the stability of its purpose, 'guarded' by the membership in the niche and the trust placed in it by the community of stakeholders it represents.

As discussed in chapter 2, trust and legitimacy are derived and generated in a process that requires a constellation of factors to piece together a model which includes proof of intent, as well as evidence of impact.[41] This is a construction that is easily fractured but not so easily re-built. The case studies in chapter 7 make the recognition of variant and evolving contexts evident in the way trust and access is allocated. An academic study of the reconstruction in Sri Lanka following the tsunami in 2004, and the post-conflict reconstruction after defeat of the LTTE in 2009, recognises the contingent nature of the aid and development environment.[42] It emphasises that a final definition of reconstruction approaches depends less on external circumstance than on developments in local politics. That is to say, practice in the environment would be influenced by the character of established or unestablished power in the local environments rather than by the norms of the international community.[43] The case studies corroborate these contingent dynamics in the accompanying political narratives. The absence of expressions linking the purpose and practices of the formal humanitarian system as auxiliary to the community of stakeholders they represent cautions against assumptions of an internationalist pattern for common action.

My book has argued consistently for achievable goals if identities in the niche are to gain the trust and confidence of the stakeholders they represent, calling for a carefully constructed balance between intent and efficiency. Chapter 5 has indicated the risks from over-exposure that an extension of purpose and an expansion of practice present. A 'Dunantist' adherence to the principles of the classical humanitarians and the solidaristic 'Wilsonian' approach that sees the consequences of the act – and not the act itself – as being the moral arbiter between good and bad are considered the two main ethical approaches in the emergency aid.[44] The difficulty is that many in the sector try to practice both and representations become confused. The solution lies in the construction of a balance in these approaches. This challenges arguments which insist on a clear separation of these identities. Rather, it calls for a recognition of the interdependence of both, representing cross-related approaches able to engage in discussion of the moral worth of each amongst the community of stakeholders. Eleanor Burt and Samuel Mansell observe that moral responsibility requires good intention. Institutional or organisational procedures on their own are not enough: 'real intentionality requires a unified consciousness'.[45] This means having agency in a space capable of holding a position that is distinct from individual desires (e.g. of the person or the state) and allows the freedom to choose an approach that coheres with the humanitarian norms of the community: the autonomy to coordinate judgements into a single system that that is 'morally relevant'.[46]

What evidence is there that identities of cooperation will gain more legitimate authority than identities of confrontation? An answer turns to the cross-disciplinary studies explored in my book reflecting the universal need for partnerships, framed in the terms of a human urge to make welcome and to be made welcomed, presented in chapter 8. This questions the view that hostile competition is a main driving-force in inter-group behaviour, citing studies in social psychology that provide empirical evidence that there is more in-group/out-group cooperation than the dominant approaches lead us to expect.[47] These studies indicate that even though there is a preferential attachment to the in-group (attachment to the I-mode), this does not imply negativity or hostility towards out-groups (attachment to the We-mode). Rather, the sustained well-being of groups significantly depends on successful cooperation with a greater collective.[48] Studies in biological and evolutionary science indicate that an empathic-helping relationship may have evolutionary roots based on kinship ties (in group) and cooperative ties with non-kin (out-group), crafting a relationship to ensure or enable the likelihood of reciprocal cooperation in the future as a reward.[49] The legitimacy of these conscious processes of a reciprocal transaction is acquired through the freedom of a voluntary choice to cooperate: a transaction rooted in the urge to survive but situated in the frame of a freedom to choose.

The strength and legitimacy of the voluntary transaction is reflected by the Kantian and Contractarian philosophical approaches discussed in chapter 6, presenting understandings of 'moral justice' (Kantian), 'justice as fairness' (Contractarian) and their tensions with Utilitarian approaches. John Rawls indicates the utilitarian flaws that extend the principle of choice for one dominant group to the whole of society (a teleological approach), but which cannot/must not be superior to the principles of justice as fairness. It must not be seen to overrule the right to common dignity and the basic capabilities to achieve this (a deontological approach). The arguments presented in my study adopt a hybrid approach that recognises a utilitarian stance in respect of the rational 'I' which seeks maximum profit from a voluntary humanitarian response to crises, but not at the expense of de-legitimising its identity to the broader community it represents, and thereby losing its trust. Therefore, just as a deontological approach towards justice as fairness does not aim to reward a pre-defined moral status or the arbitrariness of talent, so the members of the niche cannot assume legitimacy based on moral superiority. Rather, legitimacy ensues from its identity with a common purpose and the performance of shared practice, recognising a function of equal moral worth.[50] In this book I argue that the surest foundation for a popularly legitimated moral worth is identified by acts that are spontaneous, voluntary, and not driven by arbitrary endowments of skill, status and power: one which constructs the former as a platform for the 'ordinary virtues' described by Ignatieff. This is reached along a path that emphasises 'capabilities' instead of 'abilities' and is not troubled by inequalities of endowment but insists on equality of access. This resembles the 'convivial' approach used by Nyamnjoh and de Goede that sees relationships as a site of interaction rather than altercation, where convivial agency occurs.[51]

Convivial interaction means recognition of complementarity not exceptionalism. Studies have cautioned against the formation of a new 'relief elite' and the dangers of a humanitarian oligopoly using the principles and practices as a distinct market niche,[52] making the concept of humanitarian action as something they want everyone to value and enjoy but which only they are allowed to do.[53] My arguments in the book counter this with support for a Capability Approach that promotes equality of access but acknowledges the inequalities of hierarchies in society. The emphasis is on equality of access to opportunities, and not necessarily equality of status and equal entitlements, apart from the entitlement to a dignified life. Using this as an approach to direct identities in the niche, I suggest its discourse will lead to a different, less presumptive and more meaningful expression of differentiation that is not so closed or homogenising as the modern (Liberal and Marxist) expressions of global unity, giving space to a middle ground driven by a spirit of voluntary mutual engagement. This means one which is comfortable with its more modest position as an auxiliary support to humanitarian responses within the dimensions of power.

Protection against an assumption of moral superiority rests upon the auxiliary identity of the niche as being an aid and representative to the common community of stakeholders, not as being the utilitarian or realist driver of the humanitarian purpose being practised. There are moral, social and political obligations that we commonly recognise arising from the communities and traditions that shape our identity, and towards which, in its enactment, we are all auxiliary. However, the strength in the arguments presented here rests on the voluntary spirit of their identity that is freed from the moral encumbrance associated with the egotistical act of 'to be seen to perform'. This is an argument in line with Kantian notions of the right over the good, but which recognises the sense of a voluntary 'obligation' influenced by historical, social and political associations in the variety of contexts where they are made. It recognises the background narratives that account for how we rationalise our purposes, and operationalise our practices (or, in Alasdair Macintyre's formulation, 'how we behave in our practices').[54] This suggests there can be no universal blueprint and that 'best practices' can only be legitimated by an unencumbered recognition of its history, framed by a universal desire for the fundamental right to dignity and respect, and the less predictable formulation of the contexts of its practice.

RE-IDENTIFYING THE HUMANITARIAN RELATIONSHIP

The predominance of approaches influenced by the Global North in formulating the philosophy and practice of the humanitarian identity has meant not only the lack of accessible entry-points for those outside of these traditions, but also that it represents an incomplete, or partial, responsibility for a humanitarian response, since it selects only the portions with which it feels comfortable, leaving less familiar traditions excluded.[55] This concluding section turns to mapping how a revised and inclusive identity can lead towards charting access to less partial and more representative avenues in the humanitarian space. If we accept the premise that the space has not diminished, then the restricted access can be attributed to the loss of relevance in the humanitarian narrative which means that the stakeholders have become so distant they are no longer able to see how each can complement the other, resulting in a perpetual state of contest. The question is how to re-orientate the map? The solution offered by this book is an orientation of the discourse which does not approach the narrative by asking 'who do we need most?' or 'what type of actor is best?' Rather, humanitarian stakeholders – including national authorities, donors, intergovernmental entities and implementing organisations – must consider what arrangement of complementary actors is best suited to the context in question?[56] This means moving away from establishing narratives about causal links between situations of crisis and casting blame, instead focusing a lens on how these contestations in the environment are identified and represented: giving a different sense of meaning for its stakeholders beyond their identification with the socio-political and economic structures dominating the current discourse. This directs us towards a pathway that promotes engagement with and within the space, able to interact and engage with the lived experiences of vulnerable communities.[57] This requires a narrative engagement that is more representational: one which engages a prosocial process that addresses the controversy and confrontations related to the provision of humanitarian relief and restores a sense of meaning.

The new direction focuses as much on the principles of voluntary service and universality as on the principles of impartiality, neutrality and independence, all equally recognised, and all 'governed' by the over-arching principle of humanity. The re-conception of this discourse requires reconsidering the epistemology of meaning and function – of purpose and practice – that re-understands them as the pairing of 'spirit' and 'praxis', rather than as the contesting constructions often interpreted by the judgemental dichotomies of 'motive' and 'action'. This enables the discourse to shift towards one that acknowledges the cultural variations in the roles and in the structures supporting them, with recognition of the different histories and influences that craft their identities. This is not to exclude the significance that material considerations of impact and efficiency have on generating the trust called for in my book. The arguments presented have clearly indicated the critical role they play in securing a trusted identity, and recent empirical studies have confirmed this as a key indicator of trust.[58] The difference here is one of emphasis. In my articulations, 'intent' is more emphatic than 'efficiency' and this re-positioning is the impetus to drive forward a less conflicting narrative. Studies referred to in this book show that humanitarian agencies have been obliged to professionalise and so would increasingly take ownership of the 'totems' of non-profit management – efficiency, effectiveness, impact and value for money – which meant that 'effectiveness', with its focus on results, came to be the definition of success.[59] Through a results-based framework, effectiveness can be quantified, but 'meaning' can be lost in the process. My book suggests a re-positioning – or an equal-positioning – of meaning with function: of purpose with practice. In philosophical terms, this translates as the distinction between 'moral sense' and 'moral culture', raised in the introduction to this chapter to express the synthesis between the deontology of the humanitarian purpose (its 'moral culture') and the teleology of its practices (its 'moral sense').[60] Whilst arguments in my book make a distinction between purpose and practice, they see the differences as an assimilation of complementary strengths. That is to say, they are more symmetrical than asymmetrical, presenting complementary tensions that create a more 'human' space for humanitarian assistance to be rendered relevant and representative within the complexity of identities in the humanitarian arena. This constructs the humanitarian 'niche' sheltering a focused, less complex identity, anchoring a shared moral culture and harbours legitimated expressions of a moral sense. The strength of its moral bond lies in the relevance to its stakeholders and the sense of its shared representation by them and towards them: a 'spirit' of humanity, with boundaries that indicate limits and allow it to function.

Cross-disciplinary studies examined in my book have argued that Liberal and Neo-Liberal approaches in the social, economic and political realms have shaped inter-personal and inter-group identities that promote processes of commodification. This frames adherence to humanitarian principles as a material transaction, constrained by obligations to a binary vision of power and authority. These have constructed new environments but have left behind unchanged narratives. The new direction called for in my book is for a re-conception of this dynamic: one which remains 'transactional' in the sense of creating an obligation to provide the capabilities for voluntary participation in response to crises that is reciprocal and protected by the community of stakeholders it represents. This is not understood as a political, material or even a purely moral transaction but as one which recognises the spirit of shared cooperation and the natural desire to make welcome. As well as being transactional, the direction is also transformational: the new humanitarian identity is produced by the construction of changed and mutually respectful relationships between its stakeholders, creating opportunities for the prosocial dynamics of representation and trust. [61]

I have argued that there has been dishonesty – or, at best, insincerity – in the refusal to recognise the interdependence of the political and the humanitarian in the expression of power and authority: a denial of the political agency of its identity. Evidence in the case studies, as well as empirical data from studies on violence to aid workers to the funding strategies of the humanitarian system, show how each interacts to produce and be produced in environments of complex emergency and make clear the complicity of each in defining access, trust and representation. Attempts by humanitarians to declare innocence of political agency can at best be naive but are more often a display of arrogance – a complacent declaration that their level of complicity is somehow more innocent than another's. More importantly, its blind complacency has meant a failure to recognise opportunities for a middle ground where more convivial and trusted relations can occur. In order to break away from this self-imposed entrapment, its discourse needs to recognise the interconnectedness of the dynamics and divest itself of the aura of innocence. This means locating and adopting a middle ground between ruler and the ruled that acknowledges and accepts a shared identity and shared responsibility within restricted boundaries of a humanitarian crisis. It calls for a humbler identity that recognises both the limits of its authority and the breadth of its legitimacy. This is one that no longer sees humanitarians with unique and unchallenged channels to construct a humanitarian identity, formed from a universal set of practices, but is firmly set in a universalist mould of principles. Humility does not – must not – mean innocence or a devolution of responsibility. By engaging honestly with the political relationship, it can occupy a middle ground that is innocent of rulership, but not of leadership. In promoting a sense of humanitarian governance, where its status as its trustee acts as an auxiliary for access to the 'ordinary virtues', there are opportunities for a less arrogant, more modest coupling of process and outcome. The nature of governance in the niche focuses on being a speaker for the community, with access to it and deriving authority from it. It is both authorised and recognised, and inhabits a newly defined, semi-partial and autonomous place at the borderlands, described by Nyamnjoh as a place where they can simultaneously belong and not belong.[62] In my study, this translates as a boundaried space where it has the capability to act in accordance with agreed and shared principles and which – as a humanitarian on the frontier between the moral authority of the community and the politics of power – holds the authority to challenge.

Recognition of the Long-Term Vision

Re-humanising the narratives requires a gaze that looks beyond a simple glance. Defining clarity from the reflections cast by the mirrors on identity urged in chapter 8 requires careful and patient reflection. It is a process, not an event. Just as the drivers of conflict are more complex than simply a battle, then so too are those that drive its resolution. Creating space for a prosocial discourse is a process that requires the patient engagement of multiple identities, just as the places they inhabit may require multiple spaces. The solution presented has been the recognition of these diversities, binding them together through definition of a shared purpose. My study on trust and access is about this shared identity, formed from a mix of organisational trust (purpose) and institutional efficiency (practice). Legal debates about the right of access to populations in distress are prolific.[63] The challenges to accessible humanitarian response in the 1990s gave rise to the operational guidelines and codes of conduct for practitioners in the field mentioned in this book. Whilst these legal and normative debates are important, my study contributes to an equally important, more universally relevant, shift towards securing social relationships whose significance has been neglected because of the attention paid to a quest for the 'international' and misplaced universal assumptions. The arguments this book presents are to direct attention towards the creation of social bonds in a niche that promote the moral authority of its stakeholders, and that will, in time, become transferable across the broader humanitarian arena. This urges a focus towards new understandings of meaning and practice in a humanitarian space that is principled, ethical and achievable – expressive of a universalist narrative which is less arrogant, more representative, and more robust. It is a paradox that the expansion of structures and the transformation towards professionalisation and accountability of the humanitarian sector over past decades has meant its 'presence' is no longer seen to be proximate. These distanced humanitarians are not regarded as legitimate representatives of the communities at risk, nor of the stakeholders that support them. Representation in the construction proposed in my book is about identities in a humanitarian society that extend the debates beyond those around localisation which feature prominently in current attempts to redesign the sector. It calls for a different kind of paradox: one that encompasses a broader representation, occupying a simplified space that is messier and more dynamic – but is a well-disordered space.

My book has stressed the opportunities for humanitarian social order emerging from stability in the humanitarian space, anchored by the history of its principles and its joint participation in the quest for dignity and respect. Empirical evidence from field studies conducted by ALNAP have indicated the importance of a respectful relationship. These find that people who had been able to participate in crisis response and who were able to provide feedback were over three times more likely to say they had been treated with dignity and respect than people who had not.[64] The importance here is that having access to participate and be represented in the disorder of their environment gave them a sense of agency to restore order to their lives: an opportunity for fair access to the ability to choose. Examples of communities trying to make sense of the war in Bosnia were provided in chapter 8, where the freedom to choose identities to cope helped restore a sense of normality amidst abnormality. This places emphasis on participation in a space where they are made to feel relevant, and where the institutional indicators of efficiency and material impact are secondary. The arguments in my book do not call for access to rights-based entitlements which may not be achievable in every context, or which confront the established hierarchies of society. Rather, the call is for equal access to a common platform for discussion and representation. This must not be a re-formulation of hierarchies that represent positions of 'high-standing' expressed by the practice of meritocratic dignity in ideas of the Classical Greek polis which was reserved to a privileged few and generates the restricting and restrictive echoes in the chamber which my book urges to reform. It shares a more pluralist expression of the classical tradition which sees dignity as non-humiliation: the ability of 'holding one's head up in the company of others and being properly acknowledged by them'.[65] This resembles understandings of civic dignity as practiced in

Classical Athens which were seen as an intermediate stage of 'equal high standing' 'available to and protected by free citizens who have an equal opportunity to participate in a public domain of decision and action'.[66] It requires giving prominence to a social value that is not reduced to the state of the individual and yet recognises the need of a personalised expression in the collective identity of the community.[67]

Reviews of history and anthropology show that concepts of dignity and respect are themselves unstable, contingent on expressions of culture and power. The elevated status of the meritocracies of ancient Greece and the dignity of the Knights and warrior classes in mediaeval contexts elevated their status in society and access to capabilities was granted accordingly. But cultures and empires fell and these contingent avenues to access were lost. The niche argued for in my book must not be meritocratic in the Classical sense, based on a hierarchy of merit or exceptional talent. However, it is a protected space to anchor confidence and trust that is 'proofed' by experience of good intent and efficiency. It identifies with a pattern of civic merit that sees itself available to, and protected by, citizens who have an equal opportunity to participate in public action; one that is grounded in political and communal relations. The niche described in my book resembles this as a space of equal participation and trusted representation in the humanitarian environment, based on the expression of a common purpose. It avoids expressions of meritocracy except for merits accorded by the principles to which all citizens want to adhere. This requires a sensitive balance between being an auxiliary in a system of power yet having the authority to challenge when the system fails to protect access to dignity and respect: an auxiliary when it works and an anarchist when it does not. 'Real-life' legitimacy is derived from well-understood survival mechanisms in crisis, presented here as the ability to make normal amidst the traumas of an abnormal world.[68] This recognises the strengths of a 'well-disordered' society which is at once virtuous, reciprocal and rational, grounded in a stable discourse of a shared humanitarian identity and the social 'culture' surrounding it. In operational terms, this translates as the practical skills of coordination, communication and cooperation, proven to be key to the establishment of trust.[69] My study suggests it is the strength of the voluntary obligations within the boundaries of the humanitarian niche that promote a shared responsibility, and so creates the social bond which Fredrik Barth sees as a requirement for the construction of cultural identity that least exposes it to instrumental challenges.

Studies in philosophy and social psychology recognise the platforms for cooperation when communities are faced with common threats and there is a sense of mutual responsibility to respond.[70] This form of social bonding is most accessible in environments of crisis and complex emergency, where shared responses of state, non-state and civic actions (the community of stakeholders) are seen as auxiliary support to a common need and will be protected by it. The examples of first emergency response in the case studies in chapter 7 have given evidence of contexts where the community becomes the state and the opportunities for mutual trust and cooperation are at its highest. Thus, by focusing its action on a shared purpose, an individual and a collective dignity is constructed that provides cooperative access to defined humanitarian space and legitimation of the actions within it. Cooperation in the niche is sustained by adherence to its primary goal of saving lives and protecting dignity: a voluntary restraint which, my arguments suggest, diminishes the construction of a competing authority that deforms the contemporary focus on the core humanitarian principles of neutrality, impartiality and independence in contemporary humanitarian discourse.

Making Humanitarian Sense

Countering assumptions that the existing humanitarian discourse is already relevant, representative and legitimate has been central to the arguments presented in the preceding chapters. Evidence supporting calls for a new kind of engagement is provided in the latest ALNAP report on the state of the humanitarian system in which the case studies show that the humanitarian principles are 'not unerringly applied and nor do they command instant respect',[71] findings that are corroborated by the studies conducted by the Harvard Humanitarian Initiative (HHI), referred to earlier. While this does not in itself question principled action, the HHI report considers the main challenge to come from a different angle, which is from increasing state or institutional pressure that conditions alignment of humanitarian action with policy objectives. This does not indicate a reduction in humanitarian space, but rather restrictions of movement in that space, which is conditional on strategic objectives and not human identities. As a counterpoint, my study argues for the need to re-humanise the discourse and the voices within it. This recognises that a legitimate conception of the purpose of aid is not only in the practice of its delivery but in a process that sees humanitarian response as a social interaction engaging with the principles required for it to succeed.[72] We return to the arguments presented by Craig Calhoun in chapter 8, calling for the need to shift from a monocular focus on the traditions that have helped forge the dominant humanitarian narratives in the modern environments towards an acknowledgement of other traditions of solidarity that Cosmopolitan and Enlightenment approaches neglect; one that will 'complement the liberal idea of rights with a stronger sense of what binds people together'.[73] My book argues that this inclusive solidarity can be accessed through attention to more universal assumptions related to a shared spirit of voluntary service which offers opportunities to rehumanise the debates around the core principles of humanitarian action.

This supports arguments for an expansion of the interpretation of civil society presented by Bhikhu Parekh, seen as the product of relationships that are voluntarily formed by individual interests sharing a common goal: 'a world created by individuals but who have nonetheless found enough in common to bring and to hold them together for varying lengths of time and with varying degrees of mutual commitment'.[74] It mirrors the temporal nature of the niche as a socially organised humanitarian space enabled to assist and challenge in times of crisis. It is temporal in the sense of having agency at defined times and is 'incomplete' through the freely chosen limitations to its authority. But it is not discontinuous since it is able to re-continue its representation when required. As Calhoun has argued,[75] a good political order must deal fairly with the fact that most people will not be politically active most of the time, so the niche is not active most of the time but only in situations of crisis and complex emergency. This identifies the middle ground between continuity and change, one that resembles Nyamnjoh's space of conviviality, described in chapter 8.

This book has stood firmly for a position that acknowledges diversity and the opportunities emerging from creative tensions: a 'constructive anarchy' emerging from the messiness of humanity. The creative tensions that emerge will provide direction towards formation of a common prosocial space in which the expression (spirit) and the practice of humanity can regain the relevance and trust that its history had seen hopeful to promote. The creative tensions are formed by interactions between the complex identities that shared representation in the humanitarian niche must include. There is a need to caution against over-extending this discourse beyond the boundaries of its identity within a 'humanitarian culture' which risks straying into a more contested discourse around ethics and morality in the broader humanitarian-development-peace arena. It is difficult to bridge avenues to a discourse that holds more judgemental discussions around moral worth and values presented in the political, cultural and ideological environments of contemporary identity politics and the politics of identity, where contestations are fanned by access to divisive narratives. It needs care that 'humanitarian culture' does not become an ideology of its own, with the prescriptions, absolutes and essentialist associations that ideological doctrines entail, and which my study contests.

The approaches in my book are inclusive not only across disciplines in the academic sphere but are inter-relational in the philosophical and cultural sphere. Ideas presented in Rousseau's 'Social Contract' have been twinned with the Liberal-Rationalist approaches of Kant and Rawls, reflecting the counter-indications in their discussions on values, merit and worth that each present, with an aim to distil the essences for a new discourse.[76] In the same way, my study has presented the tensions and contradictions which exist at the practical level in an expanded arena, anchoring expressions of principles and practice that swing across the wider axis of rights-based activism. Common to all is the illegitimacy of a discourse that – in Rousseau's words – 'denature man' and 'take away his absolute existence, to give him a relative one'.[77] It calls for a middle ground that protects against the risks of the relative and an over-extension of the absolute. It acknowledges there are positions of human morality which are immutable and take on the character of the absolute, including adherence to humanitarian purpose and the principles of its practice. The resolution of this equation of opposites rests in the process of trust and the foundation of its relevance to the communities it serves. Talk of a 'niche' may itself appear to be too exclusive. The discourse is around the formulation of a common narrative, based on history and practice, reflecting culture and context. Rousseau observed that 'the most important laws are the laws of morals, custom and opinion'.[78] This is the contract of a humanitarian society that engages access, trust and cooperation in a prosocial space, in which new constructions of a representative humanitarian identity are formed and legitimated: the social bonds of a humanitarian service where the common identity rests on its spirit of a voluntary obligation to assist humanity.

As remarked in chapter 1, structures in the contemporary socio-political environment have changed. In his recent book on the understandings of 'praxis', Kratochwil observes that 'although sovereignty remains the recognised organizational principle, new actors, such as intergovernmental organizations (IGOs) and nongovernmental organizations (NGOs), have emerged and have undermined the state's monopoly on determining sovereignty's meaning'.[79] The arguments in my book present interpretation of this challenge to authority as one of the most significant factors leading to a lack of trust and dysfunction in the humanitarian environment. It proposes a resolution through new narratives that don't seek to define or re-define the meaning of sovereignty but provide access to a space for a cooperative, less prescriptive, discourse that expresses a shared 'organisational principle' for humanitarian action in situations of crisis. This is a discursive space which constitutes a more inclusive domain of politics that displays new organisational forms and patterns of interaction.[80] This requires re-imagining the boundaries and reconceptualising the agency of the spaces they define. Given the changed and changing structures, Kratochwil argues that 'society' is no longer represented by the units of space defined by the older patterns of construction.[81] Instead, it is formed from the processes of voluntary interaction and interdependency which emerge from the drawing of these boundaries and is more amorphous: a 'liminal' space for transaction and transformation. This book concludes that humanitarian society is an integral part of social and political society, defined within boundaries formed by a shared discourse around a common purpose. Trust in its identity rests on the agency of its discourse, one that is able both to support and to challenge the units of authority on its frontiers.

Notes

INTRODUCTION

1. In the book, I use lower case letters (e.g. voluntary service) when making general reference to these concepts in relation to humanitarian principles and upper case letters (e.g. Voluntary Service) when referring specifically to the Fundamental Principles of the Red Cross and Red Crescent Movement.

2. See Alasdair Gordon-Gibson, 'Goma 1994: Notes from the field', *Genocide Studies International,* Volume 10, no. 2 (2016): 254–267.

3. See Rebecca Walker, 'Taking a back seat: The uses and misuses of space in a context of war and natural disaster', *Journal of Human Rights,* Volume 12, no. 1 (2003). One of the interviewees in this study remarks: 'It's like there was a loss of consciousness of differences. There are the army who had to pull Tamil children from the waves, some who died themselves and the LTTE who at that point immediately rushed to help with the army. It's funny, it's like, in that crisis everyone becomes human . . . but then that was lost' (ibid: 77).

4. Often described as the 'classical' humanitarians, or *Dunantists*, named after one of the founders of the Red Cross, Henry Dunant (Barnett, 2011).

5. International Committee of the Red Cross, *The Fundamental Principles of the Red Cross and Red Crescent*, https://www.icrc.org/en/doc/assets/files/other/icrc_002_0513.pdf; Jérémie Labbé and Pascal Daudin, 'Applying the humanitarian principles: Reflecting on the experience of the International Committee of the Red Cross', *International Review of the Red Cross,* Volume 97, no. (897/898) (2016): 183–210; Marc DuBois, 'The new humanitarian basics', Working Paper. Humanitarian Policy Group/ODI (2018): 13.

6. Craig Calhoun, 'The class consciousness of frequent travelers: Toward a critique of actually existing cosmopolitanism', *The South Atlantic Quarterly,* Volume 101, no. 4 (2002): 879.

7. Calhoun, 'The class consciousness of frequent travelers'.

8. This book uses the terms 'Global North' and 'Global South' when referring to the complex economic and social inequalities in contemporary discussions about human development (see Arie Kacowicz, Globalization, Poverty, and the North-South Divide, *International Studies Review,* Volume 9 (2007): 565–580). This in preference to the terms 'Northern Hemisphere' and 'Southern Hemisphere' which were current following the report of the Independent Commission on International Development Issues (the Brandt Report), Willy Brandt, *North-South: A programme for survival* (Cambridge, Massachusetts, MIT Press, 1980).

9. For example, http://dfat.gov.au/about-us/publications/Documents/effective-governance-strategy-for-australias-aid-investments.pdf and other inter-governmental documents related to the essential practices of 'Good Governance' https://www.gov.uk/international/governance-in-developing-countries

10. Teun van Dijk, 'Critical discourse analysis', in *The Handbook of Discourse Analysis*, eds. Deborah Schiffrin, Deborah Tannen and Heidi Hamilton (Oxford: Blackwell, 2001), 352–371.

11. I purposely use the word 'community' in the context of the arguments presented in my book. An explanation of the terminology used is provided at the end of this 'Introduction'.

12. Intersectionality is a perspective that explores the interactions of social markers that shape an individual's or group's experience and emphasises the important complexity of human identity and power relations. See Adele Norris, Yvette Murphy-Erby and Anna M. Zajicek, 'An intersectional perspective in introductory sociology textbooks and the sociological imagination: A case study', *Race, Gender and Class* Volume 14, no. 1–2 (2007): 334.

13. Hugo Slim, 'Impartiality and intersectionality ICRC humanitarian law and policy ICRC weblog', 16 January 2018. https://blogs.icrc.org/law-and-policy/2018/01/16/impartiality-and-intersectionality/

14. Slim, 'Impartiality and intersectionality'. The Red Cross and Red Crescent Movement sent a message to the World Humanitarian Summit asking to recognise that there is not a single international system of humanitarian response: 'The challenge is not to fix one system but to bring together diverse capacities and systems effectively around a given context' (message to the World Humanitarian Summit, Council of Delegates of The International Red Cross and Red Crescent Movement, Geneva, 2015 https://rcrcconference.org/app//uploads/2015/03/CD15-R3-message-to-WHS_EN.pdf)

15. See debates in *The New Humanitarian* https://www.thenewhumanitarian.org/opinion/2020/1/7/triple-nexus-international-aid-Marc-DuBois

16. See, for example, Ed Schenkenberg van Mierop and Marzia Montemurro, weblog HERE-Geneva, 6 February 2020. http://here-geneva.org/keep-it-complex-stupid/

17. For example, Bertrand Badie, 'New perspectives on the international order'. https://doi.org/10.1007/978-3-319-94286; Bertrand Badie, 'Toward a theory of weakness politics: Does weakness rule the world?', *Global Society,* Volume 32, no. 2 (2018): 139–148; Andrew Williams, *Failed Imagination? The Anglo-American New World Order from Wilson to Bush* (Manchester: Manchester University Press, 2008).

18. See the introduction to a Special Issue of *Security Dialogue*, by James Der Derian and Alexander Wendt, 'Quantizing international relations': The case for quantum approaches to international theory and security practice' (February 2020).

19. Stephen Hopgood, *The Endtimes of Human Rights* (Ithaca: Cornell University Press, 2013).

20. Jenny Petersen, 'Introduction', in *The Routledge Companion to Humanitarian Action*, eds. Roger Mac Ginty and Jenny Petersen (London: Routledge, 2015), 1–9.

21. Naomi Ellemers and Alexander Haslam, 'Social identity theory', in *Handbook of Theories of Social Psychology*, eds. Paul Van Lange, Arie Kruglanski and E. Tory Higgins: 379–398 (London: SAGE, 2012).

22. Tom Tyler, Peter Degoey and Heather Smith, 'Understanding why the justice of group procedures matters: A test of the psychological dynamics of the group-value model', *Journal of Personality and Social Psychology,* Volume 70, no. 5 (1996): 913–930; Raimo Tuomela, *Social Ontology: Collective Intentionality and Group Agents* (Oxford: Oxford University Press, 2013).

23. Martha Nussbaum *Frontiers of Justice* (Cambridge MA: Belknap Press, 2006); Amartya Sen, *Commodities and Capabilities* (Oxford: Oxford University Press, 1985); Amartya Sen, *Development as Freedom* (Oxford: Oxford University, 1999). Sen regards capabilities as a measurement for quality of life; Nussbaum as an account of core human entitlements that should be applicable to all – an approach 'focusing on what people are actually able to do and to be' (*Frontiers of Justice*: 70).

24. The ICRC, founded on the initiative of a Swiss businessman, Henry Dunant and other citizens in Geneva, originated from a sub-committee of the Geneva Society of Public Utility: 'The International Committee for the Relief of Wounded in Situations of War'. The volunteer identity was symbolised by the provision of 'neutral' care to those injured in war, whose rights and protection as non-combatants were legally codified in the first Geneva Convention of 1864. David Forsythe provides a comprehensive account of the origins and function of the ICRC in *The Humanitarians: The International Committee of the Red Cross* (Cambridge: Cambridge University Press, 2005). See also François Bugnion, *The International Committee of the Red Cross and the Protection of War Victims* (Oxford: Macmillan, 2014).

25. Ivana Maček, *Sarajevo under Siege: Anthropology in Wartime* (Pennsylvania: University of Pennsylvania Press, 2009).

26. Peter Walker and Daniel Maxwell, *Shaping the Humanitarian World* (Abingdon: Routledge, 2009), 2.

27. John Borton, *Future of the Humanitarian System: Impacts of Internal Changes* (Feinstein International Center: Tufts University, 2009).

28. Hugo Slim, 'Global welfare: A realistic expectation for the international humanitarian system?' *ALNAP Review of Humanitarian Action* (2006): 19. https://www.alnap.org/system/files/content/resource/files/main/ch1-f1.pdf

29. Hugo Slim, 'By what authority? The legitimacy and accountability of non-governmental organisations'. *Journal of Humanitarian Aid* (2002): 10.

30. Walker and Maxwell, *Shaping the Humanitarian World*: 3.

31. Michel Agier, 'Humanity as an identity and its political effects (A note on Camps and humanitarian government)', *Humanity*, Volume 1, no. 1 (2010): 34.

32. Denise Rousseau, Sim Sitkin, Ronald Burt and Colin Camerer, 'Not so different after all: A cross-discipline view of trust', *The Academy of Management Review,* Volume. 23, no. 3 (1998): 393–404.

33. Rousseau et al., 'Not so different after all'. Lisa PytlikZillig and Christopher Kimbrough, 'Consensus on conceptualizations and definitions of trust: Are we there yet?' In *Interdisciplinary Perspectives on Trust,* eds. E. Shockley, T. Neal, L. PytlikZillig and B. Bornstein B. (London: Springer, 2016), 17–47.

34. Rousseau et al., 'Not so different after all'. 395.

1. HUMANITARIAN RELATIONS

1. See 'Introduction', page 11.

2. Christina Bennett, (lead author), *Time to Let Go: Remaking Humanitarian Action for the Modern Era.* (Geneva, Humanitarian Policy Group/ODI, 2016), 7.

3. See interview with Sadako Ogata in World Chronicle, 14 March 2005 https://www.un.org/webcast/pdfs/wc970.pdf. For a recent book looking at the palliative nature of humanitarian action in complex emergencies, see Kurt Mills *International Responses to Mass Atrocities in Africa* (Philadelphia: University of Pennsylvania Press, 2015).

4. Including the Sphere Guidelines and the Code of Conduct for the International Red Cross and Red Crescent Movement and Non-Governmental Organizations (NGOs) in Disaster Relief.

5. https://agendaforhumanity.org/summit

6. Stefan Stürmer and Mark Snyder, *The Psychology of Pro-Social Behavior* (Chichester: Wiley-Blackwell, 2010).

7. See Jonathan Hill and Thomas Wilson, 'Identity politics and the politics of identities', *Identities: Global Studies in Culture and Power,* Volume 10, no. 1 (2003), 1–8.

8. Cressida Heyes, 'Identity politics', in *The Stanford Encyclopedia of Philosophy (Fall 2017 Edition),* ed. Edward Zalta. https://plato.stanford.edu/archives/fall2017/entries/identity-politics/

9. Kurt Mills, *International Responses to Mass Atrocities in Africa* (Philadelphia: University of Pennsylvania Press, 2015).

10. Michel Agier and Françoise Bouchet-Saulnier, 'Humanitarian spaces: spaces of exception', in *In the Shadow of 'Just Wars': Violence, Politics, and Humanitarian Action,* ed. Fabrice Weissman (Ithaca NY: Cornell University Press, 2004), 297–313; Dorothea Hilhorst, 'Classical humanitarianism and resilience humanitarianism: Making sense of two brands of humanitarian action', *Journal of International Humanitarian Action* Volume 3, no. 15 (2018),1–12.

11. Michael Barnett and Thomas Weiss, eds., *Humanitarianism in Question; Power, Politics, Ethics.* (Ithaca: Cornell University Press, 2008): 5.

12. Antonio Donini, (lead author), *Humanitarian Agenda 2015: Final Report, The State of the Humanitarian Enterprise* (Feinstein Institute, Medford MA: Tufts University, 2008); Michael Barnett, *Empire of Humanity* (Ithaca: Cornell University Press, 2011); Antonio Donini, ed., *The Golden Fleece: Manipulation and Independence in Humanitarian Action* (Sterling VA: Kumarian Press, 2012).

13. The term 'stakeholder' holds differing associations across the arts, sciences and law. The study in this book considers a broad group of stakeholders that include people directly affected by situations of humanitarian emergency, the state and

non-state actors responding on the ground. These could include a variety of interests along the humanitarian-development spectrum.

14. For example, John Borton, *Future of the Humanitarian System: Impacts of Internal Changes* (Feinstein International Center: Tufts University, 2009).

15. Jonathan Hill and Thomas Wilson, 'Identity politics and the politics of identities', *Identities: Global Studies in Culture and Power,* Volume 10, no. 1: 1–8. DOI: 10.1080/10702890304336.

16. Mills, *International Responses to Mass Atrocities*; DuBois, 'The new humanitarian basics'.

17. Friedrich Kratochwil, *Praxis: On Acting and Knowing* (Cambridge: Cambridge University Press, 2018).

18. Hugo Slim, 'Wonderful work: Globalising the ethics of humanitarian action', in *The Routledge Companion to Humanitarian Action.*

19. In the book, I use the acronym RCRC, or 'the Movement', when discussion involves all three components of the Movement: ICRC, IFRC and the national Red Cross and Red Crescent societies. In references to any one component, their individual acronyms are used.

20. Barnett, *Empire of Humanity;* Janet Gross Stein, 'Communities of Practice', in *International Practices*, eds. Emanuel Adler and Vincent Pouliot (Cambridge: Cambridge University Press, 2011): 87–107.

21. Caroline McGoldrick, 'The future of humanitarian action: an ICRC perspective', *International Review of the Red Cross,* Volume 93, no. 884 (2011): 976; Bennett, *Time to Let Go*: 46.

22. For example, Michael Duffield, *Global Governance and the New Wars: The Merging of Development and Security* (London: Zed Books, 2001); Oliver Richmond, 'The globalization of responses to conflict and the peacebuilding', *Cooperation and Conflict, 39/129* (2004); Andrew Williams, *Liberalism and War: The Victors and the Vanquished* (Abingdon: Routledge, 2006); Vivienne Jabri, *War and the Transformation of Global Politics* (Basingstoke: Palgrave Macmillan, 2007).

23. Bennett, *Time to Let Go,* 68.

24. Fredrik Barth, ed., *Ethnic Groups and Boundaries. The Social Organization of Culture Difference* (Long Grove, Ill: Waveland Press, 1998).

25. Richard Bernstein, *Beyond Objectivism and Relativism: Science, Hermeneutics, and Praxis* (London: Blackwell, 1983), 2.

26. Bernstein, *Beyond Objectivism and Relativism,* 2–3.

27. Bernstein engages with discussion around 'the practice of engaged fallibalistic pluralism', seen as inclusive practices which are not always right, but right enough (Bernstein, ibid).

28. Thomas Weiss, *Military-Civilian Interactions: Intervening in Humanitarian Crises* (Boulder: Rowman and Littlefield, 1999); Michael Barnett, 'Humanitarianism Transformed', *Perspectives on Politics,* Volume 3, no. 4 (2005): 723–740; Barnett and Weiss, *Humanitarianism in Question*, 2008.

29. Christina Bennett, 'Constructive deconstruction: Imagining alternative humanitarian action', HPG Working Paper. Humanitarian Policy Group/ODI (2018); Henry Radice, Saving ourselves? On rescue and humanitarian action. *Review of International Studies,* Volume 45, no. 3 (2019): 431–448.

30. Michel Foucault, *The Archaeology of Knowledge and the Discourse on Language*, trans. Alan Sheridan-Smith (London: Tavistock, 1972).

31. See Clare O'Farrell, *Foucault: Historian or Philosopher?* (Basingstoke: Macmillan, 1989).

32. Emanuel Adler and Vincent Pouliot, eds., *International Practices* (Cambridge: Cambridge University Press, 2011), 8. This is significant in consideration of the arguments explored more thoroughly in chapter 2, acknowledging the importance of *agency* as the driver for positive socialisation of legitimated humanitarian practices, according to their relevance within the context of each environment.

33. Adler and Pouliot, *International Practices*.

34. Adler and Pouliot, *International Practices*, 8.

35. Stephen Reicher and Alexander Haslam describe small acts with harmonious consequences that are 'often singly banal but socially consequential in combination', in 'Beyond help: A social psychology of collective solidarity and social cohesion', *The Psychology of Prosocial Behavior*, ed. by Stefan Stürmer and Mark Schneider (Chichester, UK: Wiley-Blackwell, 2010), 292.

36. Roderick Stirrat and Heiko Henkel, 'The development gift: The problem of reciprocity in the NGO world', *Annals of the American Academy of Political and Social Science,* Volume 554: 66–80 (1997).

37. Stürmer and Snyder, *The Psychology of Prosocial Behavior*, 5.

38. Stürmer and Snyder, *The Psychology of Prosocial Behavior*, 6.

2. VOLUNTARY SERVICE

1. Helmut Anheier and Lester Salamon, 'Volunteering in Cross-National Perspective: Initial Comparisons', *Duke University, Law and Contemporary Problems,* Volume 62, no. 4 (1999): 43.

2. United Nations General Assembly (UNGA), 2002. Resolution 56/38, Recommendations on support for volunteering http://dag.un.org/bitstream/handle/11176/237258/A_RES_56_38-EN.pdf?sequence=3&isAllowed=y

3. Anheier and Salamon, *Volunteering in Cross-National Perspective*, 49.

4. Anheier and Salamon, *Volunteering in Cross-National Perspective*, 43.

5. Pictet became Director General of the ICRC in 1966. From 1967 to 1979, he was elected a member of its Assembly (Governing Board) serving as the vice president from 1971 to 1979. His book *Les Principes de la Croix-Rouge* (Red Cross Principles), published in 1955, guided formulation of the Fundamental Principles of the Red Cross/Crescent Movement which were adopted at the 20th International Conference in Vienna, 1965. The use of the term 'Red Cross' to designate the International Red Cross and Red Crescent Movement, remained predominant on most official documentation until the renaming of the League of Red Cross Societies as the League of Red Cross and Red Crescent Societies in 1983. See François Bugnion, 'The International Conference of the Red Cross and Red Crescent: Challenges, key issues and achievements', *International Review of the Red Cross*, Volume 91, no. 876 (2009): 675–712.

6. Jean Pictet, 'The Fundamental Principles of the Red Cross', *International Review of the Red Cross,* 19 (1979): 135. In his commentary, Pictet clearly acknowledges the risks inherent in unremunerated or uncompensated voluntary service, when 'amateurism' can lead to a tolerance of indiscipline, poorly defined authority and a damaging dispersion of responsibilities. Until the 1970s, field staff for ICRC were selected from a core of volunteers, most from the Swiss business and civil service sectors. The selection and training process consisted of one-day's interview in Geneva before being sent to the field, for a period normally no more than three months. In 1970, a more rigorous recruitment process was introduced, and field delegates were hired for renewable assignments lasting around six months. Starting in 1974, thirty permanent delegates were hired for a period of five years, and this pattern became the norm (Marie-Luce Desgrandchamps, ' "Organising the unpredictable": the Nigeria – Biafra war and its impact on the ICRC', *International Review of the Red Cross* (2012): 1409–1432). A review of procedures for identification and appointment of delegates began in 2011, looking to provide a more mobile (less headquarter centred) structure with a focus on access and local knowledge, and is a process currently underway (author's discussions, ICRC Geneva, April 2018).

7. Stürmer and Snyder, *The Psychology of Prosocial Behavior*, 5.

8. See chapter 3.

9. Anheier and Salamon, *Volunteering in Cross-National Perspective*.

10. Shaun Hazeldine and Matt Baillie Smith, *IFRC Global Review of Volunteering* (Geneva: IFRC, 2015), 9.

11. Hazeldine and Baillie Smith, *IFRC Global Review of Volunteering*. Definitions containing elements of these three pillars abound in documentation on the humanitarian sector (e.g. see the United Nations Volunteers [UNV]). *Transforming Governance*. United Nations Development Programme, State of the World's Volunteerism Report (2015). https://www.unv.org/swvr/2015-state-worlds-volunteerism-report-swvr-transforming-governance and United Nations Volunteers (UNV). *The Thread That Binds: Volunteerism and Community Resilience*. United Nations Volunteers, State of the World's Volunteerism Report (2018). https://www.unv.org/sites/default/files/UNV_SWVR_2018_English_WEB.pdf However, the study by Hazeldine and Baillie Smith makes it clear that there are a variety of factors that were challenging these definitions and other norms of volunteering as accepted in most developed countries (*IFRC Global Review of Volunteering*, 28–29).

12. Worldwide, the Red Cross and Red Crescent Movement has more than twelve million active volunteers https://media.ifrc.org/ifrc/what-we-do/volunteers/

13. The 20th International Conference of the Red Cross proclaimed the following Fundamental Principles on which Red Cross action is based. *Humanity*: The Red Cross, born of a desire to bring assistance without discrimination to the wounded on the battlefield, endeavours to prevent and alleviate human suffering wherever it may be found. *Impartiality*: It makes no discrimination as to nationality, race, religious beliefs, class or political opinions. *Neutrality*: In order to continue to enjoy the confidence of all, the Red Cross may not take sides in hostilities or engage at any time in controversies of a political, racial, religious or ideological nature. *Independence*: The Red Cross is independent. The National Societies, while auxiliaries in the humanitarian services of their governments and subject to the laws of their respective countries,

must always maintain their autonomy so that they may be able at all times to act in accordance with Red Cross principles. *Voluntary Service*: The Red Cross is a voluntary relief organisation not prompted in any manner by desire for gain. *Unity*: There can be only one Red Cross Society in any one country. It must be open to all. It must carry on its humanitarian work throughout its territory. *Universality*: The Red Cross is a worldwide institution in which all societies have equal status and share equal responsibilities and duties in helping each other. (ICRC, *The Fundamental Principles of the Red Cross and Red Crescent*). For a commentary on the Fundamental Principles, see Pictet, 'The Fundamental Principles'.

14. Pictet, 'The Fundamental Principles', 135 (emphasis added).

15. Use of the term 'International Red Cross and Red Crescent Movement' became prominent in official RCRC documentation following the renaming of the League of Red Cross Societies as the League of Red Cross and Red Crescent Societies in 1983. (See Bugnion, *The International Conference of the Red Cross and Red Crescent*. Also, note 14 in chapter 6.).

16. Pictet, 'The Fundamental Principles', 129.

17. In German, the term 'Ehrenamt' is used, indicating 'honorary position'.

18. Pictet, 'The Fundamental Principles', 46.

19. Rebecca Gill, 'The rational administration of compassion: The origins of British relief in war', *Le Mouvement Social*, Volume 227, no. 2 (2009), 9–26.

20. Caroline Abu Sa'Da and Xavier Crombé, 'Volunteers and responsibility for risk-taking: Changing interpretations of the Charter of Médecins Sans Frontières', *International Review of the Red Cross*, Volume 97, no. 897/898 (2016): 136.

21. Abu Sa'Da and Crombé, *Volunteers and responsibility*, 136.

22. https://www.msf.org.uk/our-charter

23. The study notes that there are various categories of volunteers recognised in French law. See https://www.associations.gouv.fr/les-differentes-formes-de-volontariat.html

24. Abu Sa'Da and Crombé, *Volunteers and responsibility*, 136.

25. Hazeldine and Baillie Smith, *IFRC Global Review of Volunteering*, 11.

26. Anheier and Salamon, *Volunteering in Cross-National Perspective*, 49.

27. Anheier and Salamon, *Volunteering in Cross-National Perspective*, 43.

28. Anheier and Salamon, *Volunteering in Cross-National Perspective*, 44.

29. Hazeldine and Baillie Smith, *IFRC Global Review of Volunteering*, 24.

30. ICRC, *The Fundamental Principles of the Red Cross and Red Crescent* (italics added).

31. Paul Dekker and Loek Halman, eds., *The Values of Volunteering: Cross-Cultural Perspectives* (London: Plenum, 2003).

32. Elinor Ostrom, 'Toward a behavioral theory linking trust, reciprocity and reputation', in *Trust and Reciprocity. Interdisciplinary Lessons from Experimental Research*, eds. Elinor Ostrom and James Walker (New York: Russell Sage, 2003), 19–79. (italics added).

33. Studies in evolutionary psychology are supported by cross-disciplinary studies in evolutionary biology. In his study on the evolutionary drivers behind altruism, David Sloan Wilson presents one of the key debates in evolutionary theory that revolves around group-level functional organisation. Arguments rotate around considerations of what Wilson labels 'selfish' behaviour and 'altruistic' behaviour.

In the former, relative fitness is increased within the group, and in the latter 'when it increases the fitness of the group but places the individual at a relative fitness disadvantage within the group' (David Sloane Wilson, *Does Altruism Exist?* New Haven: Yale University Press, 2015, 22). His study provides scientifically verified explanations as to what, in evolutionary terms, enables 'this contrasting dynamic to support Darwinian theories of survival of the fittest.

34. Leeuwen and Täuber, 'The strategic side of out-group helping', 81.

35. Duffield, *Global Governance and the New Wars*; Hilhorst, 'Classical humanitarianism and resilience humanitarianism'.

36. Charles Taylor, 'Modern Social Imaginaries', *Public Culture,* Volume 14, no. 1 (2002): 91–124.

37. Sami Halabi and Arie Nadler, 'Receiving help: Consequences for the recipient', in *The Psychology of Pro-Social Behavior*, eds. Stefan Stürmer and Mark Snyder (Chichester, UK: Wiley-Blackwell, 2010), 121–138.

38. Jennifer Rubenstein, *Between Samaritans and States* (Oxford: Oxford University Press, 2015), 115.

39. See 'Introduction', note 23.

40. For example, community platforms with the International Association of Professionals in Humanitarian Assistance (PHAP https://phap.org/), and the Centre of Competence for Humanitarian Negotiation (CCHN https://frontline-negotiations.org/).

41. For example, the case studies on Lebanon and Somalia in the British Red Cross project, Principles in Action, available at https://www.redcross.org.uk/about-us/what-we-stand-for. Also the studies by the Harvard Humanitarian Initiative https://hhi.har vard.edu/ referred to later in this book. Volunteers working with the Emergency Medical Services of the Syrian Red Crescent were afforded popular protection from affected communities in the face of hostile approaches from authorities and armed groups during humanitarian response to the conflict in Syria (author's personal notes and diaries).

42. Arnold van Gennep, *The Rites of Passage* (Chicago: University of Chicago Press, 1960), originally published in French 1909. Victor Turner's essay, 'Betwixt and Between: The Liminal Period in Rites de Passage', in *The Forest of Symbols* (Ithaca NY: Cornell University Press, 1967).

3. EVOLVING EXPRESSIONS OF HUMANITARIAN SPACE

1. Henry Radice, *The Politics of Humanity: Humanitarianism and International Political Theory* Ph.D. thesis, London School of Economics (2010). Quoted with the kind permission of the author.

2. Radice, *The Politics of Humanity*, 40

3. Radice, *The Politics of Humanity*, 10.

4. International Review of the Red Cross (The Review), 'Applying the Fundamental Principles of the Red Cross and Red Crescent: a subject for continued thought'. *International Review of the Red Cross,* Volume 29, no. 273 (1989): 503.

5. John Borton, *Future of the Humanitarian System: Impacts of Internal Changes* (Feinstein International Center, Tufts University, 2009), 4; Bennett, *Time to Let Go*: 5; Claude Bruderlein, ed. *Field Manual on Frontline Humanitarian Negotiation* (Geneva: Centre of Competence on Humanitarian Negotiation 2018), 341.

6. See Michael Duffield, *Development, Security and Unending War: Governing the World of People*. (Cambridge: Polity Press, 2007); Barnett, *Empire of Humanity*.

7. Bennett, *Time to Let Go*; Paul Currion, 'Network humanitarianism', Working Paper: Constructive Deconstruction: Imagining Alternative Humanitarian Action. Humanitarian Policy Group/ODI (2018).

8. Bertrand Taithe, 'Humanitarian History?' in *The Routledge Companion to Humanitarian Action*, 62.

9. Austen Davis, 'Accountability and Humanitarian Actors: Speculations and Questions', *Humanitarian Exchange Issue 24* (2003).

10. Borton, *Future of the Humanitarian System*; Bennett, *Time to Let Go*.

11. ALNAP, *The State of the Humanitarian System* (London: ODI, 2018), 32.

12. Randolph Kent and Sophie Evans, 'Humanitarian Futures' in *The Routledge Companion to Humanitarian Action*, 387–402; Hugo Slim, 'Doing the right thing: Relief agencies, moral dilemmas and moral responsibility in political emergencies and war', *Disasters,* Volume 21, no. 3 (1997): 245.

13. Alan Stewart, 'Humanity at a Price: Erasmus, Bude, and the Poverty of Philology', in *At the Borders of the Human: Beasts, Bodies and Natural Philosophy in the Early Modern Period*, edited by Erika Fudge, Ruth Gilbert and Susan Wiseman (Basingstoke: Macmillan, 1999), 9–25.

14. Iain Wilkinson, 'The problem of understanding modern humanitarianism and its sociological value', *International Social Science Journal*, Volume 65 (2016): 65–78.

15. The word 'ubuntu' derived from a Nguni (isiZulu) aphorism: *Umuntu Ngumuntu Ngabantu*, which can be translated as 'a person is a person because of or through others' (James Khomba and Ella Kangaude-Ulaya, 'Indigenisation of corporate strategies in Africa: Lessons from the African Ubuntu philosophy', *China-USA Business Review,* Volume 12, no. 7/121 (2013): 673). See also Geraldine Fraser-Moleketi, 'Towards a common understanding of corruption in Africa', *Public Policy and Administration*, Volume 24/3 (2009), 331–338.

16. Khomba and Kangaude-Ulaya, *Indigenisation of Corporate Strategies in Africa*, 673.

17. Clifford Orwin, *The Humanity of Thucydides* (Princeton: Princeton University Press, 1997), 9.

18. Samuel Moyn, *The Last Utopia: Human Rights in History* (Cambridge: Belknap Press, 2010), 15.

19. Bertrand Taithe, '"Cold calculation in the faces of horrors?" Pity, Compassion and the making of humanitarian protocols', in *Medicine, Emotion and Disease, 1700–1950*, ed. Fay Alberti (London: Palgrave Macmillan, 2006), 93.

20. Taithe, 'Cold calculation', 93.

21. Wilkinson, *The problem of understanding modern humanitarianism*; Fuyuki Kurasawa, 'The sentimentalist paradox: on the normative and visual foundations of humanitarianism', *Journal of Global Ethics,* Volume 9/2 (2013): 201–214.

22. Taithe, 'Cold calculation', 87.

23. Eleanor Davey, John Borton and Matthew Foley, 'A history of the humanitarian system: Western origins and foundations,' Humanitarian Policy Group Working Paper (London: ODI, 2013).

24. Davey, Borton and Foley, 'A history of the humanitarian system', 5. According to some scholars, zakat does not really qualify as being the equivalent of humanitarian aid in modern terms, since 'it is obligatory and payable only to Muslim beneficiaries who are specified in the Qur'an' (Masood Hayder, referring to the Qur'an, Sura 9, verse 60). Hayder goes on to say that 'Sadaqa, especially one particular kind designated as sadaqat al-tatawwu' (alms of spontaneity) is voluntary and can be given to Muslim and non-Muslim alike without further specification of their status or need. This type of sadaqa is therefore more akin to humanitarian aid in modern terms' (Masood Hayder, 'Humanitarianism and the Muslim World'. *The Journal of Humanitarian Assistance*. Feinstein International Center, Tufts University (2007). https://sites. tufts.edu/jha/archives/52). See also Jasmine Moussa, 2014; and Jonathan Benthall, 'Charity' in Cambridge Encyclopedia of Anthropology (2017) www.anthroencyclo pedia.com/entry/charity

25. Moyn, *The Last Utopia*, 220.

26. Moyn, *The Last Utopia*.

27. Moyn, *The Last Utopia*, 225.

28. Michael Barnett and Thomas Weiss, *Humanitarianism Contested. Where Angels Fear to Tread* (London: Routledge, 2011).

29. Currion, 'Network humanitarianism'.

30. Charles Taylor, *Sources of the Self: The Making of the Modern Identity* (Cambridge: Cambridge University Press, 1989). Wilkinson, *The problem of understanding modern humanitarianism*.

31. Taylor, *Sources of the Self*, 191.

32. Taylor, *Sources of the Self*, 191.

33. Taylor, *Sources of the Self*, 28. Taylor and others (e.g. Hannah Arendt, Alasdair MacIntyre and Martha Nussbaum) identify a common axis around understandings of a 'full' life that centre around 'dignity' and 'respect' as articulations of the common good.

34. Barnett, *Empire of Humanity*.

35. The practice extended beyond the established identities/territories of the European colonial/imperial powers of the time. For example, American Protestant missionary humanitarianism had been active in the Near East since the early 1820s. For a comprehensive account, see Davide Rodogno, 'Beyond relief: A sketch of the Near East Relief's humanitarian operations, 1918–1929'. *Monde(s), no. 6 (2014): 45–64.

36. Alasdair Gordon-Gibson, *Humanitarian Space – The quest for a protected niche in the global arena*. (MPhil thesis, University of St Andrews, 2015).

37. Hilhorst, 'Classical humanitarianism and resilience humanitarianism', 4.

38. Dualta Roughneen, *Humanitarian Subsidiarity: A New Principle?* (Cambridge: Cambridge Scholars Publishing, 2017).

39. Taylor, *Sources of the Self*.

40. Paul Harvey, 'International humanitarian actors and governments in areas of conflict: Challenges, obligations, and opportunities', *Disasters, 37 (Supplement 2)* (2013): S167.

41. The state's primary responsibility in responding to disasters is clearly recognised in law and in statements of principle. For example, UN General Assembly

Resolution 46/182, article 4 (19th December 1991) stipulates: 'Each State has the responsibility first and foremost to take care of the victims of natural disasters and other emergencies occurring on its territory. Hence, the affected State has the primary role in the initiation, organization, coordination, and implementation of humanitarian assistance within its territory'. http://www.un.org/documents/ga/res/46/a46r182.htm

42. Barnett, *Empire of Humanity*, 21.

43. David Rieff, *A Bed for the Night: Humanitarianism in Crisis* (London: Random House, 2002); Kurt Mills, 'Neo-humanitarianism: The role of international humanitarian norms and organizations in contemporary conflict', *Global Governance,* Volume 11, no. 2 (2005): 161–183; Mills, *International Responses*.

44. Taylor, *Sources of the Self*, 28.

45. Wilkinson, *The problem of understanding modern humanitarianism,* 73. See also Michael Barnett, *The International Humanitarian Order* (London: Routledge, 2010).

46. For example, Duffield, *Global Governance and the New Wars; Development, Security and Unending War*; Barnett, *The International Humanitarian Order*; Barnett and Weiss, *Humanitarianism Contested*; Roger Mac Ginty, *International Peacebuilding and Local Resistance: Hybrid Forms of Peace* (London: Palgrave, 2011).

47. https://www.agendaforhumanity.org/summit

48. Wilkinson, *The problem of understanding modern humanitarianism.* While recognising the critiques of modern humanitarianism, Wilkinson takes the view that these are insufficient for the task of opening up modern humanitarianism to sociological insight: 'there is a danger here that in setting humanitarianism purely as a matter for critique, we fail to recognise the extent to which, nevertheless, it remains a vital element in our attempts at human understanding and in the critical thinking that seeks to advance this as a common cause' (ibid, 73).

49. Ben Jones and Marie-Juul Petersen, 'Instrumental, narrow, normative? Reviewing recent work on religion and development', *Third World Quarterly,* Volume 32, no. 7 (2011): 1292–1306.

50. See Rieff, *A Bed for the Night*; Stephen Hopgood, *The Endtimes of Human Rights* (Ithaca: Cornell University Press, 2013). Also, Kurt ver Beek, 'Spirituality: A development taboo', *Development in Practice,* 10/1 (2000).

51. Jones and Petersen, 'Instrumental, Narrow, Normative?'.

52. These are analysed more fully in my examination of Social Identity Theory, in Chapter 4.

53. Anthony Redmond considers that the levels of control and accountability are what most distinguishes understandings of the differences between the amateur and professional: Anthony Redmond, 'Professionalisation of the Humanitarian Response', in *The Routledge Companion to Humanitarian Action,* 403–416.

54. Peter Walker and Larry Minear, 'One for all and all for one: Support and assistance models for an effective IFRC', *A Report for the International Federation of Red Cross and Red Crescent Societies (Executive Summary & Conclusions)* (Feinstein International Center, Tufts University, 2004), 6.

55. Peter Rogers, 'Family is NOT an institution: Distinguishing institutions from organisations in social science and social theory', *International Review of Sociology,* Volume 27, no. 1 (2017): 129.

56. Rogers, 'Family is NOT an institution', 129.

57. Others include churches, schools, colleges, reformatories and asylums, as well as guilds, banks, trade unions and corporations (Rogers, 'Family is NOT an institution', 129).

58. Rogers, 'Family is NOT an institution'.

59. Ernest Burgess and Harvey Locke. *The Family: From Institution to Companionship* (Oxford: American Book Co, 1945), quoted in Rogers, 'Family is NOT an institution', 129.

60. https://media.ifrc.org/ifrc/who-we-are/national-societies/national-societies-directory/ In the book I use upper case 'National Societies' when referring to the member societies of the International Red Cross and Red Crescent Movement, unless lower case is used in textual extracts (such as in the Case Studies, Chapter 7) or quotations.

61. International Federation of Red Cross and Red Crescent Societies (IFRC), 2007. Constitution (Original 1987, revised and adopted by 16th session of the General Assembly, Geneva, November 2007). https://www.ifrc.org/Global/Governance/ Statutory/Constitution_revised-en.pdf

62. Rogers, 'Family is NOT an institution', 132.

63. For example, Médecins Sans Frontières (MSF) comprises twenty-four sections with five operations centres (OCs) worldwide (Belgium, France, Holland, Spain and Switzerland). 'The OCs can act independently but all layers of MSF interconnect and are formally bound as one movement by a shared name, a shared commitment to the MSF Charter and principles, and shared membership of MSF International' https:// www.msf.org.uk/msf-movement. Save the Children and Oxfam are amongst several other large NGOs with an international structure and associations for membership. For a study on intra-organisational dynamics in humanitarian action, see Webster and Walker, 'One for All and All for One'.

64. The definition of volunteerism used in the UN report refers to 'activities . . . undertaken of free will, for the general public good and where monetary reward is not the principal motivating factor' (United Nations Volunteers, State of the World's Volunteerism Report. *Transforming Governance*. United Nations Development Programme [2015]: xiv https://www.unv.org/swvr/2015-state-worlds-volunteerism-report-swvr-transforming-governance).

65. United Nations Volunteers, *Transforming Governance*: xv.

66. The ICRC emphasises that its work should not devolve the legitimate authorities in a country from their responsibility towards its own populations. The legal personality of the RCRC National Societies as *auxiliaries* to the state in disaster response gives emphasis to this position.

67. Tilman Schwarze, *Space, Violence and Resistance: A Lefebvrian Analysis of Everyday Life on Chicago's South Side.* (PhD Thesis, University of St Andrews, 2020).

68. Rebecca Gill, *The Rational Administration of Compassion: The Origins of British Relief in War. Le Mouvement Social*, Volume 227, no. 2 (2009): 25.

69. United Nations Volunteers, *Transforming Governance*: xiv.

70. UN General Assembly Resolution 46/182, article 4, 1991 https://undocs.org/ A/RES/46/182

71. Karolina Kluczewska, 'How to translate "Good Governance" into Tajik? An American Good Governance Fund and norm localisation in Tajikistan', *Journal of Intervention and Statebuilding* (2019): 1–20.

72. Kluczewska, 'How to Translate "Good Governance" into Tajik', 4.

73. Kluczewska, 'How to Translate "Good Governance" into Tajik', 8; 10.

74. United Nations Volunteers, *Transforming Governance*, xxii.

75. See Colin Rochester, Angela Paine and Steven Howlett, eds., *Volunteering & Society in the 21st Century* (Basingstoke: Palgrave Macmillan, 2010); United Nations Volunteers, *Transforming Governance*; Hazeldine and Baillie Smith, *IFRC Global Review of Volunteering*.

76. Hazeldine and Baillie Smith, *IFRC Global Review of Volunteering*. UNV, *Transforming Governance*. United Nations Volunteers (UNV). *The Thread That Binds: Volunteerism and Community Resilience*. United Nations Volunteers, State of the World's Volunteerism Report (2018).

77. See, for example, https://www.ifrc.org/en/what-we-do/volunteers/volunteering-policy/

78. United Nations Volunteers, *Transforming Governance*.

79. United Nations Volunteers, *Transforming Governance*, xxv.

80. Abu Sa'da and Crombé, *Volunteers and Responsibility*.

81. Abu Sa'da and Crombé, *Volunteers and Responsibility*, 134.

82. Abu Sa'da and Crombé, *Volunteers and Responsibility*, 135.

83. Abu Sa'da and Crombé, *Volunteers and Responsibility*, 136.

84. Personal discussions, Geneva, May 2018.

85. Georg Hegel, 'Die Vernunft in der Geschichte', in *Collected Essays*, ed. Johannes Hoffmeister (1955), cited in Charles Taylor, *Hegel* (Cambridge: Cambridge University Press, 1975), 380.

86. Taylor, *Hegel*, 384.

87. Taylor, *Hegel*, 386.

88. Taylor, *Hegel*, 388.

89. Jean-Jacques Rousseau, *The Social Contract*, Translated by Maurice Cranston (2nd edition), (London: Penguin [1762] 2004). Further discussions on Rousseau's formulation of the social contract are presented in chapter 8.

90. Michael Sandel, ed., *Liberalism and Its Critics* (Oxford: Blackwell, 1984).

91. For example, a notable aspect of the *karma* theory in Buddhism is merit transfer. A person accumulates merit not only through intentions and ethical living but is also able to gain merit from others by exchanging goods and services, such as through dana (charity to the Buddhist community) and acts of voluntary service. Almsgiving (*zakat*) is one of the five pillars of Islam and is predominantly a voluntary decision, given to private or religious collectors, rather than state-sponsored structures. Notions of voluntary service feature prominently in the sacred texts of the Qur'an and the Hadith. Charity and voluntary service, or *utsarga*, is prominent in the Hindu tradition (see Jasmine Moussa, *Ancient Origins, Modern Actors: Defining Arabic Meanings of Humanitarianism*, (Geneva, Humanitarian Policy Group/ODI, 2014); Masitoh Ahmad et al., 'The role of religion in higher education funding: Special reference to Hinduism and Buddhism in Malaysia'. *GJAT*, Volume 6, no. 1/69 (2016) http://www.gjat.my/gjat062016/10420160601.pdf).

92. In his book *The Dark Sides of Virtue*, David Kennedy urges the dominant paradigm of the Global North to abandon the complacency and indifference emerging from institutional certainty of the 'enchanted tools' belonging to the modern humanitarian world (David Kennedy, *The Dark Sides of Virtue: Reassessing International Humanitarianism* (Princeton University Press Kennedy, 2004), xviii; 21–35 and 352.

93. Taylor, *Hegel,* 416.

94. For example, see Donini et al., *Humanitarian Agenda 2015*; Barnett, *Empire of Humanity*; Donini, *The Golden Fleece.*

4. THE SOCIAL IDENTITY OF THE NICHE

1. Charles Taylor, 'Interpretation and the sciences of man', *The Review of Metaphysics,* Volume 25, no. 1 (1971), 30.

2. Tom Tyler and Peter Degoey, 'Trust in organizational authorities. The influence of motive attributions on willingness to accept decisions', in *Trust in Organizations: Frontiers and Theory of Research,* eds. Roderick Kramer and Tom Tyler (London: SAGE, 1996), 336.

3. Tyler and Degoey, *Trust in Organizational Authorities*, 333–336.

4. It is important to note that there is a wide body of scholarship which counters assumptions that behavioural traits identified in studies of western, educated, industrialised, rich and democratic (WEIRD) societies are representative of human populations across the world. Analyses of comparative databases in the behavioural sciences indicate that WEIRD subjects are frequent outliers and are not representative of the species (Joseph Henrich, Steven Heine and Ara Norenzayan, 'The weirdest people in the world?', *Behavioral and Brain Sciences,* 33 (2010).

5. Tyler and Degoey, *Trust in Organizational Authorities*, 334–335.

6. Tuomela, *Social Ontology.*

7. Louise Amoore and Alexandra Hall, 'The clown at the gates of the camp: Sovereignty, resistance and the figure of the fool', *Security Dialogue,* Volume 44/2 (2013): 93–110; Giorgio Agamben, *Homo Sacer: Sovereign Power and Bare Life* (Stanford: Stanford University Press, 1998).

8. Amoore and Hall, 'The clown at the gates of the camp', 93.

9. Arguments comparing this with the liminal spaces in anthropology are presented in chapter 9.

10. Amoore and Hall, 'The clown at the gates of the camp', 96.

11. Raimo Tuomela. *Social Ontology: Collective Intentionality and Group Agents* (Oxford: Oxford University Press, 2013). The Oxford English Dictionary (John Simpson and Edmund Weiner, eds. 1989) defines cooperation as 'The action of cooperating i.e. of working together towards the same end, purpose or effect'.

12. See Tuomela's analysis of the team-game results in *Social Ontology*, 179–213.

13. Tuomela. *Social Ontology*, 147–148.

14. Tyler and Degoey, *Trust in Organizational Authorities*, 340.

15. Tyler and Degoey, *Trust in Organizational Authorities*; Theodore Schatzki, Karin Knorr Cetina and Eike von Savigny, eds., *The Practice Turn in Contemporary Theory* (London: Routledge, 2001); Tuomela, *Social Ontology.*

16. See Tyler and Degoey, *Trust in Organizational Authorities*; Matthew Stevens, 'The collapse of social networks among Syrian refugees in urban Jordan', *Contemporary Levant,* Volume 1, no. 1 (2016): 51–63.

17. Roderick Kramer and Tom Tyler, eds., *Trust in Organizations: Frontiers and Theory of Research* (London: SAGE, 1996).

18. Noel Calhoun, 'With a little help from our friends: a participatory assessment of social capital among refugees in Jordan', *New issues in refugee research. UNHCR research paper* no. 189 (2010) https://www.unhcr.org/research/working/4ca0a0109/little-help-friends-participatory-assessment-social-capital-among-refugees.html; Stevens, 'The collapse of social networks among Syrian refugees in urban Jordan'.

19. Stevens, 'The collapse of social networks among Syrian refugees in urban Jordan'.

20. Maček, *Sarajevo under Siege.*

21. Walter Powell and Paul DiMaggio, *The New Institutionalism in Organisational Analysis* (Chicago: University of Chicago Press, 1991)

22. Tyler and Degoey, *Trust in Organizational Authorities,* 348.

23. Enid Welsford, *The Fool: His Social and Literary History* (London: Faber and Faber, 1935). Modern analogies might be linked to the political lampooning through perceived foolishness in series like the Simpsons in the United States. Chapter 7 makes reference to satirical characters who featured in the narratives during the conflict in the former Yugoslavia.

24. Ted Honderich, ed., *Oxford Companion of Philosophy* (Oxford: Oxford University Press, 1995), 31.

25. Honderich, *Oxford Companion of Philosophy,* 30. Tuomela presents a similar argument for a non-hierarchical leadership within a 'we-mode' group to avoid disharmony within a pro-group 'I-mode', comparing it to the conductor of an orchestra who directs but does not dictate the phrasing and tempo of the music, where musical harmony can be directed from dissonant phrasing (*Social Ontology*: 161).

26. The centrality of the individual in communitarian theory is in opposition to traditional Marxist 'determinism' and state socialism, when power is highly centralised, and so represents a decentralisation of action, but distinct from anarchy and liberal 'free will'. According to Sandel (*Liberalism and Its Critics*), this is a 'prescriptive' argument in the sense that life will be better if collective, community and public values guide us. My study prefers a 'descriptive' argument that emphasises a need for cooperation, expressed as 'voluntary service' working inside an autonomous niche but also as 'interdependent' holistic structures.

27. The Oxford Companion to Philosophy states that 'value communitarianism' refers to two things, first, the commitment to collective values, such as trust, reciprocity and solidarity. 'These cannot be enjoyed by individuals as such – each person's enjoyment depends on others' enjoyment. In other words, they depend on a threshold of "intersubjectivity". Second, the commitment to public goods – facilities and practices designed to help members of the community develop their common and hence their public lives' (Honderich, *Oxford Companion to Philosophy,* 143).

28. John Turner, 'Towards a cognitive redefinition of the social group', in *Social Identity and Intergroup Relations*, ed. Henri Tajfel (Cambridge: Cambridge University Press, 1982): 29.

29. Turner, 'Towards a cognitive redefinition of the social group', 31.

30. Turner, 'Towards a cognitive redefinition of the social group', 31.

31. Rupert Brown, *Group Processes: Dynamics within and between Groups,* 2nd edition (London: Blackwell, 2000), 28.

32. O'Farrell, *Foucault: Historian or Philosopher?,* 37.

33. O'Farrell, *Foucault: Historian or Philosopher?*, 39.

34. United Nations Development Programme and United Nations Population Fund (UNDP/UNFPA), United Nations Volunteers: Report of the Administrator (2002) http://web.undp.org/execbrd/pdf/dp02-18e.pdf

35. Taylor, *Interpretation and the Sciences of Man,* 30.

36. Later expressions in the Enlightenment theories emerging from the debates on natural law and international relations of the seventeen century (Hobbes; Grotius; Locke) and eighteenth century (Rousseau; Kant; Bentham), which form much of the modern Western traditions of philosophical thought, refer in some form to the construction of a 'social contract' which view that a person's moral and political obligations are dependent upon a contract or agreement among them to form the society in which they live.

37. Taylor, *Hegel.*

38. Rubenstein, *Between Samaritans and States.*

39. Henry Radice, 'Saving ourselves? On rescue and humanitarian action', in *Review of International Studies,* Volume 45, no. 3 (2019): 433.

40. Calhoun, 'The class consciousness of frequent travelers', 880.

41. Taylor, *Hegel,* 386 (italics added).

42. For more than 150 years, the ICRC and Red Cross and Red Crescent societies have pioneered volunteering and organised volunteers for humanitarian assistance, to alleviate suffering and poverty. Worldwide, the Red Cross and Red Crescent Movement is able to mobilise more than seventeen million volunteers (Hazeldine and Baillie Smith, *IFRC Global Review of Volunteering*) with around twelve million regularly active https://media.ifrc.org/ifrc/what-we-do/volunteers/

43. United Nations Volunteers (UNV), *Transforming Governance*: xiv.

44. Complementarity of roles is seen as important in the RCRC Movement. '[The] ICRC's modus operandi is not the right way for everyone. "Neutral, impartial and independent" is not the solution to every problem or situation, but it is useful in specific contexts. It shows the need to implement distinct, complementary and separate activities and roles. [The] ICRC will strive to maintain its principled stand. This does not preclude others from engaging in peace-building and human rights. Yet, distinction is needed and we should not confuse these different approaches' (Labbé and Daudin, *Applying the Humanitarian Principles,* 209–10, quoting from a speech given by ICRC President, Peter Maurer, December 2012).

45. Nussbaum, *Frontiers of Justice,* 82.

46. Calhoun, 'The class consciousness of frequent travelers', 16. See also the study on Civil Service Organisations, Jessica Braithwaite and Amanda Licht, 'The Effect of Civil Society Organizations and Democratization Aid on Civil War Onset', *Journal of Conflict Resolution,* Volume 64, no. (6) (2020). https://doi.org/10.1177/0022002719888684

47. Dekker and Halman, *The values of volunteering,* 10. An example of this from personal experience has been broader social inclusion of the Syrian Red Crescent and UN volunteer membership since the start of the conflict in Syria, in 2011. This stems in part from demographic reasons (displacement of the urban elite who formed the traditional base of recruitment) but also from a wider recognition of its humanitarian identity (author's diaries and field notes, 2016).

48. Vivien Burr, *Social Constructionism* (3rd Edition) (London: Routledge, 2015), 163.

49. Nussbaum, *Frontiers of Justice*, 43–44.

50. Nussbaum, *Frontiers of Justice*, 44.

51. Nussbaum, *Frontiers of Justice*, 37.

52. Supporting Nussbaum's rejection of what she calls 'the fiction of a contract for mutual advantage in the state of nature' that leaves aside the essential natural rights, benevolence and human dignity (*Frontiers of Justice,* 45).

53. Nussbaum, *Frontiers of Justice*, 92.

54. Nussbaum advocates for a Capability Approach to include entitlements for animals and other living species. See also Martha Nussbaum, 'Human capabilities and animal lives: Conflict, wonder, law: A Symposium', *Journal of Human Development and Capabilities,* 18 No. 3 (2017): 317–321.

55. Nussbaum, *Frontiers of Justice*, 93.

56. Charles Taylor, 'Modern social imaginaries', *Public Culture*, Volume 14, no. 1 (2002): 91–124.

57. Nussbaum, *Frontiers of Justice*, 160.

58. Gérard Prunier, *Africa's World War: Congo, the Rwandan Genocide, and the Making of a Continental Catastrophe* (Oxford: Oxford University Press, 2009); Mills, *International Responses to Mass Atrocities.*

59. Nussbaum, *Frontiers of Justice*, 293.

60. *Between Samaritans and States.*

61. Jennifer Wolch, *The Shadow State: Government and Voluntary sector in Transition* (New York: The Foundation Center, 1990): 210

62. Rubenstein provides, as an example, the decision by MSF France to stop its humanitarian assistance programme in Goma, 1994, when it considered that a decision to remain and assist in the relief programme to refugees in the camps would be too much of a compromise of its principles for humanitarian action. MSF's autonomy and proven record on the field ('intent and efficiency') meant trust in its judgement, and public opinion remained positive (see Rubenstein, *Between Samaritans and States*, 109–114).

63. Rubenstein, *Between Samaritans and States*. For an example of the negative effects from this sort of competition for space, see Alasdair Gordon-Gibson, 'Goma 1994: Notes from the field'. *Genocide Studies International,* Volume 10, no. 2 (2016): 254–267.

64. 'Just as a conventional government cannot walk away from its citizens, insofar as NGOs function as governments, they cannot walk away from its citizens' (Rubenstein, *Between Samaritans and States,*105).

65. Jeffrey Murer, 'Political violence: Benjamin, Bourdieu, and the law', in *Oxford Handbook of U.S. National Security,* eds. Derek Reveron, Nikolas Gvosdev and John Cloud (New York: Oxford University Press, 2018), 495–508.

66. Carl Schmitt, *The Concept of the Political* (Chicago: University of Chicago Press, 2007), in Murer, 2018: 493.

67. Murer, 'Political violence', 494.

68. Murer, 'Political violence'.

69. Murer, 'Political violence'.

70. Murer, ''Political violence'. 500.

5. RISKS AND OPPORTUNITIES

1. David Kennedy, *The Dark Sides of Virtue: Reassessing International Humanitarianism* (Princeton: Princeton University Press, 2004): xiv.

2. Kennedy, *The Dark Sides of Virtue*, ibid.

3. Kennedy, *The Dark Sides of Virtue*, xv.

4. Kennedy, *The Dark Sides of Virtue*, 236.

5. Kennedy, *The Dark Sides of Virtue*, 237.

6. Juha Käpylä and Denis Kennedy, 'Cruel to care? Investigating the governance of compassion in the humanitarian imaginary', *International Theory*, Volume 6, no. 2 (2014): 255–292.

7. Alex de Waal, *Famine Crimes: Politics and the Disaster Relief Industry in Africa* (Bloomington: Indiana University Press, 1997); Tony Vaux, *The Selfish Altruist* (London: Earthscan, 2001); Fiona Terry, *Condemned to Repeat? The Paradox of Humanitarian Action* (Ithaca: Cornell University Press, 2002).

8. Pierre Bourdieu, 'The social space and the Genesis of groups', *Theory and Society*, Volume 14, no. 6 (1985): 724.

9. Murer refers to the risks of symbolic violence which he sees 'is the expression of discursive and normative power that normalizes and perhaps even justifies structural and physical violence' (*Political Violence*, 496) and is tied to the concept of symbolic power. Hammond (2008) has expressed this in the form of performative violence, that she sees as a context-specific attack on humanitarianism to 'spoil' and 'discredit' its moral high ground. See Laura Hammond, 'The power of holding humanitarianism hostage and the myth of protective principles', in *Humanitarianism in Question*, 177.

10. Norbert Götz, 'Rationales of Humanitarianism: The Case of British Relief to Germany, 1805–1815', *Journal of Modern European History*, Volume 12, no. 2 (2014): 199.

11. See Caroline Moorehead, *Dunant's Dream: War, Switzerland and the History of the Red Cross* (London: Harper Collins, 1998); Sébastien Farré and Yan Schubert, 'L'illusion de l'objectif. Le délégué du CICR Maurice Rossel et les photographies de Theresienstadt'. *Le Mouvement Social*, Volume 2, no. 227 (2009): 65–83.

12. Farré and Schubert, *L'illusion de l'objectif*, 65. Original text in French: 'Relais entre donateur et victime, il tend à incarner l'esprit militant des nouvelles organisations caritatives en renonçant à se taire pour réveiller une conscience citoyenne et mondiale'.

13. See Naomi Klein on 'Disaster capitalism', *TIME* interview by Katie Rooney (2007), available at http://content.time.com/time/arts/article/0,8599,1666221,00.html See also, Antonio Donini, 'The far side: The meta functions of humanitarianism in a globalised world', *Disasters*, 34, special edition 2 (2010): S220–S237.

14. See de Waal, *Famine Crimes*; Rieff, *A Bed for the Night*; Linda Polman, *War Games: The Story of Aid and War in Modern Times* (London: Penguin, 2011).

15. Donini, 'The far side'; Donini, *The Golden Fleece*; Currion, *Network Humanitarianism*.

16. ALNAP, *The State of the Humanitarian System*. London: ODI, 2018. https://sohs.alnap.org/system/files/content/resource/files/main/SOHS%202018%20full%20report%20online.pdf. The report notes that growing numbers of national humanitarian workers appeared to drive this increase, while the number of international staff remained stable.

17. The OECD Development Committee Report, 2018 provides a snapshot of the multiple donor interests https://www.oecd.org/dac/DCR2018-Leave-No-one-Behind. PDF

18. Such as the 1999 International Convention for the Suppression of the Financing of Terrorism, or UN Security Council Resolution 1373, approved in September 2001 (see Emanuela-Chiara Gillard, *Recommendations for Reducing Tensions in the Interplay Between Sanctions, Counterterrorism Measures and Humanitarian Action* (London: Chatham House, 2017).

19. Gillard, *Recommendations for Reducing Tensions.*

20. Gillard, *Recommendations for Reducing Tensions.*

21. Such as the UK 'designated areas offence' which gives the government powers to designate all or part of a country illegal for UK nationals and residents to enter or remain in that area https://www.bond.org.uk/news/2019/01/counter-terrorism-bill-aid-workers-to-be-exempt-from-damaging-law

22. Costas Douzinas, 'The many faces of humanitarianism', *Parrhesia, No. 2* (2007): 3.

23. Douzinas, 'The many faces of humanitarianism', 3–4.

24. Douzinas, 'The many faces of humanitarianism', 3.

25. Douzinas, 'The many faces of humanitarianism', 16.

26. Götz, *Rationales of Humanitarianism.*

27. Mark Duffield, *Development, Security and Unending War: Governing the World of Peoples* (Cambridge: Polity Press, 2007).

28. Schiffrin, Tannen and Hamilton, *The Handbook of Discourse Analysis.*

29. Martha Nussbaum, *Love's Knowledge – Essays on Philosophy and Literature* (Oxford, UK: Oxford University Press, 1992).

30. Barnett and Snyder, 'The grand strategies of humanitarianism', in *Humanitarianism in Question*, 143–171.

31. Henry Dunant, *A Memory of Solferino* (Geneva: International Committee of the Red Cross, [1862] 1986).

32. ICRC Archive, ACICR B AG 012–014. Original text in French: 'Le CICR s'est toujours montré très jaloux de son indépendance vis-à-vis de la Confédération Helvétique. Celle-ci, de son côté, a toujours respecté cette indépendance'.

33. ICRC Archive, ACICR B AG 012–014, page 2.

34. John Twigg and Irina Mosel, 'Emergent groups and spontaneous volunteers in urban disaster response', *Environment & Urbanization,* Volume 29, no. 2 (2017): 449. The authors define emergent groups as 'individual citizens coming together to deal collectively with disasters, forming new and informal groups to do so' (*Emergent groups*, 445).

35. Twigg and Mosel, *Emergent groups* (italics inserted). The study is careful to note that whilst emergent activity is mostly altruistic in these environments, and in

the public interest, people can self-organise spontaneously for private interests, such as obtaining emergency items for their own use or protecting private property. The study provides reports of organised looting following an earthquake in Chile, in 2010 (*Emergent groups*, 453).

36. Graham Hancock, *The Lords of Poverty: The Power, Prestige, and Corruption of the International Aid Business* (Atlantic Monthly Press, 1989); Linda Polman, *War Games: The Story of Aid and War in Modern Times* (London: Penguin, 2011).

37. For example, following the Indian Ocean tsunamis, 2004 http://www.island. lk/2006/02/12/features10.html and the earthquake in Haiti, 2010 https://www.pri.org/ stories/2012-01-11/haiti-two-years-after-earthquake-where-did-money-go

38. Radice, *The Politics of Humanity*; Kurt Mills, 'The postmodern tank of the humanitarian international', *Journal of Social Justice*, 18 (2013): 261–267; Hugo Slim, 'Wonderful work: Globalising the ethics of humanitarian action', 13–25.

39. Rebecca Gill, *The Rational Administration of Compassion: The Origins of British Relief in War. Le Mouvement Social*, Volume 227, no. 2 (2009): 9–26; Polman, *War Games*; Daniel McCall and Ana Iltis, 'Health care voluntourism: Addressing ethical concerns of undergraduate student participation in global health volunteer work', *HEC Forum*, Volume 26 (2014): 285–297.

40. Gill, *The Rational Administration of Compassion*, 17.

41. ACICR B AG 013–001, document D199.

42. ACICR B AG 013–002.

43. Larissa Fast, 'Mind the gap: Documenting and explaining violence against aid workers'. *European Journal of International Relations*, Volume 16 (2010): 1–25.

44. See John Tsukayama, By any means necessary: *An interpretive phenomenological analysis study of post 9/11 American abusive violence in Iraq* (Ph.D. thesis, University of St Andrews, 2014).

45. Emmanuel Tronc, Rob Grace and Anaïde Nahikian, 'Humanitarian access obstruction in Somalia: Externally imposed and self-inflicted dimensions', *Humanitarian Action at the Frontlines: Field Analysis Series. Harvard Humanitarian Initiative* (2018).

46. Sorcha O'Callaghan and Leslie Leach, 'The relevance of the Fundamental Principles to operations: learning from Lebanon', *International Review of the Red Cross*, 95/890 (2013): 287–307; Labbé and Daudin, *Applying the Humanitarian Principles*; Karen Beekman, 'From Fundamental Principles to individual action: Making the principles come alive to promote a culture of non-violence and peace', *International Review of the Red Cross*, Volume 97, no. 897/898 (2016): 263–293; Ed Schenkenberg van Mierop, *Local Humanitarian Actors and the Principle of Impartiality* (Geneva: HERE, 2017). See *International Review of the Red Cross, 'Principles Guiding Humanitarian Action'*, Volume 97, no. (897/898) (2015) for a comprehensive collection of contemporary studies on the humanitarian principles.

47. United Nations OCHA defines impartiality as 'humanitarian action must be carried out on the basis of need alone, giving priority to the most urgent cases of distress and making no distinctions on the basis of nationality, race, gender, religious belief, class or political opinions' https://docs.unocha.org/sites/dms/Documents/ OOM_HumPrinciple_English.pdf

48. Ed Schenkenberg van Mierop, 'Local humanitarian actors and the principle of impartiality', in *Based on Need Alone? Impartiality in Humanitarian Action* MSF Germany; Caritas Germany; Diakonia (2018): 60–71. http://chaberlin.org/wp-content/uploads/2019/02/humhilfe-studie-unparteilichkeit_2018_Mierop_EN.pdf

49. Schenkenberg van Mierop, 'Local humanitarian actors', 4.

50. ACICR B AG 012–014.

51. Theodore Sarbin, 'The narrative as root metaphor for psychology' in Burr, *Social Constructionism*, 162.

52. Burr, *Social Constructionism*, 165

53. Referring to Mary Gergen, *Feminist Reconstructions in Psychology* (London: SAGE, 2001).

54. The ICRC Delegation in Baghdad was targeted for attack in 2003. There are incidents of violence and kidnapping of staff in Syria and Afghanistan and on other Red Cross/Crescent operations around the world (see Abby Stoddard, Adele Harmer and Monica Czwarno, *Aid Worker Security Report 2017. Behind the Attacks: A Look at the Perpetrators of Violence against Aid Workers*. Humanitarian Outcomes (2017).

55. W Richard Scott, *Institutions and Organizations* (2nd edition) (London: Foundations for Organizational Science/Sage, 2001).

56. Scott, *Institutions and Organizations*, 60–61.

57. Scott, *Institutions and Organizations*, 50.

58. Scott, *Institutions and Organizations*; Adler and Pouliot, *International Practices*; Burr, *Social Constructionism*.

59. Douzinas, 'The many faces of humanitarianism', 3.

60. Richard Little, 'Britain's Response to the Spanish Civil War: investigating the implications of foregrounding practice for English School thinking' in *International Practices*, eds. Adler and Pouliot (Cambridge: Cambridge University Press, 2011), 179.

61. Bourdieu, *The Social Space and the Genesis of Groups*.

62. See for example, Christina Bennett, 'Constructive deconstruction: Imagining alternative humanitarian action', Working Paper. Humanitarian Policy Group/ODI (2018).

63. Marie Juul Petersen, *For Humanity or for the Umma? Aid and Islam in Transnational Muslim NGO* (London: Hurst, 2015).

64. Dorothea Hilhorst, 'Being good at doing good? Quality and accountability of humanitarian NGOs', *Disasters,* Volume 26/3 (2002): 193–212.

65. Martha Finnemore, 'Rules of war and wars of rules: The International Red Cross and the restraint of state violence', in *Constructing World Culture: International Non-Governmental Organizations since 1875*, eds. John Boli and George Thomas (Stanford, CA: Stanford University Press, 1999): 149–165.

66. Slim, *Doing the Right Thing,* 244.

67. Tronc, Grace and Nahikian, *Humanitarian Access*, 2.

68. Esther van Leeuwen and Suzanne Täuber, 2010. The strategic side of outgroup helping. In *The Psychology of Prosocial Behavior*, 81.

69. Roderick Kramer, 'Trust and distrust in organizations: Emerging perspectives, enduring questions'. *Annual Review of Psychology*, Volume 50 (1999), 569–598.

70. Helmut Anheier and Jeremy Kendall, 'Interpersonal trust and voluntary associations: examining three approaches', *British Journal of Sociology,* Volume 53, no. 3 (2002): 352.

71. Anheier and Kendall, 'Interpersonal trust and voluntary associations', 355.

72. ACICR B AG 012–013, document G-332/61. Original text: 'en tout temps et partout dans le monde, la Croix-Rouge n'a qu'une seule et même signification: C'est de lutter contre la souffrance et la mort, et d'assurer la dignité de l'homme, sans distinction'. This formed the text of the Fundamental Principle of Humanity, proclaimed at the Vienna Conference in 1965 (see Chapter 2, note 13).

6. THE SPIRIT OF HUMANITY

1. Prominent amongst these are the *Red Cross and Red Crescent Code of Conduct* and the *Humanitarian Charter and Minimum Standards in Humanitarian Response (the* Sphere Guidelines). See chapter 2.

2. Donini, 'The far side'.

3. Duffield, *Global Governance and the New Wars*; Donini, 'The far side'.

4. See Peter Walker and Susan Purdin, 'Birthing sphere'. *Disasters*, 28/2 (2004): 100–111; Peter Walker, 'Cracking the code: The genesis, use and future of the Code of Conduct'. *Disasters,* 29/4 (2005): 323–336.

5. For details of the Fundamental Principles of the Movement and how these are referred to in the book, see 'Introduction', note 1 and chapter 2, note 13.

6. The League of Red Cross Societies, founded in 1919, and renamed in 1983 as the League of Red Cross and Red Crescent Societies, became the IFRC in 1991.

7. Pictet, *The Fundamental Principles,* 135.

8. The ICRC, founded on the initiative of a Swiss businessman, Henry Dunant, and other citizens in Geneva, originated from a sub-committee of the Geneva Society of Public Utility: 'The International Committee for the Relief of Wounded in Situations of War' (Forsythe, *The Humanitarians,* 17). David Forsythe's study provides a comprehensive account of the origins and function of the ICRC.

9. Gustave Moynier, 'Comité International: ce que c'est que le croix rouge'. *Bulletin International des Sociétés de la Croix -Rouge,* vol. 6, nbr 21 ([1875] 2009): 1–8; ICRC, *The Fundamental Principles of the Red Cross and Red Crescent*.

10. ICRC, *The Fundamental Principles of the Red Cross and Red Crescent*. For a comprehensive account of the evolution of the Movement structures and the role of the International Conferences, see François Bugnion, 'The International Conference of the Red Cross and Red Crescent: challenges, key issues and achievements', *International Review of the Red Cross*, Volume 91, no. 876 (2009): 675–712.

11. ICRC, *The Fundamental Principles of the Red Cross and Red Crescent*. Pictet lists the Fundamental Principles in his study as: Humanity, Equality, Due Proportion, Impartiality, Neutrality, Independence and Universality. The Organic Principles are: Selflessness, Free Service, Voluntary Service, Auxiliarity, Autonomy, Multitudinism, Equality of National Societies, Unity, Solidarity and Foresight. For a definition of each, see Jean Pictet, *The Principles of the Red Cross* (Geneva: ICRC, 1956), 14. Original publication in French, *Les Principes de la Croix Rouge* (1955).

12. Pictet, 1956. This became formalised in the 1965 proclamation as: 'Humanity. The Red Cross, born of a desire to bring assistance without discrimination to the wounded on the battlefield, endeavours to prevent and alleviate human suffering

wherever it may be found. Its purpose is to protect life and health and to ensure respect for the human being. It promotes mutual understanding, friendship, cooperation and lasting peace amongst all peoples'.

13. Pictet, *The Fundamental Principles*, 144; 155. In a study on the re-appraisal of the role of the Red Cross commissioned by the League of Red Cross Societies in 1971, the research design states that 'the first principle of Humanity can be considered as a normative goal' (ACICR B AG 012–010, page 2). It is, however, careful to note that 'even the standard set by a normative goal in a global organisation have different values at different places' (ibid).

14. The use of the term 'Red Cross' to designate the International Red Cross and Red Crescent Movement remained predominant on most official documentation until the renaming of the League of Red Cross Societies as the League of Red Cross and Red Crescent Societies in 1983 (see Bugnion, *The International Conference of the Red Cross and Red Crescent*).

15. ICRC, *The Fundamental Principles of the Red Cross and Red Crescent*, 17.

16. See, for example, Rachel Cohon, 'Hume's moral philosophy', in *The Stanford Encyclopedia of Philosophy*, ed. Edward Zalta (2018). https://plato.stanford.edu/entries/hume-moral/

17. Patrick Hayden, *Political Evil in a Global Age: Hannah Arendt and International Theory* (London: Routledge, 2009).

18. Immanuel Kant, 'Groundwork of the metaphysics of morals: A German-English edition', ed. Jens Timmermann, English trans. Mary Gregor (Cambridge University Press, [1786] 2011). E Book, available at: https://www-cambridge-org.ezproxy.st-andrews.ac.uk/core/books/immanuel-kant-groundwork-of-the-metaphysics-of-morals/B91AC5779FCA0698B074C81C0D09DA48

19. League of Red Cross Societies (LRCS), *Guide on Red Cross Volunteer Service* (Geneva: LRCS, 1952), 8. An observation repeated at a presentation on voluntary service to the United Nations (undated, page 8. In International Federation of Red Cross and Red Crescent Archives, folder 'services League 1935–1970').

20. The Standing Commission was established in 1928 as a means to direct the work of the Red Cross Movement and acts as Trustee for the Movement between International Conferences (Bugnion, 2009). It did not have jurisdictional or executive power.

21. ACICR B AG 012–010. Original text in French: 'Codifier, c'est limiter. Il existe un esprit Croix Rouge et à ce propos comme Carl Burkhardt observe: *Ubi Spiritus, ibi Libertas* et c'est ceci qui doit guider et inspirer le Croix Rouge'. Boissier's reference comes from the Latin version of the Second Letter of St Paul to the Corinthians, Chapter 3, Verse 17. See Émile Gebhart, 1887. *La Renaissance Italienne et la philosophie de l'histoire: la théorie de Jacob Burckhardt* (e-book, 2013, available at https://www.gutenberg.org/files/43196/43196-h/43196-h.htm (page 116).

22. ACICR B AG 011–012. Original text: 'La Croix Rouge, institution volontaire, animée de l'esprit de service, ne vise que l'intérêt humanitaire des personnes. Elle ne tire aucun profit de ses activités'.

23. Juan de Rueda, in Minutes of Working Group for the revision of the Red Cross Principles, 24 March 1959 (underlining in original). ACICR B AG 011–012,

document 7 JP/JMM, pages 1–2). Original text: 'Tout le monde parle des principes et personne au fond n'a formulée ce que c'est un principe. On le confond souvent avec des descriptions, des buts ou des règles. On ne se tient pas à l'idée créatrice de ce que c'est un principe. Il est certain que le principe se trouve sur le plan des idées pures et pour atteindre ce plan, il y a certainement diverses façons de procéder, mais dans tous les cas la force qui doit être manifestée pour atteindre ce plan, ne peut être que la bonne volonté, soit pour le travail, en dehors de la personnalité, soit pour la réflexion ou la méditation en dehors toujours des questions personnelles. En réalité on n'invente rien, on découvre ce qui existe et qui est applicable. En conséquence, il me semble qu'un Principe c'est la base et le point de départ d'une idée générale qui d'abord est perceptible par quelques-uns puis elle est admissible et pour finir elle devient évidente, d'abord pour l'élite et ensuite pour la plupart des gens qui se penchent sur un problème'.

24. ACICR B AG 011–012, document 7 JP/JMM. Original text: 'La Croix Rouge participe donc de quelques principes dont elle ne prétend pas d'avoir le monopole, mais son caractère particulier est comme si elle avait des tranches de ces principes'.

25. ACICR B AG 011–012.

26. ACICR B AG 012–010. 26 National Societies responded, out of which fourteen approved the text presented by the Working Group, and twelve submitted in-depth comments (ten of these are documented in written responses, though the submission from the Swedish Red Cross includes comments from the Norwegian and Danish Red Cross Societies).

27. Moynier, *Bulletin International des Sociétés de la Croix-Rouge,* 5. Original text: 'Les sociétés de peuples belligérants ne peuvent pas toujours, malgré leur désir, porter secours à ceux de leurs nationaux blessés ou malades qui sont capturés par l'ennemi, mais elles compensent ce désavantage en donnant leurs soins, avec un égal empressement, a tous les malheureux qui tombent entre leurs mains, sans distinction de nationalité. Il en résulte une véritable et touchante mutualité, un échange de services qui assure à tout blessé un traitement convenable, quelle que soit la société qui ait à s'occuper de lui'.

28. Pictet, *The Principles of the Red Cross*, 93.

29. ACICR B AG 012–010, document D 610, 25 August 1960. See note 26 of this chapter.

30. Whilst the replies from the American Red Cross and Canadian Red Cross do not include Voluntary Service in their condensed list of four Fundamental Principles, the notion of Voluntary Service as inherent in the principle of Humanity is implied.

31. ACICR B AG 012–010, document D 610, pages 2–3

32. The word 'Samaritans' is frequently used within discussions and narratives amongst the voluntary sector of the period to indicate persons acting out of good will and compassion. The Argentine Red Cross society uses the term in reference to its own volunteers (Minutes from the study group to discuss the peacetime activities of Red Cross volunteers, Paris 28 and 29 May 1935. In IFRC archives, Box 999534).

33. ACICR B AG 012–010, document D 610, page 7.

34. ACICR B AG 012–010, document D 610, page 12. Questions around recompense and recovery of costs arise frequently in the documents studied in the Red Cross archives and these continue to be issues of debate in the Movement (Hazeldine and Baillie Smith, *IFRC Global Review of Volunteering*. See also Yves Biegbeder, *The role and status of international humanitarian volunteers and organizations: the right and duty to humanitarian assistance*. Dordrecht: Nijhoff, 1991).

35. ACICR B AG 012–010, document D 610, page 12.

36. AICR B AG 012–010, document D 610, page 13.

37. ACICR B AG 012–010, document D 610, page 13.

38. ACICR B AG 012–010, document D 610, page 14.

39. Tensions related to the 'Free Gift' indicated by the Japanese Red Cross are features that occur frequently in studies within Social Anthropology, referred to in chapter 1. See Stirrat and Henkel, 1997. A letter from Japanese Red Cross/Inoue to ICRC Tokyo/R. J Wilhelm highlights its political flavour in Communist states and remarks that 'in the coming century the Free Service will be in great vogue' (15/08/1960, document G/410/60 in ACICR B AG 013–001).

40. ACICR B AG 012–010, document D 610, page 4.

41. Comparisons might be made to discussions around the amateur character of the Olympic Games which were current (and often controversial) at this period and which held symbolic importance during the period of the Cold War. See Seth Brown, 'De Coubertin's Olympism and the Laugh of Michel Foucault: Crisis Discourse and the Olympic Games', *Quest,* Volume 64, no. 3 (2012): 150–163; Dikaia Chatziefstathiou, *The changing nature of the ideology of Olympism in the modern Olympic era*, (PhD thesis, Loughborough University, 2005).

42. The Commission tasked to study the role of the ICRC noted the need for a complementary representation of the continuity from the professional ICRC Directorate and the 'amateur' perspectives of the Assembly in the *Conseil du Présidence* ACICR B AG 012–019, (document JP/JMM doctrine 8, 1967).

43. ACICR B AG 012–010, document D 610, page 21, underlining in original. Original text: 'Lorsque la volonté de servir existe, elle suppose l'esprit de service. Nous progressons donc d'un pas et diminuons la distance qui sépare une disposition de l'esprit de l'acte secourable'.

44. ACICR B AG 012–010, document D 610, page 16.

45. ACICR B AG 012–010, document D 610, page 16 (underlining in original).

46. Julia Pacitto and Elena Fiddian-Qasmiyeh, *Writing the 'Other' into humanitarian discourse Framing theory and practice in South-South humanitarian responses to forced displacement*. Oxford University Refugee Studies Centre, Working Paper series no. 93. (2013): 6.

47. See Kratochwil, *Praxis,* 18.

48. Kratochwil, *Praxis*. Kratochwil makes reference to studies on the communicative behaviour of bees and wolves.

49. Kratochwil, *Praxis*,11.

50. Kratochwil, *Praxis,* 24.

51. Karl von Frisch, *The Dance Language and Orientation of Bees*. (Cambridge MA: Harvard University Press, 1993).

52. Kratochwil, *Praxis*, 26, quoting John Searle, *The Construction of Social Reality* (London: Penguin, 1995).

53. The text proposed in 1959, under the heading 'Democratic and unique character', reads: 'In each state there can only be one Red Cross Society. This shall be directed by one central body, its membership open to all nationals of the country concerned and its activities extending to the whole territory. The Society must be constituted on a democratic basis'.

54. The Fundamental Principle of Unity proclaimed at the Vienna Conference reads: 'There can be only one Red Cross Society in any one country. It must be open to all. It must carry on its humanitarian work throughout its territory'.

55. In its submission, the Swedish Red Cross present these as: humanity, non-discrimination (impartiality), independence and neutrality. ACICR B AG 012–010, 8–9.

56. ACICR B AG 012–010, document D 610, 9.

57. Chexbres, 1971–1972. Referred in the documentation as 'Le Projet de Cannes' (The Cannes Project). ACICR B AG 012–068.02.

58. ACICR B AG 012–020, document MBB/EJ, page 2. Original text: 'Il n'y a que trois critères, à mon avis, qui soient vraiment importants: 1. 'Quel est l'intérêt des victimes' par opposition à l'intérêt publicitaire ou 'politique'? 2. Une fois une action lancée ou avant même de la lancer, il faut chaque fois se poser la question: 'N'y-at-il vraiment aucune autre instance qui puisse faire tout aussi bien, sinon mieux que le CICR?' 3. 'N'y-a-t-il vraiment aucun autre intermédiaire acceptable ou à même d'agir?'. The first criterion listed is a formulation of Pictet's 'Golden Rule': 'Whenever the Red Cross is faced with a dilemma, one must ask oneself where the interest of the victim lies' (Pictet, *The Principles of the Red Cross,* 91; 95; 97).

59. Original French 1954. English translation 1956.

60. ACICR B AG 012–020.06, document D946.

61. ACICR B AG 011–012, document JP/JMM no. 7, page 3. The Standing Commission comprised two participants from the ICRC (Frédéric Siordet and Jean Pictet) and two from the League (Henry Dunning and Wilfred Phillips) supported by a member of the Mexican Red Cross (Juan de Rueda), engaged as a special advisor for the Movement.

62. ACICR B AG 011–012, document JP/JMM no. 7, 2.

63. ACICR B AG 011–012, document JP/JMM no. 7, 4. Original text in French: 'Le but actuel de la Commission est de rédiger une déclaration aussi simple que possible, pouvant être adoptée par tout le monde, même si dans chaque pays on donne aux mots un sens légèrement différent'.

64. Masutaro Inoue, Japanese Red Cross, Essay Two, 'The Organic Principles of the Red Cross, in ACICR B AG 011–012), with ref to Pictet, *The Principles of the Red Cross*, 10 and 93.

65. with ref to Pictet, *The Principles of the Red Cross*, 98.

66. with ref to Pictet, *The Principles of the Red Cross*, 149.

67. Inoue, *The Organic Principles of the Red Cross*, 1–2 (underlining in original).

68. Masutaro Inoue, Japanese Red Cross, Essay One, page 3. In ACICR B AG 011–12.

69. with ref to Pictet, *The Principles of the Red Cross*, 98 and 107.

70. with ref to Pictet, *The Principles of the Red Cross*, 107.
71. with ref to Pictet, *The Principles of the Red Cross*, 130.
72. with ref to Pictet, *The Principles of the Red Cross*, 126.
73. Inoue, *The Organic Principles of the Red Cross*, 4 (underlining in original). The Japanese Red Cross/Inoue is careful to note: 'auxiliary means to help the State. It does not mean that the organisation should be subsidised by the State' (ibid, referring to Pictet, *The Principles of the Red Cross*, 127).
74. Pictet, *The Principles of the Red Cross*, 97.
75. Pictet, *The Principles of the Red Cross*, 41 and *passim*.
76. Pictet, *The Principles of the Red Cross*, 127; 153.
77. Pictet, *The Principles of the Red Cross*, 128.
78. ACICR B AG 013–001. Original text 'Elle serait stérile comme une fleur coupée de ses racines, elle peut être belle, mais elle fanera inexorablement'.
79. 'Veiller à l'unité entre doctrine et action; idéal et réalité'.
80. 'comme l'expression d'une aspiration implicite chez la plupart des peuples'.
81. Rodolfo Olgiati, report 11th October 1955, in ACICR B AG 013–002.
82. Donald Tansley, *Final Report: An Agenda for Red Cross – Re-appraisal of the Role of the Red Cross* (Geneva: ICRC, 1975).
83. Tansley, *Final Report,* 35, in *The Review*, 1989, 501.
84. *The ICRC, the League and the Tansley Report* (Geneva, 1977: 49), in *The Review,* 1989, 501.
85. Pictet, *The Principles of the Red Cross,* 107.
86. Michael Sandel, *Justice: What's the Right Thing to Do?* (London: Penguin, 2009): 107.
87. ACICR B AG 013–001, (underlining in original document). Original text: 'J'écarterai donc tout effort de rendre acceptable la Croix-Rouge par son utilité; cet aspect déploie encore suffisamment ses efforts dans l'application concrète des actions de Croix-Rouge, mais l'introduction de l'élément d'utilité dans la doctrine fondamentale de la Croix Rouge détruirait l'âme de celle-ci, car l'élément caractéristique de la Croix-Rouge est l'action désintéressée, pour le reste c'est une belle manifestation d'égoisme social et collectif, pour autant qu'il n'y a pas la collaboration bénévole, constituant un véritable sacrifice'.
88. Masutaro Inoue, Japanese Red Cross, Essay Three, in ACICR B AG 011–012.
89. Kratochwil, *Praxis.*
90. For example, the Projet de Cannes, see note 57 of this chapter.
91. ACICR B AG 012–020.
92. ACICR B AG 012–068.02, document CP/YC, 29.3.71
93. ACICR B AG 012–068.02, (underlining in original). Original text: 'Les Croix-Rouges nationales, qui sont des auxiliaires du gouvernement, sont devenues des éléments importants de la vie sociale, sur lesquels le gouvernement doit pouvoir compter. Il en va de même pour le CICR qui, nolens volens, est devenu un organe de la communauté internationale qui, lorsque certaines circonstances sont réunies, doit agir'.
94. ACICR B AG 012–019.
95. See Tessa Morris-Suzuki, 'Defining the boundaries of the Cold War nation: 1950s Japan and the other within', *Japanese Studies*, Volume 26, no. 3 (2006): 303–316.

96. Pictet, *The Principles of the Red Cross,* 93.

97. For example, the representative from the USSR called for clear statements about the pacifist character of the Movement during meetings of the Standing Commission reviewing the statutes in preparation for a meeting of the Council of Delegates in Prague, 1961. These followed tense debates over revisions of the statutes during the International Conferences at Toronto, 1952 and New Delhi, 1957. See François Bugnion, 'The International Conference of the Red Cross and Red Crescent: Challenges, key issues and achievements', *International Review of the Red Cross,* Volume 91, no. 876 (2009): 675–712.

98. International Conference, Toronto, Resolution 10 and Resolution 12, in ACICR B AG 151–010.

99. Minutes, Plenary Session 6–11–1957, Doc 512/5. ACICR B AG 151–021.02.

100. Pictet, *The Principles of the Red Cross,* 111.

7. CASE STUDIES

1. A complex emergency can be defined as a humanitarian crisis in a country, region or society where there is a total or considerable breakdown of authority resulting from internal or external conflict, and which requires an international response that goes beyond the mandate or capacity of any single agency or the ongoing UN country programme (UNHCR https://www.unhcr.org/uk/partners/partners/3ba88e7c6/coordination-complex-emergencies.html).

2. John Telford, John Cosgrave and Rachel Houghton, *Joint Evaluation of the International Response to the Indian Ocean Tsunami: Synthesis Report* (London: Tsunami Evaluation Commission, 2006).

3. Jan Egeland, in Michael Barnett and Thomas Weiss, *Humanitarianism Contested. Where Angels Fear to Tread* (London: Routledge 2011): xxi.

4. Gordon-Gibson, *Humanitarian Space,* 45.

5. Dorothea Hilhorst and Bram Jansen, 'Humanitarian space as arena: A perspective on the everyday politics of aid', *Development and Change,* Volume 41, no. 6 (2010): 1117–1139.

6. Formed originally as information for an email list in 1995 by members of the Sri Lankan Tamil community residing in the United States, it has been accused of having a Tamil nationalist and pro-LTTE bias. It was widely used as a source of information by foreign journalists, diplomats and others before being banned by the Sri Lankan government in 2009.

7. A search of key term shows a distinct reduction in commentaries on the tsunami after March 2005. All the articles reviewed are available online: http://www.thesundayleader.lk/archive/ http://www.island.lk/ and https://www.tamilnet.com/

8. Such as 'international community' (nine results); 'Tamil community' (two results); 'fishing community (six); 'community action' (four results).

9. Excluding references to 'Trust Funds' and proper names such as 'The Syria Trust'.

10. *Sunday Leader,* Spotlight, 2 January 2005.

11. *Sunday Island,* News, 2 January 2005.

12. *Sunday Leader*, Spotlight, 9 January 2005.

13. *Sunday Leader*, Spotlight, 16 January 2005.

14. These were for rescue and relief (TAFRER), for reconstruction and rehabilitation (TAFREN) and logistics, law and order (TAFLOL).

15. *Sunday Leader*, Spotlight, 16 January 2005.

16. Sunday Leader, Spotlight, 16 January 2005.

17. 'Liberation Tigers of Tamil Eelam', founded in 1976 as a militant organisation to create an independent state of Tamil Eelam in the north and east of the island.

18. *The Sunday Leader* ran a series of articles aimed at exposing what it regarded as the abuse of power by the government, international organisations and NGOs.

19. *Sunday Leader*, Spotlight, 9 January 2005.

20. Whilst most refer to abuse of political or institutional authority, some articles refer to the risks of physical abuse and the exposure of vulnerable groups. See, for example, http://www.thesundayleader.lk/archive/20050320/spotlight.htm#Tents

21. Sunday Island, *News*, 26 June 2005.

22. The People's Liberation Front, a political party formed in 1965 that combined a commitment to Marxism-Leninism with extreme nationalist positions. See David Lewis, 'The myopic Foucauldian gaze: discourse, knowledge and the authoritarian peace', *Journal of Intervention and Statebuilding, 11/1* (2017): 21–41.

23. Priya Deshingar and M Aheeyar, *Remittances in Crisis: Sri Lanka after the Tsunami*. Humanitarian Policy group/ODI (2006). There were approximately 1.2 million migrants from Sri Lanka in 2004 who sent around $1.5 billion back home. The level of remittances was anticipated to be $1.7 billion in 2005 (Deshingar and Aheeyar, *Remittances in crisis*, citing figures from the World Bank).

24. TamilNet, 09 January 2005.

25. TamilNet, 09 January 2005.

26. TamilNet, 24 January 2005.

27. TamilNet, 29 June 2005.

28. TamilNet, 09 May 2005.

29. TamilNet, 31 December 2004.

30. TamilNet, 02 March 2005.

31. John Telford, John Cosgrave, and Rachel Houghton, *Joint Evaluation of the International Response to the Indian Ocean Tsunami: Synthesis Report* (London: Tsunami Evaluation Commission, 2006). Formed in 2005, the TEC was a multi-agency initiative where participants collaborated on evaluations of the tsunami response in order to benefit learning in the sector. http://www.tsunami-evaluation.org/Introduction+to+the+TIC/index.html

32. http://www.tsunami-evaluation.org/The+TEC+Synthesis+Report/Full+Report.htm. IFRC operations updates are available at https://www.ifrc.org/en/publications-and-reports/appeals/?ac=&at=6&c=&co=&dt=1&f=2005&re=&t=2005&ti=&zo=SP3

33. 'Humanitarian Values' occurs 35 times and refers to the IFRC integrated promotion of the Movement's seven Fundamental Principles into its programme activities and recovery plan: https://www.ifrc.org/en/what-we-do/principles-and-values/

34. Sri Lanka Red Cross Society.
35. IFRC, *Operations Update no. 58*, 16.
36. IFRC, *Operations Update no. 57*, 13.
37. Community Based Disaster Preparedness, one of the IFRC programmatic themes.
38. IFRC, *Operations Update no. 58*, 14.
39. IFRC *Operations Update no. 57*, 28.
40. IFRC *Operations Update no. 58*, 37.
41. IFRC *Operations Update no. 58*, 38.
42. IFRC *Operations Update no. 58*, 43.
43. Telford, Cosgrave, and Houghton, *Synthesis Report*. Hereafter referred as the 'TEC report' or 'the report'.
44. TEC report.
45. TEC report, 31.
46. TEC report, 23.
47. Article 19 of the Universal Declaration of Human Rights
48. TEC report, 112.
49. TEC report,118. Good Humanitarian Donorship (GHD), a donor forum which facilitates advancement of its collective principles and good practices https://www.ghdinitiative.org/ghd/gns/home-page.html. The Sphere Standards https://spherestandards.org/wp-content/uploads/Sphere-Handbook-2018-EN.pdf and Red Cross Code of Conduct https://www.icrc.org/en/doc/assets/files/publications/icrc-002-1067.pdf
50. TEC report, 23.
51. The TEC report notes since its focus is on process rather than results, the evaluations differentiate systematically between good and less good practice, and link this to specific agencies. It is careful to observe that they are used to illustrate general points and should not be understood as a statement of overall performance.
52. TEC report, 30.
53. TEC report, 18.
54. Hugo Slim and Lorenzo Trombetta, *Syria Crisis Common Context Analysis*. Co-ordinated Accountability and Lessons Learning (CALL) Initiative. IASC Inter-Agency Humanitarian Evaluations Steering Group, New York (2014).
55. IFRC Operations Updates July–December 2012, Syria Crisis Emergency appeal n° MDRSY003; Slim and Trombetta, *Syria Crisis*.
56. Outright political dissent or criticism of the regime was not tolerated, but there was criticism of government performance in official and unofficial media, see Khalid Abu-Ismail, Omar Imady, Aljaz Kuncic and Osama Nojoum (Lead Authors), *Syria at War: Five Years on*. UN ESCWA and University of St Andrews (2016): 9.
57. This study was commissioned by the Inter-Agency Humanitarian Evaluations Steering Group. Members of the Steering Group are ALNAP, FAO, IFRC, OCHA, UNHCR, UNICEF, WFP, WHO and World Vision International.
58. See Slim and Trombetta, *Syria Crisis*; Raymond Hinnebusch and Tina Zintl, 2014. *Syria from Reform to Revolt, Volume 1: Political Economy and International Relations*. Syracuse University Press; Hinnebusch, R, 2020. Identity and state formation in multi☐sectarian societies: Between nationalism and sectarianism in Syria. *Nations and Nationalism*, 26:138–154. See also note 55 of this chapter.

59. Slim and Trombetta, *Syria Crisis: 19.*

60. In June, the Sri Lankan government signed a document to set up the post-tsunami operational management structure (P-TOMS). The structure was designed to act as a mechanism to receive funds and monitor projects that would benefit those affected by the tsunami in the areas of northern and eastern Sri Lanka held by the LTTE (IFRC *Operations Update, 57*).

61. 'Entrusted' occurs four times in relation to the assignment of political/military authority to members of the Alawite clan and supporters of the regime.

62. Stirrat and Henkel, *The Development Gift*; Roderick Stirrat, 'Competitive Humanitarianism: Relief and the tsunami in Sri Lanka', *Anthropology Today,* Volume 22, no. 5 (2006); Hilhorst, 'Classical humanitarianism and resilience humanitarianism'.

63. A meeting of ASEAN Foreign Ministers shortly after the cyclone struck Myanmar led to an agreement to form the Tripartite Core Group (TCG), comprising the government of Myanmar (Chair), ASEAN and the UN, to act as an ASEAN-led mechanism to facilitate trust, confidence and cooperation between Myanmar and the international community in the urgent humanitarian relief and recovery work after Cyclone Nargis hit Myanmar.

64. Gordon-Gibson, *Humanitarian Space, 58.*

65. In the case of Sri Lanka, the period analysed coincides with approaching national elections and each publication targets a particular political and social demographic.

66. Mateja Peter, *International Authority in Statebuilding*, Chapter 2 (pending publication). Paper presented at University of St Andrews, School of International Relations, February 2020. Quoted with the kind permission of the author.

8. RE-HARBOURING THE HUMANITARIANS

1. Barnett and Snyder, 'The grand strategies of humanitarianism', in *Humanitarianism in Question*, 2008, 146.

2. Andrew Selth, 'Even paranoids have enemies: Cyclone Nargis and Myanmar's fears of invasion', *Contemporary Southeast Asia: A Journal of International and Strategic Affairs,* Volume 30, no. 3 (2008), 379–402.

3. Rebecca Barber, 'The responsibility to protect the survivors of natural disaster: Cyclone Nargis, a case study' *Journal of Conflict & Security Law,* Volume 14, no. 1 (2009), 3–34.

4. Robert Turner, Jock Baker, Zaw Myo Oo and Naing Soe Aye, *Inter-Agency Real Time Evaluation of the Response to Cyclone Nargis*, UN OCHA (2008). https://www.unocha.org/sites/unocha/files/dms/Documents/IA_RTE_Nargis_Response_Final_Report_with_pics%5B1%5D.pdf

5. Author's experience as head of operations for IFRC in Myanmar at the time.

6. These were in public health; water and sanitation; psycho-social support, shelter and reconstruction (IFRC Emergency Appeal https://www.ifrc.org/docs/appeals/11/MDRMM002_OU_30.pdf).

7. Even if many of the military and government authorities were not originally from the region, all who were resident there at the time had been affected by the crisis.

8. Cooperation was increased once MRCS, together with IFRC, established operational centres in the townships affected by the disaster.

9. Slim and Trombetta, *Syria Crisis,* 42–45. Public recognition of the humanitarian services provided by SARC branches and volunteers had progressively grown since their response to the Zeyzoun Dam collapse in Homs governorate in 2002. This was followed by response to support refugees and displaced third country nationals at the start of the war in Iraq in 2003; response to refugees and third country nationals fleeing the conflict in Lebanon, in 2006 and the provision of public health services and livelihoods support to vulnerable Syrians affected by the drought which began in 2009 and severely affected rural communities in the north and east of the country (IFRC Operations Updates; author's field reports and personal diaries. See also chapter 2, note 41).

10. See Ger Duijzings, *Religion and the Politics of Identity in Kosovo* (London: Hurst, 2000) and Mary Kaldor, *New and Old Wars* (Cambridge: Polity Press, 2012).

11. Author's personal diaries, Sarajevo.

12. Kaldor, *New and Old Wars,* 41.

13. Maček, *Sarajevo under Siege.*

14. Maček, *Sarajevo under Siege,* xi–xii.

15. Maček, *Sarajevo under Siege.* Self-deprecating humour was common amongst Sarajevans during the siege and amongst citizens elsewhere in Bosnia and Herzegovina during the conflict. These often featured the characters of Mujo, Suljo and Fata making jokes that reflected a short, humorous analysis of that time (author's personal diaries). See also Kreševljaković http://balkans.aljazeera.net/vijesti/humor-under-siege-mujo-dont-jump-around-youll-get-hungry and Maček, *Sarajevo under Siege,* 51–54.

16. See Howard Adelman and Astrid Suhrke, 'Early warning and response: why the international community failed to prevent the genocide', *Disasters,* Volume 20, no. 4 (1996): 295–304; John Eriksson, *Synthesis report, The International Response to Conflict and Genocide: Lessons from the Rwanda Experience. Joint Evaluation of Emergency Assistance to Rwanda* (London: Danida and ODI, 1996).

17. Mills, *Mass Atrocities.*

18. The first major influx of refugees fleeing the mass atrocities in Rwanda numbered around 200,000 into the Ngara district of Tanzania at the end of April 1994 (rising to a figure of around 500,000 a year later), then 300,000 to Bukavu in eastern Zaire. Between the 14th and 18th of July more than a million refugees fled across the border into Zaire, with around 850,000 settling in and around the town of Goma (Eriksson, *Synthesis Report*: 1996).

19. Mills, *Mass Atrocities:* 80. Mills makes a distinction between what he considers as the cynical political motivations behind this response and the humanitarian drive to alleviate the suffering and remarks clearly that his use of the term 'palliation' 'is in no way meant to devalue the work of humanitarians' (ibid: 22).

20. Eriksson, *Synthesis Report*: 25.

21. Gordon-Gibson, *Notes from the Field,* 256

22. Author eyewitness, Kibumba camp, Goma, 1994. Personal diaries.

23. IFRC, World Disasters Report, 2015. Available at https://www.ifrc.org/en/publications-and-reports/world-disasters-report/. The report gives an example of

volunteers from the Afghan Red Crescent working with local 'Grandmothers' Committees' in promoting behavioural change amongst young adolescents through increasing awareness on reproductive health issues and access to maternal and child healthcare services (Box 1.1 pages 14–17).

24. Michael Ignatieff, *The Ordinary Virtues: Moral Order in a Divided World*, (Cambridge MA: Harvard University Press, 2017).

25. Ignatieff, *Ordinary Virtues*. Ignatieff lists these as tolerance, forgiveness, trust, reconciliation and resilience (ibid: 26) (which latter he combines elsewhere in his study as 'respect').

26. Ignatieff, *Ordinary Virtues, 18*.

27. Ignatieff, *Ordinary Virtues, 27*.

28. My arguments here were prompted by discussions presented by Michael Sandel, on BBC Radio 4, 'Morality in the 21st Century', broadcast 03–09–2019.

29. Ignatieff, *Ordinary Virtues, 52*.

30. ICRC President, Cornelio Sommaruga, expressed this passionately in his address at the 75th anniversary of the foundation of the IFRC: 'It is tragically pointless to be united and universal if the Movement fails to be effective. But it cannot be effective unless we know what is expected of us, what specific task is assigned to each one of us' *International Review of the Red Cross,* no. 300, 1994, 282. https://www.cambridge.org/core/services/aop-cambridge-core/content/view/80C91A14B2B 6931214254ECA55EFC358/S0020860400078165a.pdf/address_by_the_president_ of_the_international_committee_of_the_red_cross_mr_cornelio_sommaruga.pdf. In his work on creative approaches to the study of asymmetrical power, Bertrand Badie advocates a need for new rules and new thinking that are better adapted to the conflicts of twenty-first century, and observes that 'inter-social relations are now the framework for the conduct of international action' (*New Perspectives on the International Order,* 11).

31. Richard Bernstein, *Beyond Objectivism and Relativism: Science, Hermeneutics, and Praxis* (London: Blackwell, 1983), 2.

32. Adler and Pouliot, eds., *International Practices*, 13.

33. Adler and Pouliot, eds., *International Practices*, 15.

34. Taylor, *Hegel*.

35. See Eleanor Burt and Samuel Mansell, 'Moral agency in charities and business orporations: Exploring the constraints of law and regulation', *Journal of Business Ethics*: 1–15 (2017). In their study of 'moral agency' in charities and business corporations, Burt and Mansell observe that literature on the topic agree 'that if an organisation has agency, it necessarily has purposes of its own that may differ from the separate goals of its members' (ibid, 5).

36. Ian Clark, Sebastian Kaempf, Christian Reus-Smit and Emily Tannock, 'Crisis in the laws of war? Beyond compliance and effectiveness', *European Journal of International Relations,* Volume 24, no. (2) (2018): 319–343.

37. Manuel Castells, *The Power of Identity* (Oxford: Blackwell, 1997).

38. Denise Rousseau, Sim Sitkin, Ronald Burt and Colin Camerer, Not so Different after All: A Cross-Discipline View of Trust. *The Academy of Management Review,* Volume 23, no. 3 (1998): 393–404.

39. See Kaldor, *New and Old Wars*. Also, Ian Clark Sebastian Kaempf, Christian Reus-Smit and Emily Tannock. 'Crisis in the laws of war? Beyond compliance and effectiveness', *European Journal of International Relations,* Volume 24. no. 2 (2018): 321.

40. Clark et al. *Crisis in the laws of war?*, 329.

41. Paul Collier and Anke Hoeffler, 'Greed and grievance in civil war' *Oxford Economic Papers, 56* (2004): 563–595; James Fearon and David Laitin, 'Ethnicity, insurgency, and civil war', *The American Political Science Review*, Volume 97, no. 1 (2003): 75–90.

42. Ayesha Siddiqi, Disasters in conflict areas: finding the politics. In *Disasters,* 42(S2): S161–S172 (2018); Ayesha Siddiqi and Jose Canuday, 'Stories from the frontlines: decolonising social contracts for disasters', *Disasters,* Volume 42, no. S2: S215–S238 (2018).

43. Meike de Goede, *Consuming Democracy: Local Agencies & Liberal Peace in the Democratic Republic of Congo* (Leiden: African Studies Centre, 2015); Francis Nyamnjoh, 'Incompleteness: Frontier Africa and the currency of conviviality', *Journal of Asian and African Studies*, Volume 52, no. 3 (2017), 53–270.

44. de Goede, *Consuming democracy:*20.

45. Nyamnjoh, *Incompleteness*, 255.

46. Roger Mac Ginty and Andrew Williams, *Conflict and Development* (London: Routledge, 2009); Roger Mac Ginty, 'Everyday peace: Bottom-up and local agency in conflict-affected societies', *Security Dialogue,* Volume 45, no. 6 (2014): 548–564; Oliver Richmond, 'Rescuing peacebuilding? Anthropology and peace formation' *Global Society* (2018); Hilhorst, 'Classical humanitarianism and resilience humanitarianism'. See also documents and statements appearing from the World Humanitarian Summit, 2016. https://research.un.org/en/whs.

47. de Waal, *Famine Crimes*; Maček, *Siege of Sarajevo*; Hilhorst, 'Classical humanitarianism and resilience humanitarianism'.

48. Siddiqi and Canuday, 'Stories from the frontlines'.

49. See Arnold van Gennep, *The Rites of Passage*.

50. van Gennep, *The Rites of Passage*; Victor Turner, 'Betwixt and between: The liminal period in Rites de Passage', in *The Forest of Symbols* (Ithaca NY: Cornell University Press, 1967): 93–111.

51. See Udeh Fernando and Dorothea Hilhorst, 'Everyday practices of humanitarian aid: Tsunami response in Sri Lanka', *Development in Practice,* Volume 16, no. 3/4: (2006), 292–302; John Telford and John Cosgrave, 'The international humanitarian system and the 2004 Indian Ocean earthquake and tsunamis'. *Disasters,* Volume 31, no. 1 (2007) 1–28; IFRC *World Disasters Report*, 2015 and Hilhorst, 'Classical humanitarianism and resilience humanitarianism'.

52. For example, see World Humanitarian Summit, 2016; Christina Bennett, (lead author), *Time to Let Go*; Schenkenberg van Mierop, *Local Humanitarian Actors and the Principle of Impartiality*.

53. IFRC *World Disaster Report, 2015*: 14.

54. For example, see Rousseau et al., *Not so Different after All*.

55. The text of the IFRC mission statement formulated in its 'Strategy 2010' reads: 'to improve the lives of vulnerable people by mobilizing the power of humanity'.

See Stephen Davey, 'Strategy 2010: All change at the feds?', *Humanitarian Exchange, 17,* Humanitarian Practice Network/ODI (2000): 45 https://reliefweb.int/sites/reliefweb.int/files/resources/FD00207B505C8577C1257376004FCF79-odihpn-oct2000.pdf

56. https://spherestandards.org/wp-content/uploads/Sphere-Handbook-2018-EN.pdf and https://www.icrc.org/en/doc/assets/files/publications/icrc-002-1067.pdf See Chapter One, note 4.

57. Magnus Frostenson, Humility in business: A contextual approach. *Journal of Business Ethics,* Volume 138 (2016), 91–102.

58. Rob Nielsen and Jennifer Marrone, 'Humility: Our Current Understanding of the Construct and its Role in Organizations', *International Journal of Management Reviews,* Volume 20 (2018): 807.

59. See Nussbaum, *Frontiers of Justice*; Maček, *Siege of Sarajevo.* Also, Hugo Slim, *ICRC Partnerships, Today and Tomorrow, in conflict and disaster,* a speech given at the 5th Singapore Red Cross Conference on the theme of partnerships and volunteerism for humanity, 20 July 2019. https://www.icrc.org/en/document/icrc-partnerships-today-and-tomorrow-conflict-and-disaster

60. Badie, *New Perspectives on the International Order, 9.*

61. Oliver Richmond, 'Rescuing peacebuilding? Anthropology and peace formation. *Global Society,* Volume 32 (2018), 221–239.

62. For a review and timelines of the outbreak see http://www.who.int/csr/disease/ebola/one-year-report/sierra-leone/en/

63. Richmond, *Rescuing Peacebuilding?* 4.

9. CHANGING THE SOCIAL ORDER

1. Bertrand Badie, *New Perspectives on the International Order* (English translation William Snow), The Sciences Po Series in International Relations and Political Economy (Palgrave Macmillan, 2019), vi. The Peace of Westphalia, signed in 1648, marked the end of the Thirty Years War in Europe and established a new international order that replaced an imperial political system with the sovereignty of territorial states.

2. Badie argues for engagement with what he refers to as the effective 'deviant' or 'delinquent', which promotes the agency of the excluded, *New Perspectives on the International Order,* 29.

3. For example, Karin Fierke and Nicola Mackay, 'To "see" is to break an entanglement: Quantum measurement, trauma and security', *Security Dialogue* (2020), 1–17.

4. Heyes, 'Identity politics'.

5. Patricia Collins and Sirma Bilge, *Intersectionality* Cambridge: Polity Press, (2016). See Hugo Slim, Impartiality and Intersectionality ICRC Humanitarian Law and Policy ICRC weblog, 16 January 2018. https://blogs.icrc.org/law-and-policy/2018/01/16/impartiality-and-intersectionality/

6. Williams, *Failed Imagination,* 182.

7. Roderick Kramer, 'Trust and distrust in organizations: Emerging perspectives, enduring questions', *Annual Review of Psychology*, Volume 50 (1999); Anheier and Kendall, 'Interpersonal trust and voluntary associations', 343–362.

8. Barth, *Ethnic Groups and Boundaries*.

9. Barth, *Ethnic Groups and Boundaries*, 11.

10. Barth, *Ethnic Groups and Boundaries*, 14.

11. Anaïs Rességuier, 'The moral sense of humanitarian actors: an empirical exploration', in *Disasters,* Volume 42/1 (2018): 63.

12. Rességuier, *The Moral Sense of Humanitarian Actors*.

13. Nicholas Cater and Peter Walker, eds., *International Federation of Red Cross and Red Crescent Societies, World Disasters Report* (Oxford: Oxford University Press, 1997), 140–146.

14. IFRC, *Focus on local actors, the key to humanitarian effectiveness*, 24.

15. See Larissa Fast, 'Securitization and threats to humanitarian workers' in *The Routledge Companion to Humanitarian Action*, 313–332; Sean Healy and Sandrine Tiller, Where is everyone? Responding to emergencies in the most difficult places. Publication by MSF, 2014 https://www.msf.org/sites/msf.org/files/msf-where iseveryone_-def-lr_-_july.pdf

16. Loh and Heiskanen, 'Liminal sovereignty practices: Rethinking the inside/outside dichotomy', *Cooperation and Conflict*, Volume 55, no. 3 (2020): 284–304. DOI: 10.1177/0010836720911391.

17. Loh and Heiskanen see non-state agencies and NGOs operating in an interstitial space 'which usually entails co-existence with the system' (*Liminal sovereignty practices*, 299), providing the work of Amnesty International as an example.

18. Taylor, *Hegel*, 412.

19. Taylor, *Hegel*.

20. Taylor, *Hegel*, 412.

21. Calhoun, 'The class consciousness of frequent travelers'.

22. Francis Nyamnjoh, 'Incompleteness: Frontier Africa and the currency of conviviality', *Journal of Asian and African Studies,* Volume 52, no. 3 (2017): 259.

23. Nyamnjoh, *Incompleteness*, 260.

24. Bjørn Thomassen, 'The uses and meanings of liminality', *International Political Anthropology,* Volume 2, no. 1 (2009), 5–28.

25. Thomassen, *The Uses and Meanings of Liminality*, 6.

26. Bjørn Thomassen, 'Revisiting liminality: The danger of empty spaces', in *Liminal Landscapes: Travel, Experience and Spaces In-between*, eds. Hazel Andrews and Les Roberts (London: Routledge, 2012), 21.

27. Thomassen, 'The uses and meanings of liminality', 18.

28. See Erik Abild, 'Creating humanitarian space: A case study of Somalia', *New Issues in Refugee Research, Research Paper No. 184*. Refugee Studies Centre, University of Oxford (2009).

29. Abild, 'Creating humanitarian space', 27.

30. Kennedy, *The Dark Sides of Virtue*, 328.

31. Ali Ansari, *These Islands: A Letter to 'Britain'* (London: Haus Publishing, 2018).

32. Ansari, *These Islands*, 66.

33. DuBois, 'The new humanitarian basics', 13.

34. DuBois, 'The new humanitarian basics', 26.

35. See Hugo Slim, 'Not philanthropy but rights: The proper politicisation of humanitarian philosophy', *The International Journal of Human Rights,* Volume 6/2 (2002): 14.

36. In 2013, the RCRC Movement initiated a process looking at building on strengths from the diversity of its membership (Strengthening Movement Coordination and Cooperation https://www.icrc.org/en/doc/assets/files/red-cross-crescent-move ment/council-delegates-2013/cod13-r4-3movement-coordination-adopted-eng.pdf

37. Red Cross and Red Crescent Movement, *Strengthening Movement Coordination and Cooperation (SMCC): Optimizing the Movement's humanitarian response.* Progress report. Council of Delegates, Geneva (2015) http://rcrcconference.org/app// uploads/2015/03/CoD15_SMCC_report-FINAL-EN.pdf

38. Rousseau, *The Social Contract.*

39. RCRC, *Strengthening Movement Coordination.*

40. See RCRC, *Strengthening Movement Coordination,* 8.

41. Hugo Slim, 'By what authority? The legitimacy and accountability of non-governmental organisations', *Journal of Humanitarian Aid* (2002); ALNAP, *The State of the Humanitarian System.*

42. Elly Harrowell and Alpaslan Özerdem, 'Negotiating reconstruction: Understanding hybridity in Sri Lanka's post-disaster and post-conflict reconstruction processes', *Peacebuilding,* Volume 8 (2018): 218–239.

43. Harrowell and Özerdem, 'Negotiating reconstruction', 19.

44. IFRC, *World Disaster Report, 2015,* 141.

45. Eleanor Burt and Samuel Mansell, 'Moral agency in charities and business corporations: Exploring the constraints of law and regulation', *Journal of Business Ethics,* Volume 1–15 (2017): 6.

46. Burt and Mansell, *Moral Agency in Charities and Business.*

47. Stürmer and Snyder, *The Psychology of Pro-Social Behavior,* 6.

48. Stürmer and Snyder, *The Psychology of Pro-Social Behavior.*

49. David Sloan Wilson, *Does Altruism Exist? Culture, Genes and the Welfare of Others.* (New Haven: Yale University, 2015); Kratochwil, *Praxis.*

50. According to Rawls, the distribution of shares that result from power, merit, talent and so on do not correlate to moral worth, since their endowments are arbitrary from a moral point of view (John Rawls, *A Theory of Justice* (revised edition) (Cambridge MA: Belknap Press, [1971] 1999), 274.

51. de Goede, *Consuming Democracy,* 27.

52. Julia Pacitto and Elena Fiddian-Qasmiyeh, 'Writing the "Other" into humanitarian discourse Framing theory and practice in South-South humanitarian responses to forced displacement'. Oxford University Refugee Studies Centre, Working Paper series no. 93 (2013): 6–7.

53. Slim, 'Wonderful work'.

54. Alasdair MacIntyre, *After Virtue: A Study in Moral Theory* (2nd Edition) (London: Duckworth, 1985).

55. Bennett, *Time to Let Go.*

56. Bennett, *Time to Let Go,* 64.

57. See Ayesha Siddiqi, 'Disasters in conflict areas: Finding the politics', *Disasters,* Volume 42, special edition 2 (2018): S162.

58. Bennett, *Constructive Deconstruction;* Stoddard, Harmer and Czwarno Stoddard, *Aid Worker Security Report 2017*; ALNAP, *The State of the Humanitarian System.*

59. Juliana Fiori, Fernando Espada, Jessica Field and Sophie Dicker, *The Echo Chamber: Results, Management and the Humanitarian Affairs Agenda.* London, Humanitarian Affairs Team and Humanitarian and Conflict Response Institute (2016): 37.

60. Rességuier, *The Moral Sense of Humanitarian Actors*, 62–63.

61. Hugo Slim, 'ICRC partnerships, today and tomorrow, in conflict and disaster', Speech given at the 5th Singapore Red Cross Conference on the theme of partnerships and volunteerism for humanity, 20 July 2019. https://www.icrc.org/en/document/icrc-partnerships-today-and-tomorrow-conflict-and-disaster

62. Nyamnjoh, *Incompleteness*, 260.

63. Rohan Hardcastle and Adrian Chua, 'Humanitarian assistance: Towards a right of access to victims of natural disasters', *International Review of the Red Cross,* no. 325 (1998); Gareth Evans, 'The responsibility to protect: Rethinking humanitarian intervention. (Proceedings of the Annual Meeting)' *American Society of International Law,* Volume 98 (2004): 8–89; François Bugnion, *The International Committee of the Red Cross and the Protection of War Victims* (Oxford: Macmillan, 2014).

64. ALNAP, *State of the Humanitarian System,* 161

65. Josiah Ober, 'Meritocratic and civic dignity in Greco-Roman antiquity' in *Cambridge Handbook on Human Dignity*, eds. Marcus Düwell, Jens Braarvig, Roger Brownsword and Dietmar Mieth (Cambridge, UK: Cambridge University Press, 2010), 53.

66. Ober, 'Meritocratic and civic dignity'.

67. Ober's analysis of civic dignity in Ancient Greece offers some close parallels to the arguments my study presents for definition of identities in the humanitarian niche. For example, he explains its defence against meritocracy as the collective responsibility of a clearly defined set of people, the citizens, who do not share personal ties: 'It is in their interest as persons who may in turn be threatened by the arrogance of the strong, as persons concerned with the defence of their own dignity, and as persons who recognize that defence of dignity requires the aid of fellow citizens. Civic dignity is thus at once virtuous, reciprocal and rational' (*Meritocratic and civic dignity*: 56). He observes that sustaining a regime of respect and recognition among an extensive population of diverse individuals entails the virtue of self-restraint, since as citizens, 'we ought voluntarily to restrain ourselves from self-aggrandizing actions that compromise another's dignity' (ibid,57).

68. See Maček, *Siege of Sarajevo.*

69. Claude Bruderlein, ed., *Field Manual on Frontline Humanitarian Negotiation.* Centre of Competence on Humanitarian Negotiation (2018). https://frontline-negotiations.org/wp-content/uploads/2018/11/CCHN-Field-Manual-3.pdf

70. See the collected essays in Düwell et al. *The Cambridge Handbook of Human Dignity.*

71. ALNAP, *State of the Humanitarian System,* 17.

72. See ALNAP, *State of the Humanitarian System,* 253.

73. Calhoun, 'The class consciousness of frequent travelers', 881.

74. Bhikhu Parekh, 'The cultural particularity of liberal democracy', *Political Studies XL, Special Issue* (1992): 163.

75. Calhoun, 'The class consciousness of frequent travelers'.

76. My arguments and reflections on Rousseau in this Chapter owe much to the paper 'The Moral Psychology of The Social Contract: Rousseau's Republican Citizenship', presented by Dr Robin Douglass at the University of St Andrews School of History, November 2018. Quoted with the kind permission of the author.

77. 'Good social institutions are those that best know how to denature man, to take his absolute existence from him in order to give him a relative one and transport the *I* into the common unity, with the result that each individual believes himself no longer one but a part of the unity and no longer feels except within the whole', *Emile*, in *The Collected Writings of Rousseau*, 13 vols, eds. Roger D. Masters and Christopher Kelly. Hanover, NH: University Press of New England, 1990–2010, cited by Robin Douglass (see note 76 of this chapter).

78. Douglass, *The Moral Psychology of The Social Contract* referring to Rousseau, 'On the social contract, or principles of political right', in *The Collected Writings of Rousseau*, vol. ii: 12.

79. Kratochwil, *Praxis*, 47.

80. Kratochwil, *Praxis*, 45.

81. Kratochwil, *Praxis*, 47.

Bibliography

Abild, Erik. 'Creating humanitarian space: A case study of Somalia'. *Refugee Survey Quarterly,* Volume 29, no. 3 (2010): 67–102.

Abu Sa'Da, Caroline and Xavier Crombé. 'Volunteers and responsibility for risk-taking: Changing interpretations of the Charter of Médecins Sans Frontières'. *International Review of the Red Cross,* Volume 97, no. 897/898 (2016): 133–155.

Acharya, Amitav and Barry Buzan, eds. *Non-Western International Relations Theory: Perspectives on and beyond Asia.* London: Routledge, 2010.

Adelman, Howard and Astrid Suhrke. 'Early warning and response: Why the international community failed to prevent the genocide'. *Disasters,* Volume 20, no. 4 (1996): 295–304.

Adler, Emanuel and Vincent Pouliot, eds. *International Practices.* Cambridge, UK: Cambridge University Press, 2011.

Agamben, Giorgio. *Homo Sacer: Sovereign Power and Bare Life.* Stanford, CA: Stanford University Press, 1998.

Agier, Michel. 'Humanity as an identity and its political effects (A note on Camps and humanitarian government)'. *Humanity,* Volume 1, no. 1 (2010): 29–45.

Agier, Michel and Françoise Bouchet-Saulnier. 'Humanitarian spaces: Spaces of exception'. In *In the Shadow of "Just Wars": Violence, Politics, and Humanitarian Action,* edited by Fabrice Weissman, 297–313. Ithaca, NY: Cornell University Press, 2004.

Alberti, Fay, ed. *Medicine, Emotion and Disease, 1700–1950,* 79–99. London: Palgrave Macmillan, 2006.

Amoore, Louise and Alexandra Hall. 'The clown at the gates of the camp: Sovereignty, resistance and the figure of the fool'. *Security Dialogue,* Volume 44, no. 2 (2013): 93–110.

Anheier, Helmut and Jeremy Kendall. 'Interpersonal trust and voluntary associations: examining three approaches'. *British Journal of Sociology,* Volume 53, no. 3 (2002): 343–362.

Anheier, Helmut and Lester Salamon. 'Volunteering in cross-national perspective: Initial comparisons'. *Duke University, Law and Contemporary Problems,* Volume 62, no. 4 (1999): 43–65.

Ansari, Ali. *These Islands: A Letter to 'Britain'.* London: Haus Publishing, 2018.

Bach, Lee. 'Heuristic scholar: Heuristic inquiry and the heuristic scholar'. *Counterpoints,* Volume 183 (2002) 91–102.

Badie, Bertrand. 'Toward a theory of weakness politics: Does weakness rule the world?' *Global Society,* Volume 32/2 (2018): 139–148. https://doi.org/10.1080/13600826.2018.1438991

Badie, Bertrand. 'New perspectives on the international order' (*The Sciences Po Series in International Relations and Political Economy, 2019.* Translated from the French edition, *Nous ne sommes plus seuls au monde: Un autre regard sur l'ordre international,* La Découverte, 2016. https://doi.org/10.1007/978-3-319-94286

Baert, Patrick and Felipe Da Silva. *Social Theory in the 20th Century and Beyond* (2nd Ed.). London: Polity Press, 2010.

Barber, Rebecca. 'The responsibility to protect the survivors of natural disaster: Cyclone Nargis, a case study'. *Journal of Conflict & Security Law,* Volume 14, no. 1 (2009): 3–34.

Barnett, Michael. 'Humanitarianism transformed'. *Perspectives on Politics,* Volume 3, no. 4 (2005): 723–740.

Barnett, Michael. *The International Humanitarian Order.* London: Routledge, 2010.

Barnett, Michael. *Empire of Humanity.* Ithaca, NY: Cornell University Press, 2011.

Barnett, Michael and Martha Finnemore. 'The politics, power, and pathologies of international organizations'. *International Organization,* Volume 53, no. 04 (1999): 699–732.

Barnett, Michael and Jack Snyder. 'The grand strategies of humanitarianism'. In *Humanitarianism in Question,* edited by Michael Barnett and Thomas Weiss. Ithaca, NY: Cornell University Press, 2008: 143–171.

Barnett, Michael and Peter Walker. 'How to make relief more accountable'. *Foreign Affairs,* Volume 94, no. 4 (2005): 130–141.

Barnett, Michael and Thomas Weiss, eds. *Humanitarianism in Question; Power, Politics, Ethics.* Ithaca, NY: Cornell University Press, 2008.

Barnett, Michael and Thomas Weiss. *Humanitarianism Contested. Where Angels Fear to Tread.* London: Routledge, 2011.

Barth, Fredrik, ed. *Ethnic Groups and Boundaries. The Social Organization of Culture Difference.* Long Grove, IL: Waveland Press, 1998.

Beekman, Karen. 'From fundamental principles to individual action: Making the principles come alive to promote a culture of non-violence and peace'. *International Review of the Red Cross,* Volume 97 897/898 (2016): 263–293.

Bennett, Andrew. 'The mother of all 'isms: Causal mechanisms and structured pluralism in International Relations theory'. *European Journal of International Relations,* Volume 19, no. 3 (2013): 459–481.

Bennett, Jon (principal author). *Coordination of international humanitarian assistance in tsunami-affected countries.* London: Tsunami Evaluation Committee, 2006.

Benthall, Jonathan. 'The Red Cross and Red Crescent Movement and Islamic Societies, with Special Reference to Jordan'. *British Journal of Middle Eastern Studies*,
Volume 24, no. 2 (1997): 157–177.

Benthall, Jonathan. 'Charity'. In *Cambridge Encyclopedia of Anthropology*. https://
www.anthroencyclopedia.com/entry/charity

Bernstein, Richard. *Praxis and Action: Contemporary Philosophies of Human Activity*. Philadelphia: University of Pennsylvania Press, 1971.

Bernstein, Richard. *Beyond Objectivism and Relativism: Science, Hermeneutics, and
Praxis*. London: Blackwell, 1983.

Biegbeder, Yves. *The Role and Status of International Humanitarian Volunteers and Organizations: The Right and Duty to Humanitarian Assistance*. Dordrecht: Nijhoff, 1991.

Blondel, Jean-Luc. "The Fundamental Principles of the Red Cross and Red Crescent:
Their origin and development." *International Review of the Red Cross*. No. 283
(1991): 349–357.

Borton, John. 'The international response to conflict and genocide: Lessons from the
Rwanda Experience, Study 3, humanitarian aid and effects'. *Steering Committee
of the Joint Evaluation of Emergency Assistance to Rwanda*. London: Danida and
ODI, 1996.

Borton, John. *Future of the Humanitarian System: Impacts of Internal Changes*. Medford, MA: Feinstein International Center, Tufts University, 2009.

Bourdieu, Pierre. 'The Social Space and the Genesis of Groups'. *Theory and Society*,
Volume 14, no. 6 (1985): 723–744.

Braithwaite, Jessica and Amanda Licht, 'The effect of civil society organizations and
democratization aid on civil war onset', *Journal of Conflict Resolution*, Volume
64, no. 6 (2020).

Brandt, Willy. *North-South: A Programme for Survival: Report of the Independent
Commission on International Development Issues*. Cambridge, MA: MIT Press,
1980.

Brenner, Neil and Stuart Elden. 'Henri Lefebvre on State, Space, Territory'. *International Political Sociology*, no. 3 (2009): 353–377.

Brown, Chris. 'The promise and record of international institutions'. *International
Relations* (2019): 1–14.

Brown, Rupert. *Group Processes: Dynamics within and between Groups* (2nd Ed.).
London: Blackwell, 2000.

Brown, Rupert and Samuel Gaertner. *Blackwell Handbook of Social Psychology:
Intergroup Processes*. Oxford, UK: Blackwell, 2001.

Brown, Seth. 'De Coubertin's Olympism and the Laugh of Michel Foucault: Crisis
discourse and the Olympic Games', *Quest*, Volume 64, no. 3 (2012): 150–163.

Bugnion, François. 'The International Committee of the Red Cross and the Development of International Humanitarian Law'. *Chicago Journal of International Law*,
Volume 5, no. 1 (2004): 191–215.

Bugnion, François. 'The International Conference of the Red Cross and Red Crescent: challenges, key issues and achievements'. *International Review of the Red
Cross*, Volume 91, Number 876 (2009): 675–712.

Bugnion, François. 'Birth of an idea: the founding of the International Committee of the Red Cross and of the International Red Cross and Red Crescent Movement'. *International Review of the Red Cross,* Volume 94, no. 888 (2012): 1299–1338.

Bugnion, François. *The International Committee of the Red Cross and the Protection of War Victims*. Oxford, UK: Macmillan, 2014.

Burr, Vivien. *Social Constructionism* (3rd Ed.). London: Routledge, 2015.

Burt, Eleanor and Samuel Mansell. 'Moral agency in charities and business corporations: Exploring the constraints of law and regulation'. *Journal of Business Ethics* (2017): 1–15.

Buzan, Barry. '"Change and insecurity" reconsidered'. *Contemporary Security Policy,* Volume 20, no. 3 (1999): 1–17.

Calhoun, Craig. 'The class consciousness of frequent travelers: Toward a critique of actually existing cosmopolitanism'. *The South Atlantic Quarterly,* Volume 101, no. 4 (2002): 869–897.

Calhoun, Noel. 'With a little help from our friends: a participatory assessment of social capital among refugees in Jordan'. *New issues in refugee research. UNHCR research paper* 189 (2010).

Carvalho, Anabela. 'Media(ted) discourse and society: Rethinking the framework of critical discourse analysis'. *Journalism Studies,* no. 9 (2008): 161–177.

Castells, Manuel. *The Power of Identity.* Oxford, UK: Blackwell, 1997.

Cater, Nicholas and Peter Walker, eds. *International Federation of Red Cross and Red Crescent Societies, World Disasters Report.* Oxford, UK: Oxford University Press, 1997.

Chu, Jonathan. 'A clash of norms? How reciprocity and International Humanitarian Law affect American opinion on the treatment of POWs'. *Journal of Conflict Resolution* (2018): 1–25.

Clark, Ian; Sebastian Kaempf; Christian Reus-Smit and Emily Tannock. 'Crisis in the laws of war? Beyond compliance and effectiveness'. *European Journal of International Relations,* Volume 24, no. 2 (2018): 319–343.

Clegg, Stewart, David Courpasson and Nelson Phillips. *Power and Organizations.* London: SAGE, 2006.

Collier, Paul and Anke Hoeffler. 'Greed and grievance in civil war'. *Oxford Economic Papers,* Volume 56 (2004): 563–595.

Collins, Patricia and Sirma Bilge. *Intersectionality.* Cambridge, UK: Polity Press, 2016.

Currion, Paul. 'Network humanitarianism. Constructive deconstruction: Imagining alternative humanitarian action'. Humanitarian Policy Group, Working Paper. London: ODI, 2018.

Cunningham, Andrew. *International Humanitarian NGOs and State Relations: Politics, Principles and Identity.* London: Routledge, 2018.

Dana, Karam. 'Confronting injustice beyond borders: Palestinian identity and nonviolent resistance'. *Politics, Groups, and Identities,* Volume 6, no. 4 (2018): 529–552.

Davey, Eleanor; John Borton and Matthew Foley. 'A history of the humanitarian system: Western origins and foundations'. Humanitarian Policy Group, Working Paper. London: ODI, 2013.

Dekker, Paul and Loek Halman, eds. *The Values of Volunteering: Cross-Cultural Perspectives.* London: Plenum, 2003.

de Goede, Meike. *Consuming Democracy: Local Agencies & Liberal Peace in the Democratic Republic of Congo.* Leiden: African Studies Centre, 2015.

Desgrandchamps, Marie-Luce. ' "Organising the unpredictable": the Nigeria – Biafra war and its impact on the ICRC'. *International Review of the Red Cross,* Volume 94, no. 888 (2012): 1409–1432.

Deshingar, Priya and Mohamed Aheeyar. *Remittances in Crisis: Sri Lanka after the Tsunami.* London: Humanitarian Policy group/OD, 2006.

De Torrente, Nicolas. 'Humanitarian Action under Attack: Reflections on the Iraq War'. *Harvard Human Rights Journal,* Volume 17 (2004a): 1–30.

De Torrente, Nicolas. 'Humanitarianism sacrificed: Integration's false promise'. *Ethics and International Affairs* Volume 18, no. 2 (2004b): 3–12.

de Waal, Alex. *Famine Crimes: Politics and the Disaster Relief Industry in Africa.* Bloomington: Indiana University Press, 1997.

Donini, Antonio. 'The far side: The meta functions of humanitarianism in a globalised world', *Disasters,* Volume 34, Special Edition 2 (2010): S220–S237.

Donini, Antonio, ed. *The Golden Fleece: Manipulation and Independence in Humanitarian Action.* Sterling VA: Kumarian Press, 2012.

Donini, Antonio, Larry Minear and Peter Walker. 'The future of humanitarian action: Mapping the implications of Iraq and other recent crises'. *Disaster,* Volume 28, no. 2 (2004): 190–204.

Donini, Antonio, Larry Minear and Peter Walker. 'Between cooptation and irrelevance: Humanitarian action after Iraq'. *Journal of Refugee Studies* Volume 17, no. 3 (2004): 260–272.

Donini, Antonio, Larissa Fast, Greg Hansen, Simon Harris, Larry Minear, Tasneem Mowjee and Andrew Wilder. *Humanitarian Agenda 2015: Final Report, the State of the Humanitarian Enterprise.* Medford MA: Tufts University, Feinstein International Center, 2008.

Douzinas, Costas. 'The Many Faces of Humanitarianism'. *Parrhesia,* no. 2 (2007): 1–28.

DuBois, Marc. 'The new humanitarian basics'. Humanitarian Policy Group, Working Paper. London: ODI, 2018. https://www.odi.org/sites/odi.org.uk/files/resource-documents/12201.pdf

Duffield, Mark. *Global Governance and the New Wars: The Merging of Development and Security.* London: Zed Books, 2001.

Duffield, Mark. *Development, Security and Unending War: Governing the World of Peoples.* Cambridge, UK: Polity Press, 2007.

Duijzings, Ger. *Religion and the Politics of Identity in Kosovo.* London: Hurst, 2000.

Dunant, Henry. *A Memory of Solferino.* Geneva: International Committee of the Red Cross, [1862]1986.

Dunne, Tim, Lene Hansen and Colin Wight. 'The end of International Relations theory? University of Copenhagen, Denmark'. *European Journal of International Relations,* Volume 19, no. 3 (2013): 405–442.

Dunne, Tim, Milja Kurki and Steve Smith, eds. *International Relations Theories.* Oxford, UK: Oxford University Press, 2007.

Dutton, Jane, Janet Dukerich and Celia Harquail. 'Organizational images and member identification'. *Administrative Science Quarterly,* Volume 39 (1994): 239–263.

Düwell, Marcus, Jens Braarvig, Roger Brownsword and Dietmar Mieth, eds. *The Cambridge Handbook of Human Dignity: Interdisciplinary Perspectives.* Cambridge, UK: Cambridge University Press, 2014.

Elcheroth, Guy and Stephen Reicher. *Identity, Violence and Power: Mobilising Hatred, Demobilising Dissent.* London: Palgrave Macmillan, 2017.

Ellemers, Naomi and Alexander Haslam, 'Social identity theory'. In *Handbook of Theories of Social Psychology*, edited by Paul Van Lange, Arie Kruglanski and E. Tory Higgins: 379–398. London: SAGE, 2012.

Eriksson, John. *Synthesis report, the International Response to Conflict and Genocide: Lessons from the Rwanda Experience. Joint Evaluation of Emergency Assistance to Rwanda.* London: Danida and ODI, 1996.

Evans, Gareth. 'The responsibility to protect: Rethinking humanitarian intervention'. (Proceedings of the Annual Meeting). *American Society of International Law,* Volume 98 (2004): 78–89.

Fairclough, Norman. *Analyzing Discourse.* London: Routledge, 2003.

Farré, Sébastien and Yan Schubert. 'L'illusion de l'objectif. Le délégué du CICR Maurice Rossel et les photographies de Theresienstadt'. *Le Mouvement Social,* Volume 2, no. 227 (2009): 65–83.

Fassin, Didier. 'Beyond good and evil? Questioning the anthropological discomfort with morals', *Anthropological Theory,* Volume 8, no. 4 (2008): 333–344.

Fast, Larissa. 'Mind the gap: Documenting and explaining violence against aid workers', *European Journal of International Relations,* 16 (2010): 1–25.

Fast, Larissa. *Aid in Danger: The Perils and Promise of Humanitarianism.* Philadelphia: University of Pennsylvania Press, 2014.

Fast, Larissa. 'Securitization and Threats to Humanitarian Workers' in *The Routledge Companion to Humanitarian Action*, edited by Roger Mac Ginty and Jenny Peterson, 313–321. London: Routledge, 2015.

Fearon, James and David Laitin. 'Ethnicity, insurgency, and civil war'. *The American Political Science Review,* Volume 97, no. 1 (2003): 75–90.

Fernando, Udeh and Dorothea Hilhorst. 'Everyday practices of humanitarian aid: Tsunami response in Sri Lanka'. *Development in Practice,* Volume 16, no. 3–4 (2006): 292–302.

Fierke, Karin and Nicola Mackay. 'To "see" is to break an entanglement: Quantum measurement, trauma and security'. *Security Dialogue* (2020): 1–17.

Finnemore, Martha. *National Interests in International Society.* Ithaca, NY: Cornell University Press, 1996.

Finnemore, Martha. 'Rules of war and wars of rules: The International Red Cross and the restraint of state violence'. In *Constructing World Culture: International Non-Governmental Organizations since 1875*, edited by and George Thomas, 149–165. Stanford, CA: Stanford University Press, 1999.

Finnemore, Martha. *The Purpose of Intervention: Changing Beliefs about the Use of Force.* Ithaca, NY: Cornell University Press, 2003.

Fiori, Juliana, Fernando Espada, Jessica Field and Sophie Dicker. *The Echo Chamber: Results, Management and the Humanitarian Affairs Agenda.* London: Humanitarian Affairs Team and Humanitarian and Conflict Response Institute, 2016.

Forsythe, David. 'International humanitarian assistance: The role of the Red Cross', *Buffalo Journal of International Law,* Volume 3 (1996): 235–260.

Forsythe, David. The International Committee of the Red Cross and humanitarian assistance – A policy analysis. *International Review of the Red Cross*, no. 314 (1996): 63–96.

Forsythe, David. *The Humanitarians: The International Committee of the Red Cross.* Cambridge, UK: Cambridge University Press, 2005.

Forsythe, David. 'The ICRC: A unique humanitarian protagonist'. *International Review of the Red Cross,* Volume 89, no. 865 (2007).

Forsythe, David. 'On contested concepts: Humanitarianism, human rights, and the notion of neutrality', *Journal of Human Rights,* Volume 12, no. 1 (2013): 59–68.

Forsythe, David and Barbara Ann Rieffer-Flanagan. *The International Committee of the Red Cross: A Neutral Humanitarian Actor.* London: Routledge, 2007.

Foucault, Michel. *Madness and Civilization: A History of Insanity in the Age of Reason.* Translated by Richard Howard. London: Tavistock, 1970.

Foucault, Michel. *The Order of Things,* English translation by Tavistok. London: Tavistock, 1970.

Foucault, Michel. *The Archaeology of Knowledge and the Discourse on Language.* Translated by Alan Sheridan-Smith. London: Tavistock, 1972.

Fraser-Moleketi, Geraldine. 'Towards a common understanding of corruption in Africa'. *Public Policy and Administration,* Volume 24, no. 3 (2009): 331–338.

Frostenson, Magnus. 'Humility in business: A contextual approach'. *Journal of Business Ethics,* 138 (2016): 91–102.

Fukuyama, Francis. *The End of History and the Last Man.* London: Penguin, 1992.

Fukuyama, Francis. *Identity: Contemporary Identity Politics and the Struggle for Recognition.* London: Profile Books, 2018.

Fürsich, Elfriede. 'In defense of textual analysis'. *Journalism Studies,* Volume 10, no. 2 (2009): 238–252.

George, Alexander and Andrew Bennett. *Case Studies and Theory Development in the Social Sciences.* Cambridge, MA: MIT Press, 2005.

Gill, Rebecca. 'The Rational Administration of Compassion: The Origins of British Relief in War'. *Le Mouvement Social,* Volume 227, no. 2 (2009): 9–26.

Gillard, Emanuela-Chiara. *Recommendations for Reducing Tensions in the Interplay Between Sanctions, Counterterrorism Measures and Humanitarian Action.* London: Chatham House, 2017.

Gordon, Stuart and Antonio Donini. 'Romancing principles and human rights: Are humanitarian principles salvageable?' *International Review of the Red Cross,* Volume 97, no. 897/898 (2016): 77–109.

Gordon-Gibson, Alasdair. 'Goma 1994: Notes from the field'. *Genocide Studies International,* Volume 10, no. 2 (2016): 254–267.

Götz, Norbert. 'Rationales of humanitarianism: The case of British relief to Germany, 1805–1815'. *Journal of Modern European History,* Volume 12, no. 2 (2014): 186–199.

Gross Stein, Janet. 'Communities of practice'. In *International Practices* edited by Emanuel Adler and Vincent Pouliot, 87–107. Cambridge, UK: Cambridge University Press, 2011.

Halabi, Samer and Arie Nadler. 'Receiving help: Consequences for the recipient'. In *The Psychology of Pro-Social Behavior,* edited by Stefan Stürmer and Mark Snyder, 121–138. Chichester, UK: Wiley-Blackwell, 2010.

Hancock, Graham. *The Lords of Poverty: The Power, Prestige, and Corruption of the International Aid Business.* New York: Atlantic Monthly Press, 1989.

Hansen, Lene. *Security as Practice. Discourse Analysis and the Bosnian War*. London: Routledge, 2006.

Hammond, Laura. 'The power of holding humanitarianism hostage and the myth of protective principles'. In *Humanitarianism in Question: Politics, Power, Ethics*, edited by Michael Barnett and Thomas Weiss, 172–195. Ithaca, NY: Cornell University Press, 2008.

Hardcastle, Rohan and Adrian Chua. 'Humanitarian assistance: Towards a right of access to victims of natural disasters'. *International Review of the Red Cross*, no. 325 (1998).

Harroff-Tavel, Marion. 'The International Committee of the Red Cross and the promotion of international humanitarian law: Looking back, looking forward'. *International Review of the Red Cross, 96 (895/896)* (2014): 817–857.

Harrowell, Elly and Alpaslan Özerdem. 'Negotiating reconstruction: Understanding hybridity in Sri Lanka's post-disaster and post-conflict reconstruction processes'. *Peacebuilding* Volume 8, no. 2 (2018): 218–239.

Harvey, Paul. 'International humanitarian actors and governments in areas of conflict: challenges, obligations, and opportunities'. *Disasters,* Volume 37 (Supplement 2) (2013): S151–S170.

Hassard, John and Denis Pym, eds. *The Theory and Philosophy of Organizations: Critical Issues and New Perspectives*. London: Routledge, 1990.

Hayden Patrick. *Political Evil in a Global Age: Hannah Arendt and International Theory*. London: Routledge, 2009.

Hayden, Patrick and Chamsy el-Ojeili, eds. *Globalization and Utopia: Critical Essays*. Basingstoke, UK: Palgrave Macmillan, 2009.

Hazeldine, Shaun and Matt Baillie Smith. *IFRC Global Review of Volunteering*, Geneva: IFRC, 2015.

Heller, Monica. 'Discourse and interaction'. In *The Handbook of Discourse Analysis,* edited by Deborah Schiffrin, Deborah Tannen and Heidi Hamilton, 250–264. Oxford, UK: Blackwell, 2001.

Henrich, Joseph, Steven Heine and Ara Norenzayan. 'The weirdest people in the world?' *Behavioral and Brain Sciences,* Volume 33 (2010): 61–135.

Hilhorst, Dorothea. 'Being good at doing good? Quality and accountability of humanitarian NGOs'. *Disasters,* Volume 26, no. 3 (2002): 193–212.

Hilhorst, Dorothea. 'Dead letter or living document? Ten years of the Code of Conduct for disaster relief'. *Disasters,* Volume 29, no. 4 (2005): 351–369.

Hilhorst, Dorothea and Bram Jansen. 'Humanitarian Space as Arena: A Perspective on the Everyday Politics of Aid'. *Development and Change,* Volume 41, no. 6 (2010): 1117–113.

Jonathan Hill and Thomas Wilson. 'Identity politics and the politics of identities'. *Identities: Global Studies in Culture and Power*, Volume 10, no. 1 (2003): 1–8. DOI: 10.1080/10702890304336

Honderich, Ted, ed. *Oxford Companion of Philosophy*. Oxford, UK: Oxford University Press, 1995.

Hopgood, Stephen. *The Endtimes of Human Rights*. Ithaca, NY: Cornell University Press, 2013.

Hsieh, Hsiu-Fang and Sarah Shannon. 'Three approaches to qualitative content analysis'. *Qualitative Health Research,* Volume 15, no. 9 (2005): 1277–1288.

Ignatieff, Michael. *The Ordinary Virtues: Moral Order in a Divided World.* Cambridge, MA: Harvard University Press, 2017.

Jabri, Vivienne. *War and the Transformation of Global Politics.* Basingstoke, UK: Palgrave Macmillan, 2007.

Jones, Ben and Marie-Juul Petersen. 'Instrumental, Narrow, Normative? Reviewing recent work on religion and development'. *Third World Quarterly,* Volume 32, no. 7 (2011): 1291–1306.

Kacowicz, Arie. 'Globalization, poverty, and the North-South divide'. *International Studies Review,* Volume 9, no. 4 (2007): 565–580.

Kaldor, Mary. *New and Old Wars.* Cambridge, UK: Polity Press, 2012.

Kant, Immanuel. *Groundwork of the Metaphysics of Morals.* German-English edition, edited by Jens Timmermann, English translation by Mary Gregor. Cambridge University Press [1786] 2011. https://www-cambridge-org.ezproxy.st-andrews.ac.uk/core/books/immanuel-kant-groundwork-of-the-metaphysics-of-morals/B91AC5779FCA0698B074C81C0D09DA48

Kapila, Mukesh. 'The Red Cross and Red Crescent'. In *The Routledge Companion to Humanitarian Action,* edited by Roger Mac Ginty and Jenny Peterson, 179–190. London: Routledge, 2015.

Käpylä, Juha and Denis Kennedy. 'Cruel to care? Investigating the governance of compassion in the humanitarian imaginary'. *International Theory,* Volume 6, no. 2 (2014): 255–292.

Karp, David and Kurt Mills. 'Human rights responsibilities of states and non-state actors'. In *Human Rights Protection in Global Politics,* edited by Kurt Mills and David Karp, 3–22. London: Palgrave.

Kennedy, David. *The Dark Sides of Virtue: Reassessing International Humanitarianism.* Princeton, NJ: Princeton University Press, 2004.

Kent, Randolph and Sophie Evans. 'Humanitarian futures'. In *The Routledge Companion to Humanitarian Action,* edited by Roger Mac Ginty and Jenny Peterson, 387–402. London: Routledge, 2015.

Khomba, James and Ella Kangaude-Ulaya. 'Indigenisation of corporate strategies in Africa: Lessons from the African Ubuntu philosophy'. *China-USA Business Review,* Volume 12, no. 7/ 121 (2013): 672–689.

Kluczewska, Karolina. 'How to translate "Good Governance" into Tajik? An American Good Governance Fund and norm localisation in Tajikistan'. *Journal of Intervention and Statebuilding* (2019): 1–20.

Kramer, Roderick. 'Trust and distrust in organizations: Emerging perspectives, enduring questions'. *Annual Review of Psychology,* Volume 50 (1999): 569–598.

Kramer, Roderick and Tom Tyler, eds. *Trust in Organizations: Frontiers and Theory of Research.* London: SAGE, 1996.

Kratochwil, Friedrich. 'Making sense of "international practices"'. In *International Practices,* edited by Emanuel Adler and Vincent Pouliot, 36–60. Cambridge, UK: Cambridge University Press, 2011.

Kratochwil, Friedrich. *Praxis: On Acting and Knowing.* Cambridge, UK: Cambridge University Press, 2018.

Kurasawa, Fuyuki. 'The sentimentalist paradox: On the normative and visual foundations of humanitarianism'. *Journal of Global Ethics,* Volume 9, no. 2 (2013): 201–214.

Lake, David. 'Why "isms" are evil: Theory, epistemology, and academic sects as impediments to understanding and progress'. *International Studies Quarterly,* Volume 55 (2011): 465–480.

Labbé, Jérémie and Pascal Daudin. 'Applying the humanitarian principles: Reflecting on the experience of the International Committee of the Red Cross'. *International Review of the Red Cross,* Volume 97, no. 897/898 (2016): 183–210.

League of Red Cross Societies. *Guide on Red Cross Volunteer Service.* Geneva: League of Red Cross Societies, 1952.

Lefebvre, Henri. *The Production of Space.* Translated by Nicholson-Smith. Oxford, UK: Blackwell, [1974] 1991.

Lewis, David. 'The myopic Foucauldian gaze: discourse, knowledge and the authoritarian peace'. *Journal of Intervention and Statebuilding,* Volume 11/1 (2017): 21–41.

Little, Richard. 'Britain's response to the Spanish Civil War: Investigating the implications of foregrounding practice for English School thinking'. In *International Practices,* edited by Emanuel Adler and Vincent Pouliot, 174–199. Cambridge, UK: Cambridge University Press, 2011.

Loh, Dylan and Jaako Heiskanen. 'Liminal sovereignty practices: Rethinking the inside/outside dichotomy'. *Cooperation and Conflict,* Volume 55, no. 3 (2020): 284–304. DOI: 10.1177/0010836720911391

Maček, Ivana. *Sarajevo under Siege: Anthropology in Wartime.* Philadelphia: University of Pennsylvania Press, 2009.

Mac Ginty, Roger. *International Peacebuilding and Local Resistance: Hybrid forms of peace.* London: Palgrave, 2011.

Mac Ginty, Roger. 'Everyday peace: Bottom-up and local agency in conflict-affected societies'. *Security Dialogue,* Volume 45, no. 6 (2014): 548–564.

Mac Ginty, Roger and Jenny Peterson, eds. *The Routledge Companion to Humanitarian Action.* London: Routledge, 2015.

Mac Ginty Roger and Andrew Williams. *Conflict and Development.* London: Routledge, 2009.

MacIntyre, Alasdair. *After Virtue: A Study in Moral Theory* (2nd Ed.). London: Duckworth, 1985.

Malkki, Lisa. 'Speechless emissaries: Refugees, humanitarianism, and dehistoricization'. *Cultural Anthropology,* Volume 11, no. 3 (1996): 377–404.

McCall, Daniel and Ana Iltis. 'Health care voluntourism: Addressing ethical concerns of undergraduate student participation in global health volunteer work'. *HEC Forum,* Volume 26 (2014): 285–297.

McGoldrick, Caroline. 'The future of humanitarian action: An ICRC perspective'. *International Review of the Red Cross,* Volume 93, no. 884 (2011): 965–991.

Merrifield, Andrew. 'Place and space: A Lefebvrian Reconciliation'. *Transactions of the Institute of British Geographers,* Volume 18, no. 4 (1993): 516–531.

Mills, Kurt. 'Neo-humanitarianism: The role of international humanitarian norms and organizations in contemporary conflict'. *Global Governance,* Volume 11, no. 2 (2005): 161–183.

Mills, Kurt. 'The postmodern tank of the humanitarian international'. *Journal of Social Justice,* 18 (2013): 261–267.

Mills, Kurt. *International Responses to Mass Atrocities in Africa*. Philadelphia: University of Pennsylvania Press, 2015.

Mills, Kurt and David Karp, eds. *Human Rights Protection in Global Politics: Responsibilities of States and Non-State Actors*. London: Palgrave Macmillan, 2015.

Moorehead, Caroline. *Dunant's Dream: War, Switzerland and the History of the Red Cross*. London: Harper Collins, 1998.

Morris-Suzuki, Tessa. 'Defining the boundaries of the Cold War nation: 1950s Japan and the other within'. *Japanese Studies*, Volume 26, no. 3 (2006): 303–316.

Moussa, Jasmine. 'Ancient origins, modern actors: Defining Arabic meanings of humanitarianism'. Humanitarian Policy Group Working Paper. London: ODI, 2014.

Moustakas, Clark. *Heuristic Research: Design, Methodology, and Applications*. Newbury Park, CA: SAGE, 1990.

Moyn, Samuel. *The Last Utopia: Human Rights in History*. Cambridge: Belknap Press, 2010.

Moynier, Gustave. 'Comité International: ce que c'est que le croix rouge'. *Bulletin International des Sociétés de la Croix -Rouge*, Volume 6, no. 21 [1875] 2009: 1–8.

Murer, Jeffrey. 'Political violence: Benjamin, Bourdieu, and the Law'. In *Oxford Handbook of U.S. National Security*, edited by Derek Reveron, Nikolas Gvosdev and John Cloud, 495–508. Oxford, UK: Oxford University Press, 2018.

Nielsen, Robert and Jennifer Marrone, 'Humility: Our current understanding of the construct and its role in organizations'. *International Journal of Management Reviews*, Volume 20 (2018): 805–824.

Niland, Norah. 'Protection and instrumentalization: The contemporary Solferino?' In *The Golden Fleece: Manipulation and Independence in Humanitarian Action*, edited by Antonio Donini, 219–240. Sterling VA: Kumarian Press, 2012.

Nussbaum, Martha. *Love's Knowledge – Essays on Philosophy and Literature*. Oxford, UK: Oxford University Press, 1992.

Nussbaum, Martha. *Women and Human Development: The Capabilities Approach*. Cambridge, UK: Cambridge University Press, 2000.

Nussbaum, Martha. *Frontiers of Justice*. Cambridge, MA: Belknap Press, 2006.

Nussbaum, Martha. *Creating Capabilities: The Human Development Approach*. Cambridge, MA: Harvard University Press, 2011.

Nussbaum, Martha. 'Human capabilities and animal lives: Conflict, wonder, law: A symposium'. *Journal of Human Development and Capabilities*, Volume 18, no. 3 (2017): 317–321.

Nyamnjoh, Francis. 'Incompleteness: Frontier Africa and the currency of conviviality'. *Journal of Asian and African Studies*, Volume 52, no. 3 (2017): 53–270.

Oakley, Barbara, Ariel Knafo, Guruprasad Madhavan and David Sloan Wilson, eds. *Pathological Altruism*. Oxford, UK: Oxford University Press, 2012.

Ober, Josiah. 'Meritocratic and civic dignity in Greco-Roman antiquity'. In *Cambridge Handbook on Human Dignity*, edited by Marcus Düwell, Jens Braarvig, Roger Brownsword and Dietmar Mieth, 53–63. Cambridge, UK: Cambridge University Press, 2010.

O'Callaghan, Sorcha and Leslie Leach. 'The relevance of the Fundamental Principles to operations: learning from Lebanon'. *International Review of the Red Cross,* Volume 95, no. 890 (2013): 287–307.

O'Farrell, Clare. *Foucault: Historian or Philosopher?* Basingstoke: Macmillan, 1989.

Orwin, Clifford. *The Humanity of Thucydides.* Princeton, NJ: Princeton University Press, 1997.

Ostrom, Elinor. 'Toward a behavioral theory linking trust, reciprocity and reputation'. In *Trust and Reciprocity. Interdisciplinary Lessons from Experimental Research,* edited by Elinor Ostrom and James Walker, 19–79. New York: Russell Sage, 2003.

Ostrom, Elinor and James Walker, eds. *Trust and Reciprocity. Interdisciplinary Lessons from Experimental Research.* New York: Russell Sage, 2003.

Pacitto, Julia and Elena Fiddian-Qasmiyeh. 'Writing the "Other" into humanitarian discourse framing theory and practice in South-South humanitarian responses to forced displacement'. Oxford University Refugee Studies Centre, Working Paper series no. 93 (2013).

Parekh, Bhikhu. 'The cultural particularity of liberal democracy'. *Political Studies,* Special Issue (1992): 160–175.

Patton, Michael. *Qualitative Research and Evaluation Methods (3rd Edition).* Thousand Oaks, CA: SAGE, 2002.

Petersen, Jenny. 'Introduction'. In *The Routledge Companion to Humanitarian Action,* edited by Roger Mac Ginty and Jenny Petersen, 1–9. London: Routledge, 2015.

Petersen, Marie-Juul. *For Humanity or for the Umma? Aid and Islam in Transnational Muslim NGO.* London: Hurst, 2015.

Philo, Greg. 'Can discourse analysis successfully explain the content of media and journalistic practice?' *Journalism Studies,* Volume 8, no. 2 (2007): 175–196.

Pictet, Jean. *The Principles of the Red Cross.* Geneva: ICRC, 1956.

Pictet, Jean. 'The Fundamental Principles of the Red Cross'. *International Review of the Red Cross,* Volume 19 (1979): 130–149. https://international-review.icrc.org/sites/default/files/S0020860400067218a.pdf

Polman, Linda. *War Games: The Story of Aid and War in Modern Times.* London: Penguin, 2011.

Powell Walter and Paul DiMaggio. *The New Institutionalism in Organisational Analysis.* Chicago, IL: University of Chicago Press, 1991.

Prunier, Gérard. *Africa's World War: Congo, the Rwandan Genocide, and the Making of a Continental Catastrophe.* Oxford, UK: Oxford University Press, 2009.

PytlikZillig, Lisa and Christopher Kimbrough. 'Consensus on conceptualizations and definitions of trust: Are we there yet?' In *Interdisciplinary Perspectives on Trust,* edited by Ellie Shockley, Tess Neal, Lisa PytlikZillig and Brian Bornstein, 17–47. London: Springer, 2016.

Radice, Henry. 'Saving ourselves? On rescue and humanitarian action'. *Review of International Studies,* Volume 45, no. 3 (2019): 431–448.

Rawls, John. 'Justice as fairness'. *Philosophical Review,* Volume 67, no. 2 (1958): 164–194.

Rawls, John. *A Theory of Justice* (revised edition). Cambridge MA: Belknap Press, 1971 [1999].

Redmond, Anthony. 'Professionalisation of the Humanitarian Response'. In *The Routledge Companion to Humanitarian Action*, edited by Roger Mac Ginty and Jenny Peterson, 403–416. London: Routledge, 2015.

Reicher, Stephen and Alexander Haslam. 'Beyond help: A social psychology of collective solidarity and social cohesion'. In *The Psychology of Prosocial Behavior*, edited by Stefan Stürmer and Mark Schneider, 289–310. Chichester, UK: Wiley-Blackwell, 2010.

Rességuier, Anaïs. 'The moral sense of humanitarian actors: An empirical exploration'. *Disasters*, Volume 42, no. 1 (2018): 62–80.

Richmond, Oliver. 'The globalization of responses to conflict and the peacebuilding'. *Cooperation and Conflict*, Volume 39/129 (2004).

Richmond, Oliver. 'Rescuing Peacebuilding? Anthropology and Peace Formation'. *Global Society* (2018).

Rieff, David. *A Bed for the Night: Humanitarianism in Crisis*. London: Random House, 2002.

Rochester, Colin, Angela Paine and Steven Howlett, eds. *Volunteering & Society in the 21st Century*. Basingstoke, UK: Palgrave Macmillan, 2010.

Rodogno, Davide. 'Beyond relief: A sketch of the Near East Relief's humanitarian operations, 1918–1929'. *Monde(s)*, no. 6 (2014): 45–64.

Rogers, Peter. 'Family is NOT an institution: Distinguishing institutions from organisations in social science and social theory'. *International Review of Sociology*, Volume 27, no. 1 (2017): 126–141.

Roughneen, Dualta. *Humanitarian Subsidiarity: A New Principle?* Cambridge, UK: Cambridge Scholars Publishing, 2017.

Rousseau, Jean-Jacques. *The Social Contract*. Translated by Maurice Cranston (2nd Edition). London: Penguin, [1762] 2004.

Rousseau, Denise, Sim Sitkin, Ronald Burt and Colin Camerer. 'Not so different after all: A cross-discipline view of trust'. *The Academy of Management Review*, Volume 23, no. 3 (1998): 393–404.

Rubenstein, Jennifer. *Between Samaritans and States*. Oxford, UK: Oxford University Press, 2015.

Sandel, Michael, ed., *Liberalism and Its Critics*. Oxford, UK: Blackwell, 1984.

Sandel, Michael. *Liberalism and the Limits of Justice* (2nd edition). Cambridge, UK: Cambridge University Press, 1998.

Sandel, Michael. *Justice: What's the Right Thing to Do?* London: Penguin, 2009.

Schatzki, Theodore, Karin Knorr Cetina and Eike von Savigny, eds. *The Practice Turn in Contemporary Theory*. London: Routledge, 2011.

Schenkenberg van Mierop, Ed. *Local humanitarian actors and the principle of impartiality*. Geneva: HERE, 2017.

Schiffrin, Deborah, Deborah Tannen and Heidi Hamilton, eds. *The Handbook of Discourse Analysis*. Oxford, UK: Blackwell, 2001.

Scott, W Richard. *Institutions and Organizations* (2nd Ed.). London: Foundations for Organizational Science/Sage, 2001.

Selth, Andrew. 'Even paranoids have enemies: Cyclone Nargis and Myanmar's fears of invasion'. *Contemporary Southeast Asia: A Journal of International and Strategic Affairs*, Volume 30, no. 3 (2008): 379–402.

Sen, Amartya. *Poverty and Famines*. Oxford, UK: Clarendon, 1981.

Sen, Amartya. *Commodities and Capabilities*. Oxford, UK: Oxford University Press, 1985.

Sen, Amartya. *Development as Freedom*. Oxford, UK: Oxford University Press, 1999.

Siddiqi, Ayesha. 'Disasters in conflict areas: Finding the politics'. *Disasters*, 42(S2) (2018): S161–S172.

Siddiqi, Ayesha and Jose Canuday. 'Stories from the frontlines: Decolonising social contracts for disasters'. *Disasters*, Volume 42, no. S2 (2018): S215–S238.

Sil, Rudra and Peter Katzenstein. 'Analytic eclecticism in the study of world politics: Reconfiguring problems and mechanisms across research traditions'. *Perspectives on Politics*, Volume 8, no. 2 (2010): 411–431.

Simpson, John and Edmund Weiner, eds. *Oxford English Dictionary (2nd edition)*. Oxford, UK: Oxford University Press, 1989.

Slim, Hugo. 'Doing the right thing: Relief agencies, moral dilemmas and moral responsibility in political emergencies and war'. *Disasters*, Volume 21, no. 3 (1997): 244–257.

Slim, Hugo. 'Not philanthropy but rights: The proper politicisation of humanitarian philosophy'. *International Journal of Human Rights*, Volume 6, no. 2 (2002): 1–22.

Slim, Hugo. *A Call to Alms: Humanitarian Action and the Art of War*. Geneva: Centre for Humanitarian Dialogue, 2004.

Slim, Hugo. 'Wonderful work: Globalising the ethics of humanitarian action'. In *The Routledge Companion to Humanitarian action*, edited by Roger Mac Ginty and Jenny Peterson, 13–25. London: Routledge, 2015.

Sommaruga, Cornelio. 'Address by the president of the International Committee of the Red Cross'. *International Review of the Red Cross*, Volume 300 (1994): 281–282.

Srivastava, Prachi and Nick Hopwood. 'A practical iterative framework for qualitative data analysis'. *International Journal of Qualitative Methods*, Volume 8, no. 1 (2009): 76–84.

Stevens, Matthew. 'The collapse of social networks among Syrian refugees in urban Jordan'. *Contemporary Levant, Volume* 1, no. 1 (2016): 51–63.

Stewart, Alan. 'Humanity at a Price: Erasmus, Bude, and the Poverty of Philology'. In *At the Borders of the Human: Beasts, Bodies and Natural Philosophy in the Early Modern Period*, edited by Erika Fudge, Ruth Gilbert and Susan Wiseman, 9–25. Basingstoke, UK: Macmillan, 1999.

Stirrat, Roderick. 'Competitive humanitarianism: Relief and the tsunami in Sri Lanka'. *Anthropology Today*, Volume 22, no. 5. (2006): 11–6.

Stirrat, Roderick and Heiko Henkel. 'The development gift: The problem of reciprocity in the NGO World'. *Annals of the American Academy of Political and Social Science*, Volume 554 (1997): 66–80.

Stürmer, Stefan and Mark Snyder. *The Psychology of Pro-Social Behavior*. Chichester, UK: Wiley-Blackwell, 2010.

Swidler, Ann. 'What anchors cultural practices'. In *The Practice Turn in Contemporary Theory*, edited by Theodore Schatzki, Karin Cetina and Eike von Savigny, 83–101. London: Routledge, 2001.

Taithe, Bertrand. ' "Cold calculation in the faces of horrors?" Pity, compassion and the making of humanitarian protocols'. In *Medicine, Emotion and Disease,*

1700–1950, edited by Fay Bound Alberti, 79–99. London: Palgrave Macmillan, 2006. https://doi.org/10.1057/9780230286030_4

Taithe, Bertrand. 'Humanitarian history?' In *The Routledge Companion to Humanitarian Action*, edited by Roger Mac Ginty and Jenny Petersen, 62–73. London: Routledge, 2015.

Tajfel, Henri, ed. *Social Identity and Intergroup Relations*. Cambridge, UK: Cambridge University Press, 1982.

Tansley, Donald. 'Re-appraisal of the role of the Red Cross'. *International Review of the Red Cross*, Volume 14, no. 155 (1974): 71–75.

Tansley, Donald. *Final Report: An Agenda for Red Cross – Re-appraisal of the Role of the Red Cross*. Geneva: ICRC, 1975.

Taylor, Charles. 'Interpretation and the sciences of man'. *The Review of Metaphysics*, Volume 25, no. 1 (1971): 3–51.

Taylor, Charles. *Hegel*. Cambridge, UK: Cambridge University Press, 1975.

Taylor, Charles. *Sources of the Self: The making of the modern identity*. Cambridge, UK: Cambridge University Press, 1989.

Taylor, Charles. 'Modern social imaginaries'. *Public Culture*, Volume 14, no. 1 (2002): 91–124.

Telford, John and John Cosgrave. *Joint Evaluation of the International Response to the Indian Ocean Tsunami: Synthesis Report*. London: Tsunami Evaluation Coalition, 2006.

Telford, John and John Cosgrave, 'The international humanitarian system and the 2004 Indian Ocean earthquake and tsunamis'. *Disasters*, Volume 31, no. 1 (2007): 1–28.

Terry, Fiona. *Condemned to Repeat? The Paradox of Humanitarian Action*. Ithaca NY: Cornell University Press, 2002.

Thomassen, Bjørn. 'The uses and meanings of liminality'. *International Political Anthropology*, Volume 2, no. 1 (2009): 1–27.

Thomassen, Bjørn. 'Revisiting liminality: The danger of empty spaces'. In *Liminal Landscapes: Travel, Experience and Spaces In-between*, edited by Hazel Andrews and Les Roberts, 21–34. London: Routledge, 2012.

Tronc, Emmanuel, Rob Grace and Anaïde Nahikian. 'Humanitarian access obstruction in Somalia: Externally imposed and self-inflicted dimensions'. *Humanitarian Action at the Frontlines: Field Analysis Series*. Cambridge MA: Harvard Humanitarian Initiative, 2018.

Tuomela, Raimo. *Social Ontology: Collective Intentionality and Group Agents*. Oxford, UK: Oxford University Press, 2013.

Turner, John. 'Towards a cognitive redefinition of the social group'. In *Social Identity and Intergroup Relations*, edited by Henry Tajfel, 15–40. Cambridge, UK: Cambridge University Press, 1982.

Turner, Robert, Jock Baker, Zaw Myo Oo and Naing Soe Aye. *Inter-Agency Real Time Evaluation of the Response to Cyclone Nargis*. United Nations Office for the Coordination of Humanitarian Affairs on behalf of the Inter Agency Standing Committee, 2008. https://www.unocha.org/sites/unocha/files/dms/Documents/IA_RTE_Nargis_Response_Final_Report_with_pics%5B1%5D.pdf

Turner, Stephen. *The Social Theory of Practices: Tradition, Tacit Knowledge and Presuppositions*. London: Polity, 1994.

Turner, Stephen, ed. *The Cambridge Companion to Weber*. Cambridge, UK: Cambridge University Press, 2000.

Turner, Victor. *The Forest of Symbols: Aspects of Ndembu Ritual*. Ithaca, NY: Cornell University Press, 1967.

Turner, Victor. *The Ritual Process: Structure and Anti-structure*. Chicago: Aldine, 1969.

Twigg, John and Irina Mosel. 'Emergent groups and spontaneous volunteers in urban disaster response'. *Environment & Urbanization*, Volume 29, no. 2 (2017): 443–458.

Tyler, Tom. 'Social Justice'. In *Blackwell Handbook of Social Psychology: Intergroup Processes*, edited by Rupert Brown and Samuel Gaertner, 344–366. Oxford, UK: Blackwell, 2001.

Tyler, Tom and Peter Degoey. 'Collective restraint in social dilemmas: Procedural justice and social identification effects on support for authorities'. *Journal of Personality and Social Psychology*, Volume 69, no. 3 (1995): 482–497.

Tyler, Tom and Peter Degoey. 'Trust in organizational authorities. The influence of motive attributions on willingness to accept decisions'. In *Trust in Organizations: frontiers and theory of research*, edited by Roderick Kramer and Tom Tyler, 331–356. London: SAGE, 1996.

Tyler, Tom, Peter Degoey and Heather Smith. 'Understanding why the justice of group procedures matters: A test of the psychological dynamics of the group-value model'. *Journal of Personality and Social Psychology*, Volume 70, no. 5 (1996): 913–930.

van Dijk, Teun. 'Critical Discourse Analysis'. In *The Handbook of Discourse Analysis*, edited by Deborah Schiffrin, Deborah Tannen and Heidi Hamilton, 352–371. Oxford, UK: Blackwell, 2001.

van Gennep, Arnold. *The Rites of Passage*. Chicago: University of Chicago Press, 1960.

van Leeuwen, Esther and Suzanne Täuber. 'The strategic side of out-group helping'. In *The Psychology of Prosocial Behavior*, edited by Stefan Stürmer and Mark Snyder, 81–99. Chichester, UK: Wiley-Blackwell, 2010.

Vaux, Tony. *The Selfish Altruist*. London: Earthscan, 2001.

ver Beek, Kurt. 'Spirituality: A development taboo'. *Development in Practice*, Volume 10, no. 1 (2000): 31–43.

Walker, Peter. 'Cracking the code: The genesis, use and future of the Code of Conduct'. *Disasters*, Volume 29, no. 4 (2005): 323–336.

Walker, Peter and Daniel Maxwell. *Shaping the Humanitarian World*. Abingdon, UK: Routledge, 2009.

Walker, Peter and Larry Minear. 'One for all and all for one: Support and assistance models for an effective IFRC'. *A Report for the International Federation of Red Cross and Red Crescent Societies* (Executive Summary & Conclusions). Medford, MA: Feinstein International Center, Tufts University, 2004.

Walker, Peter and Susan Purdin. 'Birthing Sphere'. *Disasters*, Volume 28, no. 2 (2004): 100–111.

Weinert, Matthew. *Making Human: World Order and the Global Governance of Human Dignity*. Ann Arbor: University of Michigan Press, 2015.

Weiss, Thomas. *Military-Civilian Interactions: Intervening in Humanitarian Crises*. Boulder, CO: Rowman & Littlefield, 1999.

Weiss, Thomas. *Humanitarian Business*. Cambridge, UK: Polity, 2013.

Weissman, Fabrice, ed. *In the Shadow of 'Just Wars': Violence, Politics, and Humanitarian Action*. Ithaca NY: Cornell University Press, 2004.

Welsford, Enid. *The Fool: His Social and Literary History*. London: Faber and Faber, 1935.

Wilkinson, Iain. 'The problem of understanding modern humanitarianism and its sociological value'. *International Social Science Journal*, Volume 65, (2016): 65–78.

Williams, Andrew. *Liberalism and War: The Victors and the Vanquished*. Abingdon, UK: Routledge, 2006.

Williams, Andrew. *Failed Imagination? The Anglo-American New World Order from Wilson to Bush*. Manchester, UK: Manchester University Press, 2007.

Williams, Paul, ed. *The Fool and the Trickster: Studies in Honour of Enid Welsford*. Cambridge, UK: Brewer, 1979.

Wilson, David Sloan. *Darwin's Cathedral: Evolution, Religion, and the Nature of Society*. Chicago: University of Chicago Press, 2002.

Wilson, David Sloan. *Does Altruism Exist? Culture, Genes and the Welfare of Others*. New Haven, CT: Yale University Press, 2015.

Wolch, Jennifer. *The Shadow State: Government and Voluntary Sector in Transition*. New York: The Foundation Center, 1990.

Wright, Stephen. 'Strategic collective action: Social psychology and social change'. In *Blackwell Handbook of Social Psychology: Intergroup Processes*, edited by Rupert Brown and Samuel Gaertner, 409–430. Oxford, UK: Blackwell, 2001.

ONLINE DOCUMENTS

Abu-Ismail, Khalid, Omar Imady, Aljaz Kuncic and Osama Nojoum. Syria at War: 5 years on. UN ESCWA, 2016. https://www.unescwa.org/publications/syria-war-five-years

ACAPS. Humanitarian access overview (2018). https://www.acaps.org/key_document/key_document/344

Ahmad, Masitoh, Muhammad Ahmad, Jamil Hashim and Wan Sabri Yusuf. The role of religion in higher education funding: Special reference to Hinduism and Buddhism in Malaysia. *GJAT,* Volume 6, no. 1/69 (2016). http://www.gjat.my/gjat062016/10420160601.pdf

ALNAP. The state of the humanitarian system. London: ODI, 2018. https://sohs.alnap.org/system/files/content/resource/files/main/SOHS%202018%20full%20report%20online.pdf

Davis, Austen. Accountability and humanitarian actors: Speculations and questions. *Humanitarian Exchange,* no. 24 (2003): 16–18. https://odihpn.org/wp-content/uploads/2003/10/humanitarianexchange024.pdf

Barnett, Michael and Peter Walker. 'Regime change for humanitarian aid'. *Foreign Affairs* (July 2016). https://www.foreignaffairs.com/articles/2015-06-16/regime-change-humanitarian-aid

Bennett, Christina. 'Constructive deconstruction: Imagining alternative humanitarian action'. HPG Working Paper. Humanitarian Policy Group/ODI, (2018). https://odi.org/en/publications/constructive-deconstruction-imagining-alternative-humanitarian-action/

Benthall, Jonathan. `Charity'. *In Cambridge Encyclopedia of Anthropology* https://www.anthroencyclopedia.com/entry/charity

Booth, D. and Unsworth, S. Politically smart, locally led development (2014). https://www.odi.org/sites/odi.org.uk/files/odi-assets/publications-opinion-files/9204.pdf

Bond. *Counter Terrorism Bill: Aid workers to be exempt from damaging law* (2019). https://www.bond.org.uk/news/2019/01/counter-terrorism-bill-aid-workers-to-be-exempt-from-damaging-law

Bruderlein, Claude, ed. *Field manual on frontline humanitarian negotiation*. Centre of Competence on Humanitarian Negotiation (2018). https://frontline-negotiations.org/wp-content/uploads/2018/11/CCHN-Field-Manual-3.pdf

Cohon, Rachel. 'Hume's moral philosophy', *The Stanford Encyclopedia of Philosophy*, edited by Edward Zalta (2018). https://plato.stanford.edu/entries/hume-moral/

Daccord, Yves. 'Beyond the "humanitarian #MeToo moment", the real crisis is one of power and trust' (2018). http://news.trust.org/item/20180423131126-rzqup

Davey, Stephen. 'Strategy 2010: All Change at the Feds?' *Humanitarian Exchange*, 17 (2000). http://www.odihpn.org/humanitarian-exchange-magazine/issue-17/strategy-2010-all-change-at-the-fed

Department for Aid and Trade (DFAT). *Effective Governance: Strategy for Australia's aid investments*, March 2015. Commonwealth of Australia Publication. http://dfat.gov.au/about-us/publications/Documents/effective-governance-strategy-for-australias-aid-investments.pdf

Djuraskovic, Ivana and Nancy Arthur. 'Heuristic inquiry: A personal journey of acculturation and identity reconstruction'. *The Qualitative Report*, Volume 15, no. 6 (2010): 1569–1593. https://nsuworks.nova.edu/tqr/vol15/iss6/12

Hayder, Masood. 'Humanitarianism and the Muslim World'. *Journal of Humanitarian Assistance*. Feinstein International Center, Tufts University (2007). https://sites.tufts.edu/jha/archives/52

Healy, Sean and Sandrine Tiller. Where is everyone? Responding to emergencies in the most difficult places. MSF (2014). https://www.msf.org/sites/msf.org/files/msf-whereiseveryone_-def-lr_-_july.pdf

Heyes, Cressida. 'Identity politics'. In *The Stanford Encyclopedia of Philosophy*, edited by Edward Zalta (2017). https://plato.stanford.edu/archives/fall2017/entries/identity-politics/

Hilhorst, Dorothea. 'Classical humanitarianism and resilience humanitarianism: making sense of two brands of humanitarian action'. *Journal of International Humanitarian Action*, Volume 3, no. 15 (2018). https://jhumanitarianaction.springeropen.com/articles/10.1186/s41018-018-0043-6

ICRC 1996. *The Fundamental Principles of the Red Cross and Red Crescent*. https://www.icrc.org/en/doc/assets/files/other/icrc_002_0513.pdf

ICRC, 2007. *Statutes of the Red Cross and Red Crescent Movement*. https://www.icrc.org/eng/assets/files/other/statutes-en-a5.pdf

ICRC, 2011. *Report of the 31st International Conference of the Red Cross and Red Crescent – Including the Summary Report of the 2011 Council of Delegates.*

https://www.icrc.org/en/publication/1129-report-31st-international-conference-red-cross-and-red-crescent-including-summary

ICRC, 2016. *Strengthening Movement Coordination and Cooperation.* https://www.icrc.org/en/doc/assets/files/red-cross-crescent-movement/council-delegates-2013/cod13-r4-movement-coordination-adopted-eng.pdf

International Committee of the Red Cross. Council of Delegates of the International Red Cross and Red Crescent Movement, Geneva, 23–24 November 2007. https://www.icrc.org/en/doc/resources/documents/publication/p1108.htm

Global Post, 2012. *Haiti: Two years after the earthquake, where did the money go?* https://www.pri.org/stories/2012-01-11/haiti-two-years-after-earthquake-where-did-money-go

International Federation of Red Cross and Red Crescent Societies (IFRC). Constitution (Original 1987, revised and adopted by 16th session of the General Assembly, Geneva, November 2007). https://www.ifrc.org/Global/Governance/Statutory/Constitution_revised-en.pdf

IFRC. *Operations Update 28*, 19 April 2010. https://reliefweb.int/sites/reliefweb.int/files/resources/2615D4513937FAED4925770B0010AEC0-Full_Report.pdf

IFRC. *Operations Update 29*, 30 September 2010. https://reliefweb.int/sites/reliefweb.int/files/resources/12A420853C90DBDCC12577B30033AB33-Full_Report.pdf

IFRC. *Strengthening local humanitarian action.* 31st International Conference (2011). https://fednet.ifrc.org/en/ourifrc/statutory-meetings/internationalconference/31st-international-conferencea/strengthening-local-humanitarian-action/

IFRC. Global review on volunteering (2011). https://www.ifrc.org/en/what-we-do/volunteers/global-review-on-volunteering/

IFRC. World Disasters Report, (WDR), 2015. https://www.ifrc.org/en/publications-and-reports/world-disasters-report/

International Review of the Red Cross (The Review). 'Applying the Fundamental Principles of the Red Cross and Red Crescent: a subject for continued thought'. *International Review of the Red Cross,* Volume 29, no. 273 (1989). https://international-review.icrc.org/sites/default/files/S0020860400074842a.pdf

Kapila, Mukesh. 'Humanitarians need to do less to do more', *The Guardian*, 12 January, 2017. https://www.theguardian.com/global-development-professionals-network/2017/jan/12/humanitarians-need-to-do-less-to-do-more

Kant, I. *Groundwork of the Metaphysics of Morals.* The Cambridge Kant German-English Edition, M. Gregor & J. Timmermann (Eds.). Cambridge: Cambridge University Press. E Book, [1785] 2011. https://www-cambridge-org.ezproxy.st-andrews.ac.uk/core/books/immanuel-kant-groundwork-of-the-metaphysics-of-morals/B91AC5779FCA0698B074C81C0D09DA48

Kreševljaković, Nihad. 'Humor under siege: Mujo, don't jump around, you'll get hungry'. *Al Jazeera*. http://balkans.aljazeera.net/vijesti/humor-under-siege-mujo-dont-jump-around-youll-get-hungry

Mayring, Philipp (2000). Qualitative Content Analysis. *Forum Qualitative Sozialforschung / Forum: Qualitative Social Research, 1*(2), Art. 20, http://nbnresolving.de/urn:nbn:de:0114-fqs0002204

Moynier, Gustave. Comité International: ce que c'est que le croix rouge. *Bulletin International,* Volume 6, no. 21 [1875] 2009. https://www.cambridge.org/core/

journals/bulletin-international-des-societes-de-la-croix-rouge/article/ce-que-cest-que-la-croix-rouge/07182F93914C5BE836E8C7E4E7A1D773

Norwegian Red Cross. *Executive summary, humanitarian access in Iraq.* HERE NRC Report (2017). https://www.nrc.no/resources/reports/principled-humanitarian-assistance-of-echo-partners-in-iraq/

Red Cross and Red Crescent Movement (RCRC). *Strengthening Movement Coordination and Cooperation (SMCC). Resolution CD/15/R1.* Council of Delegates of the International Red Cross and Red Crescent Movement, Geneva, 7 December 2015. http://rcrcconference.org/wp-content/uploads/2015/03/CoD15-R1-SMCC_EN.pdf

Red Cross and Red Crescent Movement (RCRC). *Strengthening Movement Coordination and Cooperation (SMCC): Optimizing the Movement's humanitarian response.* Progress report. Council of Delegates, Geneva.Doc CD/15/5 (2015) http://rcrcconference.org/app//uploads/2015/03/CoD15_SMCC_report-FINAL-EN.pdf

Schenkenberg van Mierop, Ed. 'Local humanitarian actors and the principle of impartiality'. In *Based on Need Alone? Impartiality in Humanitarian Action.* MSF Germany, Caritas Germany, Diakonia (2018): 60–71. http://chaberlin.org/wp-content/uploads/2019/02/humhilfe-studie-unparteilichkeit_2018_Mierop_EN.pdf

Schenkenberg van Mierop, Ed and Marzia Montemurro, weblog HERE-Geneva, 6 February 2020. http://here-geneva.org/keep-it-complex-stupid/

Slim, Hugo. 'By what authority? The legitimacy and accountability of non-governmental organisations'. Journal of Humanitarian Aid (2002). https://www.jha.ac/a082/

Slim, Hugo. *Marketing humanitarian space: Argument and method in humanitarian persuasion.* Geneva: Centre for Humanitarian Dialogue, 2003. https://www.alnap.org/system/files/content/resource/files/main/hd-slim-marketing-humanitarian-space.pdf

Slim, Hugo. 'Global welfare: A realistic expectation for the international humanitarian system?' *ALNAP Review of Humanitarian Action* (2006): 1–34. https://www.alnap.org/system/files/content/resource/files/main/ch1-f1.pdf

Slim, Hugo. ICRC Partnerships, Today and Tomorrow, in conflict and disaster. Speech given at the 5th Singapore Red Cross Conference on the theme of partnerships and volunteerism for humanity, 20 July 2019. https://www.icrc.org/en/document/icrc-partnerships-today-and-tomorrow-conflict-and-disaster

Slim, Hugo. *Impartiality and intersectionality.* ICRC Humanitarian Law and Policy weblog, 16 January 2018 https://blogs.icrc.org/law-and-policy/2018/01/16/impartiality-and-intersectionality/

Stoddard, Abby, Adele Harmer and Monica Czwarno. *Aid Worker Security Report 2017. Behind the Attacks: A Look at the Perpetrators of Violence against Aid Workers.* Humanitarian Outcomes. https://www.humanitarianoutcomes.org/sites/default/files/publications/awsr_2017.pdf

United Nations General Assembly (UNGA). Resolution 46/182, Strengthening of the coordination of humanitarian emergency assistance of the United Nations. Adopted 19th December 1991. https://undocs.org/A/RES/46/182

United Nations General Assembly (UNGA). Resolution 56/38, Recommendations on support for volunteering. Adopted 10th January 2002. http://dag.un.org/bitstream/handle/11176/237258/A_RES_56_38-EN.pdf?sequence=3&isAllowed=y

United Nations Volunteers (UNV). *Transforming Governance*. United Nations Development Programme, State of the World's Volunteerism Report (2015). https://www. unv.org/swvr/2015-state-worlds-volunteerism-report-swvr-transforming-governance

United Nations Volunteers (UNV). *The thread that binds: Volunteerism and community Resilience*. United Nations Volunteers, State of the World's Volunteerism Report (2018). https://www.unv.org/sites/default/files/UNV_SWVR_2018_English_WEB.pdf

Webster, Mackinnon and Peter Walker. *One for All and All for One: Intra-Organizational Dynamics in Humanitarian Action*. Feinstein International Center, Tufts University, 2009. https://fic.tufts.edu/wp-content/uploads/one-for-all-and-all-for-one-2009.pdf

MEDIA ARTICLES

Webster, Donovan. 'Haiti: Two years after the earthquake, where did the money go?' *Global Post*, 11 January 2012. https://www.pri.org/stories/2012-01-11/haiti-two-years-after-earthquake-where-did-money-go

Wijedasa, Namini. 'NGO fat cats: True, false or exaggerated?' *The Island*, 12 February 2006. http://www.island.lk/2006/02/12/features10.html

UNPUBLISHED SOURCES/MPHIL, PHD THESES

Dikaia Chatziefstathio. 'The changing nature of the ideology of Olympism in the modern Olympic era'. PhD Thesis, Loughborough University, 2005. https://dspace. lboro.ac.uk/dspace-jspui/bitstream/2134/2820/1/Thesis-2005-Chatziefstathiou.pdf

Douglass, Robin. 'The moral psychology of the social contract: Rousseau's republican citizenship'. Paper presented at the School of History, University of St Andrews, November 2018.

Gordon-Gibson, Alasdair. 'Humanitarian space – The quest for a protected niche in the global arena'. MPhil Thesis, University of St Andrews, 2015. https://research-repository.st-andrews.ac.uk/bitstream/handle/10023/11855/AlasdairGordon-Gibson MPhilThesis.pdf?sequence=2

Petersen, Marie-Juul. 'For humanity or for the Umma? Ideologies of aid in four transnational Muslim NGOs'. Ph.D. thesis, University of Copenhagen, 2011. https://www.researchgate.net/publication/256281060

Radice, Henry. 'The politics of humanity: Humanitarianism and international political theory'. Ph.D. thesis, London School of Economics, 2010. http://etheses.lse.ac.uk/1008/

Schwarze, Tilman. 'Space, violence and resistance: A Lefebvrian analysis of everyday life on Chicago's South Side'. Ph.D. thesis, University of St Andrews, 2020.

Tsukayama, John. 'By any means necessary: An interpretive phenomenological analysis study of post 9/11 American abusive violence in Iraq'. Ph.D. thesis, University of St Andrews, 2014. http://hdl.handle.net/10023/4510

Index

About the Author

Alasdair Gordon-Gibson worked for twenty-five years in the field of humanitarian response, mainly with the International Red Cross and Red Crescent Movement. He holds a degree of doctor of philosophy from the University of St Andrews.

www.ingramcontent.com/pod-product-compliance
Lightning Source LLC
Chambersburg PA
CBHW021814270326
41932CB00007B/184